THE TITANIC
AND
TODAY'S CHURCH

THE TITANIC

AND

TODAY'S CHURCH

—A Tale of Two Shipwrecks—

WARREN B. SMITH

MOUNTAIN STREAM PRESS

The Titanic and Today's Church: A Tale of Two Shipwrecks
© 2020 Warren B. Smith
Mountain Stream Press
P.O. Box 269
Fortine, MT 59918

Scripture quotations are taken from the *King James Version* and are in the public domain. Cover photo is from Wikimedia Commons and is in the public domain; photographer was F.G.O. Stuart (1843-1923). Cover design is by Mountain Stream Press. See all photo credits on page 253.

Publisher's Cataloging-in-Publication Data

Smith, Warren B.
  THE TITANIC AND TODAY'S CHURCH: A tale of two
shipwrecks / Warren B. Smith.
    264 pages cm
Includes bibliographical references and index.

  ISBN 978-0-9978982-7-9 (softbound : alk. paper) 1. Christianity 2. Titanic 3. 1912 4. Exhortation 5. New age movement

Library of Congress Control Number: 2020947465

Printed in the United States of America

With deep gratitude to all the many writers, researchers, organizations, and others who have contributed to the great body of work that informs us about the *Titanic*.

Contents

No living person should seek to dwell in thought

for one moment on such a disaster except in the

endeavor to glean from it knowledge that will

be of profit to the whole world in the future.[1]

—Lawrence Beesley
Titanic survivor

Titanic leaving Belfast

NOTE TO THE READER

This book has been many years in the making, and there have been more than a few "icebergs" to dodge along the way. Like the six radio warnings sent to the *Titanic* that last day as it approached the treacherous ice field, *The Titanic and Today's Church* is a warning about present and impending spiritual danger. And while similarities between the ship and today's church are used to make certain points, this does not in any way pretend to be a complete or exhaustive study.

It is the contention of this book that much of what calls itself today's church has become a shipwreck in progress as it inexorably heads toward total deception and complete disaster. It is a fact that after the *Titanic* hit the fatal iceberg, most people on board still believed they were on an "unsinkable" ship. A direct analogy can be made with many in today's professing church who are unaware they are also on a sinking ship that is headed for destruction.

Regarding His faithful church, Jesus stated that even "the gates of hell shall not prevail against it" (Matthew 16:18). Nevertheless, He issued a stern warning to the "many" who will say "Lord, Lord," thinking they are safely with Him and on their way to Heaven, when they actually are not. He says that "in that day" He will tell the many to "depart" from Him because He doesn't even know them (Matthew 7:21-23).

For years now, a relatively small number of believers have tried to warn today's church about the growing spiritual deception that has been in our midst. However, as the warnings increased, so did the deception. For whatever reasons, many church leaders, much like the complacent officers on the *Titanic*, have missed and/or too easily dismissed these warnings as they continue to lead the church into spiritual disaster. This book is one more warning—a midnight warning—about this growing deception.

Warren B. Smith

WHITE STAR LINE

ROYAL & STEAMERS

UNITED STATES MAIL

FIRST SAILING OF THE LATEST ADDITION TO THE WHITE STAR FLEET

The Queen of the Ocean

TITANIC

LENGTH 882½ FT.   OVER 45,000 TONS   BEAM 92½ FT.
TRIPLE-SCREWS

This, the Latest, Largest and Finest Steamer Afloat, will sail from

WHITE STAR LINE, PIER 10, SOUTHAMPTON

WEDNESDAY, APRIL 10TH.

en route to NEW YORK

Reservations of Berths may be made direct with this Office or through any of our accredited Agents

THIRD CLASS RATES ARE:

From SOUTHAMPTON, LONDON, LIVERPOOL	**£7 : 9$_s$: 0$_d$**
From QUEENSTOWN	**£6 : 10$_s$: 0$_d$**

PROLOGUE

At 11:40 p.m. on April 14, 1912, the RMS *Titanic*—the biggest, grandest ship of its time—collided with an iceberg on its maiden voyage from Southampton, England to New York City. Less than three hours later the seemingly unsinkable ship did the unthinkable—it sank to the bottom of the North Atlantic Ocean. Of the more than 2200 passengers and crew aboard, over 1500 people lost their lives. The shipwreck was one of the first global news events, and the worldwide shock was equivalent to that of the 9/11 World Trade Center disaster nearly a century later. Over the ensuing years, hundreds of books have been written about this infamous "Ship of Dreams," its lessons, and how "perfect storm" circumstances seemed to conspire to make sure that anything that could possibly go wrong, *did* go wrong.

One of those testifying at the United States Senate Inquiry regarding the disaster, described the events surrounding *Titanic's* end as "a very deceiving night."[1] Nineteen hundred years previous, Jesus Christ described the period before the world's end as a very deceiving "night." He said, "the night" is coming "when no man can work" (John 9:4). He stated that spiritual deception—not spiritual revival—would be the chief sign preceding His return (Matthew 24:3-4). He warned that "false Christs" and "false prophets" would "arise," and their deceptive "signs and wonders" would be so "great" that, "if it were possible, they shall deceive the very elect" (Matthew 24:5, 11, 24).

In reading about and reflecting upon the *Titanic* and the deadly iceberg that took it down, one is reminded of the Bible's prophetic warnings about Antichrist and his Antichrist system—the coming "beast" that will "rise up out of the sea" to deceive and destroy:

> And I stood upon the sand of the sea, and saw a beast rise up out of the sea, having seven heads and ten horns, and upon his horns ten crowns, and upon his heads the name of blasphemy. (Revelation 13:1)

It has been well-documented how design flaws, tragic oversights, false confidence, complacency, pride, greed, denial, disregarded warnings, missed messages, and unpreparedness all played a part in the *Titanic* shipwreck: How those in charge had underestimated the physical danger that was in their midst. Sadly, undiscerning church leaders today share many of these same characteristics as they similarly underestimate the spiritual danger in their midst.

While *Titanic* lookout Frederick Fleet shouted out his "Iceberg right ahead!" warning a moment too late, today's church leaders are issuing almost no warnings at all regarding spiritual deception (1 Corinthians 14:8). Yet God, through His infinite grace and prophetic Word, has already issued His "iceberg warnings" for just "such a time as this"—"Spiritual deception right ahead!" (Matthew 24:3-5), "False prophets, false teachers, false teachings right ahead!" (2 Peter 2:1), "Strong delusion with all power and signs and lying wonders right ahead!" (2 Thessalonians 2:9-11), "Deceptive peace and safety right ahead!" (1 Thessalonians 5:3), "A beast rising up out of the sea right ahead!" (Revelation 13:1).

The six wireless warnings sent to the *Titanic* on the day of its tragic collision were not warning about a possible ice field that *might* lie before them. They were warning about a specific ice field that *did* lie before them. In a similar manner, Scripture doesn't warn about a possible Antichrist figure that *might* "rise up" in the world, but about a specific Antichrist and Antichrist system that *will* "rise up" in the world. This Antichrist will be a most deceptive false Christ figure. He will not only come in his own name pretending to be

Christ (John 5:43), but he will actually oppose the true Christ—Jesus Christ—and all that He stands for (Daniel 8:25).

The *Titanic*—despite all of those "last day" warnings—did not escape its deadly encounter with the iceberg. In similar fashion, the world and a deceived professing church—despite all of the Bible's "last days" warnings—will not escape its deadly encounter with Antichrist and his Antichrist system (Revelation 13).

The Titanic and Today's Church is the story of two shipwrecks. One took place over a century ago. The other is a shipwreck in progress that is happening today. Hopefully, by looking at some of the similarities between the *Titanic* and today's church, we will become more aware of our Spiritual Adversary's schemes and "devices" (2 Corinthians 2:11), effectively "stand against" them (Ephesians 6:11), and "come out from among them" (2 Corinthians 6:17).

Finally, my brethren, be strong in the Lord, and in the power of his might. Put on the whole armour of God, that ye may be able to stand against the wiles of the devil. (Ephesians 6:10-11)

Holding faith, and a good conscience; which some having put away concerning faith have made shipwreck. (1 Timothy 1:19)

❧ 1 ❧

Dead Men Talking

Twelve months have now passed, in almost every week of which I have been cheered and comforted by messages from my boy, who is nearer and dearer to me than ever before.[1]

—William T. Stead, *Titanic* casualty
How I Know That the Dead Return (1909)

Jim was comforted by Josiah's visit, and it serves as proof that our son is not dead and gone, but merely moved to a different place to do other things for God.[2]

—Pastor Steve & Sarah Berger
Have Heart (2010)

❧ THE TITAN ❧

Maritime writer Morgan Robertson (1861-1915) described the huge and mighty vessel as "unsinkable" and "indestructible." He wrote:

She was the largest craft afloat and the greatest of the works of men. In her construction and maintenance were involved every science, profession, and trade known to civilization. . . .

In short, she was a floating city—containing within her steel walls all that tends to minimize the dangers and discomforts of the Atlantic voyage—all that makes life enjoyable.

Unsinkable—indestructible, she carried as few boats as would satisfy the laws.[3]

Robertson goes on to describe how this seemingly invincible ship collides with an iceberg and sinks to the bottom of the North Atlantic Ocean. However, the ship he was describing was not the *Titanic*—but rather a fictitious ship he called the *Titan*. This similarly named vessel was the subject of a short novel titled *Futility* that Robertson wrote in 1898—fourteen years before the *Titanic* ever set sail and almost a decade before the *Titanic*, or its name, were even conceived. *Futility* was a remarkable story in that the similarities between the *Titan* and the future *Titanic* were most uncanny.

THE SIMILARITIES

BESIDES having similar names, the *Titan* and the *Titanic* were both triple-screwed British ocean liners with three propellers and double masts. They were of similar weight and length, had a similar number of water-tight compartments, and both were capable of similar top speed. Both ships could carry around 3000 people, had a similar number of lifeboats, and both were acknowledged to be the largest ship of their time. Both were described as "practically unsinkable," yet they both sank on a cold April night after going too fast and colliding with an iceberg several hundred miles off the coast of Newfoundland. Because both ships lacked sufficient lifeboats, many people unnecessarily died.

THE DIFFERENCES

HOWEVER, even with all their amazing similarities, there were definite differences too. The *Titan* was sailing from New York to England; the *Titanic* from England to New York. It was not the *Titan's* maiden voyage as it was for the *Titanic*. The *Titan* had a full load of passengers, while the *Titanic* was just three quarters full. The *Titan* had few survivors, the *Titanic* had over seven hundred. The *Titan* sank on a foggy moonlit night, while the *Titanic* sank on a clear moonless night. The *Titan* capsized before it sank, while the *Titanic* upended and split in half before it sank.

Thus, as incredible as *Titan*'s story was in retrospect, it was a stunning foreshadowing but not a literal foretelling of future events. Morgan Robertson's *Futility* was not truly prophetic because it was not exact in all its details about the future (Deuteronomy 18:20-22). And like Pharaoh's magicians with their magically inspired signs and wonders, Robertson's inspiration was not from the one true God Almighty. His inspiration came from a much different and highly forbidden source.

THE ASTRAL WRITING-PARTNER

BIOGRAPHER John Vess reported that two of Morgan Robertson's close friends described the maritime author as a "psychic mystery" who was periodically "possessed" by a "discarnate soul" who was "a skilled writer." Vess wrote:

> Artist John O'Neill and journalist Henry W. Francis, both among Morg's close friends, described him as a "psychic mystery," apparently in the belief that his writing ability and often surprising knowledge resulted from his being possessed from time to time by a discarnate soul, a skilled writer who used Morg as a means of reaching the living world.[4]

Vess reported another source who also stated that Robertson's stories were inspired and controlled by a "demanding" unseen "spirit." The source said:

> [Morg] believed that he was under the control of a spirit that had passed over the border; of a soul who, demanding earthly expression, had seized him as its instrument.[5]

In his book *Premonitions: A Leap Into the Future*, author and psychic researcher Herbert B. Greenhouse wrote that Robertson described his supernatural assistant as an "astral writing-partner":

> Robertson called his co-author his "astral writing-partner." When he tried to coax his conscious mind into producing a story, nothing would happen and he would sit for hours at a time staring at his typewriter. Then "the mood" would come on. He would go into a trance, the present would fade away, and he would find himself in another dimension of time and space. It was in this mental state that he saw his vision of the *Titanic* and wrote about the *Titan*.[6]

Greenhouse said that toward the end of Robertson's life, his "astral writing-partner deserted him and nothing more would come out of his typewriter."[7] Robertson died in 1915, three years after the sinking of the *Titanic*. All alone, he passed away in an Atlantic City hotel room that looked out at the ocean where both the fictional *Titan* and the actual *Titanic* sank.

∾THE TITANIC∾

WILLIAM T. STEAD

William T. Stead (1849-1912) was a renowned British journalist, professing Christian, and practicing spiritualist, who was famously known for his investigative articles, books, and social activism. As a *Titanic* passenger, he was on his way to speak at a World Peace Conference in New York City at the request of American president William Howard Taft. Stead was one of the over 1500 people who perished at sea.

In 1886, twenty-six years before the *Titanic* tragedy, William Stead wrote a short story about the sinking of a huge ocean liner and the great loss of life that resulted from there being a shortage of lifeboats. He titled his story, "How the Mail Steamer Went Down in Mid Atlantic by a Survivor." It was published in the March 22, 1886 issue of the *Pall Mall Gazette* where he was the editor. Stead concluded his story with a sober warning: "This is exactly what might take place and what will take place if the liners are sent to sea short of boats."[8]

In 1892, twenty years before the sinking of *Titanic*, Stead wrote another story titled "From the Old World to the New" in the December edition of his *Review of Reviews*. It was about an ocean liner that sank after hitting an iceberg. The captain of the rescue ship was Captain Edward J. Smith, the same man who would captain the *Titanic* two decades later.[9]

In 1910, just two years before the *Titanic* disaster, William Stead delivered a lecture in London where he portrayed himself as the victim of a shipwreck who suddenly found himself "floundering in the water and calling for help."[10] Tragically, Stead turned out to be a victim of his own concern about shipwrecks and ships not carrying enough lifeboats. He was last seen reading a book in the *Titanic* library as the vessel was sinking.

AUTOMATIC WRITING

AS a professing Christian, William Stead was also involved in spiritualism—what would be referred to today as New Age Spirituality. He claimed to have a spiritual "gift" that enabled the spirit of another person to communicate through his passive writing hand in an unbiblical occult practice known as "automatic writing."[11] In particular, Stead literally and figuratively "handed" himself over to what he believed to be the discarnate spirit of a deceased friend named Julia Ames.[12] Her presumed spirit would then write through him on a variety of topics—many of them having strong spiritual implications. Stead periodically published transcripts of their collaborative writings in his *Borderland* magazine, a psychic quarterly he founded and edited from 1893-1897.

In 1897, Stead published a wider collection of these automatic writings in his book *Letters From Julia*. It was republished in 1905 under the title *After Death: Letters From Julia*. In the Preface, he vouched for the authenticity of his spiritual contact with "Julia" and insisted that it was "an absolute duty on the part of mortals to renew and keep up a loving intercourse with the loved ones who have gone before."[13] In 1909, at the request of the discarnate "Julia," William Stead established Julia's Bureau. The bureau was set up to enable people to submit questions to a select group of psychic mediums who would answer their requests. Also, in 1909, Stead's book, *How I Know That the Dead Return*, was published.

William Stead

GOD WITHIN

IN publishing the numerous "letters" written through him by "Julia," Stead hoped to normalize the occult practice of communicating with the dead. In particular, he wanted to share the spiritual information he received from "Julia" with the world at large. For example, in a meeting "Julia" said she had with "Jesus," this counterfeit "Jesus" told her he was going to teach her about "the secret things of God." He said:

> Be not afraid. It is I, who am appointed to teach thee the secret things of God.[14]

One of the "secret things" that "Jesus" told "Julia"—and that she subsequently communicated through Stead—pertained to what her "Jesus" described as "the God within." He told her that the purpose of our earthly lives was to "evoke" and "develop" the "God" who was "within" everyone and everything. Presenting this "secret" information she received from "Jesus," "Julia" wrote the following through Stead:

> The object of life is to evoke, to develop the God within.[15]

SPIRITUAL REVIVAL

THE "secret" of this immanent "God within" was presented in *After Death: Letters From Julia* under the bolded heading—"A Spiritual Revival." Through Stead, "Julia" wrote that worldwide revival—"a great spiritual awakening among the nations"—would take place in the future as humanity awakened to "the immanence of the Divine"—the "God within" themselves and their fellow man. "Julia" said:

> I was at first astonished to learn how much importance the spirits attach to the communications which they are allowed to have with those on earth. I can, of course, easily understand, because I feel it myself—the craving there is to speak to those whom you loved . . . but it is much more than this. What they tell me on all sides, and especially my dear guides, is that the time is come when there is to be a great spiritual awakening among the nations, and that the agency which is to bring this about is the sudden and conclusive demonstration, in every individual case which seeks for it, of the reality of the spirit, of the permanence of the soul, and the immanence of the Divine.[16]

And what "Julia" was allegedly taught by "Jesus" and her "guides" over a century ago about "a great spiritual awakening among the nations," closely resembles what is being taught by both New Age leaders and many church leaders today—that a great "worldwide revival" is fast approaching. New Age sources allege that this coming "revival" will eventually lead to unity, world peace, the formation of a New World Religion, and the salvation of mankind—and that it will all be founded on the "immanent" New Age teaching of the "God within"—God "in" everyone and everything.[17]

Sadly, most Christians do not realize that this unbiblical "God-in-everything" teaching has already entered today's church through best-selling "Christian" books and undiscerning church leaders. Just as surely as the sea water that flooded into and shipwrecked the *Titanic*, this

"God within" leaven continues to flow into today's church, shipwrecking the faith of those who choose to believe this dangerous false teaching.

A COURSE IN MIRACLES

ONE of William Stead's more modern spiritual counterparts was Columbia Presbyterian Hospital's Medical Psychology professor, Helen Schucman (1909-1981). She took her "inner dictation" from an inner voice that claimed to be "Jesus" from 1965-1972. The resultant work was published as *A Course in Miracles* in 1975. Highly promoted and internationally popularized by New Age authors Gerald Jampolsky and Marianne Williamson, as well as talk show host Oprah Winfrey, *A Course in Miracles* is now widely regarded as a New Age "Bible." Like "Julia's" false Jesus, Helen Schucman's "Jesus" presented the same foundational false doctrine of God "in" everyone and everything. One of the lessons from her channeled "Jesus" was to repeat and affirm the following statement:

God is in everything I see.[18]

And just like "Julia's" counterfeit "Jesus," Schucman's "Jesus" stated that our own spiritual awakening must first take place before we can "awaken"[19] the rest of the world to the "God within." However, the first commandment in the Bible is very explicit that we are not to follow other gods, which would most definitely include the false "God within" (Deuteronomy 5:7). God is the Creator, and He is distinct and separate from His creation. He is not "in" everyone and everything. He is uniquely God, and we are not God, or in any way a part of God. The Bible makes it clear that "the way of man is not in himself" (Jeremiah 10:23). It warns "whosoever shall exalt himself shall be abased" (Matthew 23:12), and that "every man at his best state is altogether vanity" (Psalm 39:5). The apostle Paul specifically warned:

For if a man think himself to be something, when he is nothing, he deceiveth himself. (Galatians 6:3)

Nevertheless, *A Course in Miracles* continues to be promoted and popularized as "new revelation" channeled from "Jesus" through Helen Schucman—just as "Julia" channeled "new revelation" from "Jesus" through *Titanic* passenger William T. Stead.

CHRISTIAN SPIRITUALIST?

AS a professing Christian, William Stead supported—with great enthusiasm—spirit-filled preachers, evangelical prayer circles, church revival, and Christianity in general. He described preachers like Welsh revivalist Evan Roberts as being among the most valuable members of the community. Stead's best-selling 75-page pamphlet, *The Welsh Revival*, promoted the revival and sold 200,000 copies in Britain and 500,000 in the United States.[20] As a result of his pamphlet, Stead was asked to speak in churches and other venues about the revival. Stead's *The Welsh Revival* is still in print today.[21]

On the other hand, as a practicing occultist/spiritualist, William Stead also supported—with great enthusiasm—psychic mediums, seances, metaphysical prayer circles, communicating with the dead, automatic writing, occult revival, and spiritualism in general. He regarded mediumship as "a precious gift"[22] and once stated, "Mediums are among the most valuable members of the community."[23] His occult books *After Death: Letters From Julia* and *How I Know That the Dead Return* are also still in print today.

Obviously, William Stead's sincere but confused spiritual beliefs contradict themselves and make no biblical sense. He let his mystical occult experiences trump the Bible's clear warnings about spiritual deception. In fact, the Bible explicitly warns about those, like Stead, who "depart from the faith" as they listen to "seducing spirits" that teach "doctrines of devils" (1 Timothy 4:1) like that of the "God within." As a professing Christian but practicing spiritualist, Stead was dangerously "double minded" (James 1:8) as he drank from two cups and ate from two tables (1 Corinthians 10:21) and served "two masters" (Matthew 6:24).

As a professing Christian, yet occult spiritualist, William T. Stead was greatly deceived. Unbeknownst to him, he was paving the way for a future New Age "Christianity" that was definitely not biblical. Stead was a direct forerunner to his present-day media counterpart Oprah Winfrey. Oprah has publicly promoted her occult/New Age beliefs as well as her social reform activities, while simultaneously professing her Christian faith; likewise, William Stead publicly promoted his occult/New Age beliefs as well as his social-reform activities, while simultaneously professing his Christian faith—both of them used their prominent media positions as universal platforms to preach and promote their "Christian" occultism and social reform; both of them seemingly sincere; both of them sincerely deceived.

As a footnote, shortly after the *Titanic* disaster and William Stead's passing, occult sources announced that "Stead" had begun to speak and write through earthly mediums—just as "Julia" had spoken and written through him.[24] Not surprisingly, the communications from the alleged "Stead" were totally consistent with occult/New Age spiritualism—not biblical Christianity. A group of friends and admirers founded the William T. Stead Memorial Center in Chicago, Illinois where resident pastor and medium, Mrs. Cecil Cook, held seances and services. In a book she co-authored about the Stead Center, she wrote:

> Mr. Stead is the directing head of the organization that bears his name, and through his ceaseless kindness and ministering efforts, many have been led to a new understanding of life. . . . And now the work of Mr. William T. Stead, that at best was only arrested temporarily by the sinking of the *Titanic*, is once more able to reach mankind.[25]

Titanic passenger William Stead was a classic example of a hybridized professing believer who was also a practicing occultist and spiritualist. While claiming to be a Christian believer, he carried within him "another Jesus," "another gospel," "another spirit," and another god (2 Corinthians 11:4). Yet, he supported the Welsh revival, wrote a best-selling pamphlet about it, and was asked to speak at church gatherings to promote the revival. Unfortunately, spiritually confused individuals like Stead can become main players in revival activities.

Stead, being asked by President William Taft to speak at a major Peace Conference in New York City, was similar to Oprah being asked to speak at Yankee Stadium after the World Trade Center disaster. Both William Stead and Oprah Winfrey are examples of two media people who have used their influence as professing Christians to promote the occult and the New Age.

While Morgan Robertson and William Stead's premonitions about the *Titanic* are intriguing, it is clear their psychic abilities were inspired by "familiar spirits"—not the One True God. The Bible acknowledges that divining spirits are real and can convey the future to some extent, as exemplified by Morgan Robertson and William Stead's stories. However, Scripture warns that while these deceiving spirits can deliver some true pronouncements, there is great spiritual danger in interacting with them in any way (Deuteronomy 13:1-3). Truths that emerge in their pronouncements may lead one to follow other pronouncements that are not true—like "Julia's" false teaching about the "immanence of the Divine"—the "God within."

THE PHILIPPIAN PSYCHIC

THE demonic reality behind spiritualistic foretelling is dramatically demonstrated in the New Testament when the apostle Paul and Silas were being hassled by a Philippian soothsayer (psychic) who was "possessed with a spirit of divination." After Paul cast the divining spirit out of her in the name of Jesus Christ, she was no longer able to do her psychic readings (Acts 16:16-19). Similarly, when Morgan Robertson's "astral writing-partner" mysteriously "departed," so did Robertson's ability to foresee future events and write effectively. Bottom line—no matter how amazing Morgan Robertson and William Stead's premonitions proved to be regarding the *Titanic* or anything else, their spiritual leadings came from a biblically forbidden occult source. They were not a "precious gift" from God. Quite the opposite. And this is why the Bible warns us to stay away from spiritualism and the occult and to "try the spirits" of whatever one is dealing with to see if they are really from God:

> Beloved, believe not every spirit, but try the spirits whether they are of God: because many false prophets are gone out into the world. (1 John 4:1)

FAMILIAR SPIRITS & NECROMANCY

WHAT Morgan Robertson and William Stead were doing was not just unbiblical—it was spiritually dangerous. They willingly entertained the unseen spirit realm by allowing themselves to be used by deceptive spirits that came as a "skilled writer" and a former "friend." In so doing, Robertson and Stead went directly against the Bible's explicit warning not to communicate with "familiar spirits" or attempt to interact in any way with those who have passed on (necromancy):

> There shall not be found among you any one that maketh his son or his daughter to pass through the fire, or that useth divination, or an observer of times, or an enchanter, or a witch, Or a charmer, or a consulter with familiar spirits, or a wizard, or a necromancer. (Deuteronomy 18:10-11)

Several years prior to William Stead's death on the *Titanic*, he claimed to have had contact with his deceased son. In his 1909 book *How I Know That the Dead Return*, he wrote:

> Twelve months ago this month of December I saw my eldest son, whom I had trained [in automatic writing] in the fond hope that he would be my successor, die at the early age of thirty-three. The tie between us was of the closest. No one could deceive me by fabricated spurious messages from my beloved son.

Twelve months have now passed, in almost every week of which I have been cheered and comforted by messages from my boy, who is nearer and dearer to me than ever before.[26]

How I Know That the Dead Return was William Stead's personal testimony of his alleged communication with his deceased son William. This spiritual communication gave him the final "proof" he needed to completely and wholeheartedly endorse, as a professing Christian, the occult practice of interacting with the dead. A century later, a Tennessee pastor and his wife also wrote a book about communicating with their deceased son—only his name was Josiah.

✜TODAY'S CHURCH✜

In 2010, Steve Berger, head pastor of the Grace Chapel megachurch in Leiper's Fork, Tennessee, wrote a book with his wife Sarah titled *Have Heart: Bridging the Gulf Between Heaven and Earth*. The book described how they claim to be in spiritual contact with their deceased son Josiah. And like *Titanic's* William Stead, the Bergers, as professing Christians, were attempting to justify and normalize the practice of interacting with the dead.

DEMONIC DECEPTION

IN *Have Heart*, the Bergers wrote that their deceased son Josiah has been directly communicating with the two of them, their children, and some of their friends. One of the chief examples in the book related to an incident that occurred during a Wednesday night worship service at their church. They described how Josiah allegedly appeared and spoke to then Assistant Pastor Jim Sterling during the service. In the book, as the congregation sang the praise song "It's Gonna Be Worth It," the Bergers had Sterling recounting his experience with Josiah. Sterling said:

As I was listening, I was praying, and I asked God one more time, "Lord, is it worth it?"

The next thing I knew, Josiah came into the sanctuary. It wasn't like he just appeared there. It was a sense of him coming into the aisle, and he got down on one knee and bent to speak into my ear. He said, "Way worth it, Mr. Jim." Then, as quickly as he came, he left . . .

I stood up and went over to my wife and told her, "Josiah was just here."[27]

The Bergers cited the incident in detail, telling readers that the visit proves that departed loved ones can communicate and interact with those on Earth. The Bergers wrote:

This visit proves that our loved ones in Heaven are spiritually active and that they care—they are aware of times that we need special encouragement. Josiah saw his friend, tired, questioning, and drained, and God granted Josiah permission to make an appearance to encourage and reassure him.[28]

However, in a phone call with Jim Sterling several years after *Have Heart* was published, Sterling said he had come to believe that what had seemed to be Josiah, was actually a demonic spirit.[29] No longer an assistant pastor at Grace Chapel, he said his conviction came after much prayer and reading of Scripture. And the Bible definitely backs him up. It describes consulting with familiar spirits and attempting to interact with the dead as "an abomination unto the LORD" (Deuteronomy 18:10-12).

While obviously being sympathetic to those who have suffered the tragic loss of a child, that sympathy cannot extend into condoning an occult practice like necromancy. No one—especially professing Christians like William Stead and the Bergers—should be involved in forbidden occult practices. In addition, the Stead and Berger books are as dangerous for what they don't say as for what they do say. The scriptural admonition to "test" and "try the spirits" cannot be found anywhere in their books (1 John 4:1-3).

Endorsing *Have Heart*

ALSO troubling are *Have Heart*'s inside front-page endorsements by pastors Greg Laurie and James Robison, *The Shack* author William Paul Young, and former U.S. Senate Majority leader Dr. Bill Frist. In promoting *Have Heart*, these endorsers seemed to legitimize what the Bergers were falsely teaching. Greg Laurie wrote that *Have Heart* "bursts with hope." He also said, "I hope this book will be a blessing to you." Part of James Robison's endorsement also appeared on the book's front cover. It said, "The Bergers show us how we can find light and life beyond death's shadow."

All of these endorsements have been featured in *Have Heart* for over a decade. The Berger's Grace Chapel and Greg Laurie's Harvest Christian Fellowship are both Calvary Chapel affiliates. However, Calvary Chapel's flagship radio program, *Pastors' Perspective,* has openly renounced what the Bergers were doing and what the endorsers were endorsing.

Pastors' Perspective

ANNE-MARIE, a friend who formerly attended the Berger's church, phoned in a question on the September 29, 2015 broadcast of *Pastors' Perspective.*[30] She was troubled about the issue of talking with the dead. Without mentioning the Bergers or their book by name, she wanted to know from a biblical perspective if talking with the dead was a "major" or "minor" issue regarding "the fundamentals of the Gospel."

Christian apologist and co-host Don Stewart replied that it was a "huge" issue and referred the caller to Deuteronomy 18 with its warning verses that forbid occult practices like talking with the dead. Stewart emphatically stated, "The dead don't speak to the living."

Stewart said if the living are spoken to, it originates from one of only two sources—a "demonic spirit" or from some type of "charade" working through "a medium." Stewart's co-host, Calvary Chapel pastor Brian Brodersen, also referred to Deuteronomy 18 and expressed his concern about this forbidden activity being promoted by professing believers. He said, "This could cause real problems in the church."

Before moving on to the next caller, program director Pastor Josh Turansky said that what had been discussed on the program was "dangerous" and "bizarre."

Morgan Robertson's "astral writing-partner," William Stead's former friend "Julia," and the Berger's son "Josiah" were all in alleged communication with the living. Over the years, we have come to expect psychics like John Edward and a host of other New Age figures to practice and promote this occult activity of communicating with the dead—but we do not expect this from professing Christians. Repeating the words of Pastor Brian Brodersen on *Pastors' Perspective* regarding those who teach and/or endorse communicating with the dead—"This could cause real problems in the church."

Chris Lawson of the Spiritual Research Network contacted Pastor Steve Berger by phone and politely questioned him about his alleged interactions with his deceased son, Josiah. Berger strongly defended what he and his family were doing. He told Lawson:

> God has made an exception at this time in history for the Berger family. We are indeed in communication with our son Josiah.[31]

Lawson also tried to talk with Pastor Greg Laurie about his endorsement of *Have Heart*. He documented his concern and his failed attempt to talk with Pastor Laurie. Lawson said:

> Out of concern for many Calvary Chapel pastors and the fellowships they oversee, and out of concern for all the people that attend Pastor Greg Laurie's Harvest Christian Fellowship, and out of concern also for the many thousands of people whom Greg Laurie has influenced through his ministry, and books, and Harvest Crusades, I made a telephone call to Greg Laurie in 2012. . . .
>
> I explained to Greg's secretary that I just had a quick question to ask him regarding his personal endorsement

of Steve Berger's book, *Have Heart: Bridging the Gulf Between Heaven and Earth.*

Greg's secretary asked if I would wait on hold, and so I did—for about 15 or 20 seconds. When the secretary came back onto the telephone, she simply said to me, "Greg is not available for comments on that book." With that, I thanked her for her time, and the telephone conversation ended.[32]

When Lawson also contacted Pastor James Robison and his son in 2012, they claimed to have never seen the manuscript and weren't sure if they even had a copy of the Bergers' book. They acknowledged that sometimes their endorsements were made based on "relationship" without ever having seen the actual book. They expressed their concern and told Lawson they would look into the matter. Eight years later, James Robison's endorsement is still on the hardcover and Kindle editions of *Have Heart.* The late Chuck Missler's original endorsement of the hardcover edition of *Have Heart* has since been removed, but it still remains in the present Kindle edition.

NEW AGE NECROMANCY

NEW Age author James Redfield followed up his mega best-selling novel *The Celestine Prophecy* with another popular novel titled *The Twelfth Insight: The Hour of Decision.* When the book's New Age seekers are desperately looking for secret knowledge that can save the world, Rachel, one of the main characters, suddenly finds herself having "a real interaction" with her deceased mother. Much like William Stead's "Julia," who stressed the great importance that spirits attach to their communications with those on Earth,[33] Rachel was told much the same thing. She said:

> All we have to do is use more of our power to tune in and have a conversation. It's never too late. And there is so much more they want to tell us.

In fact, my mother said they desperately need to speak with us, right now, at this crucial point in history. They know the real Plan for the human world, and it's time for us on this side to understand.[34]

And, of course, that plan had already been conveyed by William Stead's "Julia," by the "Jesus" of *A Course in Miracles,* and by so many other "familiar spirits" from the "other side." It is the plan for humanity to universally unite and "awaken" to the "God within."

THE LIGHT THAT WAS DARK

IN *The Light That Was Dark,* I describe how I was seduced into the New Age by a ball of light that suddenly manifested over my head in a psychic reading. I was told by the psychic that the ball of light had appeared to let me know I had a lot of help on the "other side." When I asked what she meant by "the other side," the first thing she told me was: "Family and loved ones who have passed away."[35] She added that "angels and other spirits" were also interested in helping me with my life. All I had to do was ask for their assistance. So I did. And the spirit world was more than willing as they seduced me further and further into spiritual deception—just as they had with William T. Stead, Helen Schucman, the Bergers, and countless others of us over the years. The amazing thing is that the Bible has thoroughly warned us about all this spiritual deception and how it will play out in these latter days.

Now the Spirit speaketh expressly, that in

the latter times some shall depart from the

faith, giving heed to seducing spirits, and

doctrines of devils. (1 Timothy 4:1)

❧2❧

A LITTLE LEAVEN

It has been demonstrated that because of the time *Titanic* actually took to sink, from the moment of impact, right up to the hull's break-up and sinking, that the total size of the damage would only amount to approximately 12 square feet.[1]

—Titanic.com

It need not be said that this man [Antichrist] and his kingdom are not the accidents of an hour; there is a long preparatory process. As with our Lord, so with him. There is a "fulness of time" for his appearing, and this is not till the antichristian leaven has spread through Christendom.[2]

—Pastor Samuel J. Andrews
Christianity and Anti-Christianity in Their Final Conflict (1899)

❧THE TITANIC❧

After the *Titanic* sank, it was generally believed the iceberg had sliced a 300 foot-long gash piercing the ship's hull. However, a decade after the *Titanic* was finally located in 1985, a scientific expedition found out what really happened.

The title of an April 8, 1997 *New York Times* article read—"Toppling Theories, Scientists Find 6 Slits, Not Big Gash, Sank *Titanic.*" The account that followed revealed that the shipwreck was not the result of the 300-foot-long gash previously theorized. Rather, it described how an international team of scientists, using sound waves to penetrate the mud covering much of the ship's hull, discovered the damaged area to be no more than "12-13 square feet." Proving that a little leaven can leaven the whole lump, it was concluded that it only took "a series of six thin openings" totaling less than the size of "two sidewalk squares" to sink the *Titanic* in less than three hours. The article explained:

> Peering through the mud with sound waves, the team found the damage to be astonishingly small—a series of six thin openings across the *Titanic*'s starboard hull. The total area of the damage appears to be about 12 to 13 square feet, or less than the area of two sidewalk squares.[3]

At the time of its sailing, it was almost inconceivable that the "unsinkable" *Titanic* could be shipwrecked at all, much less by an area that was no larger than the size of a refrigerator door—"two sidewalk squares." Thus, history now records that it took only a very small area—a little leaven—to totally shipwreck the biggest, grandest ship of its time. And it may be only a small teaching—a little leaven—that will totally shipwreck the faith of many of today's professing believers. This specific leaven is the same heretical Genesis 3:5 "ye shall be as gods" leaven that passed from the serpent to Eve and from the deceptive spirit "Julia" to *Titanic* casualty William Stead. This leaven being the heretical leaven of the "God within."

THE GREAT HERETICAL IDEA

IN her 1980 best-selling book *The Aquarian Conspiracy*, the late New Age author Marilyn Ferguson introduced what she called a "great heretical idea." She wrote:

Usually at the point of crisis, someone has a great heretical idea. A powerful new insight explains the apparent contradictions. It introduces a new principle . . . a new perspective. By forcing a more comprehensive theory, the crisis is not *destructive* but *instructive*.[4] (italics hers)

This "great heretical idea" was described by Ferguson as "the oldest heresy"—the "God" who is "in" everything—the "God within."[5] She postulated that a small number of individuals holding fast to the "great heretical idea" of the "God within," could one day "be yeast enough to leaven a whole society." She wrote:

The premonition was recorded, from time to time, that a minority of individuals would someday be yeast enough to leaven a whole society. Serving as a magnet culture, they would attract order around them, transforming the whole.[6]

Ferguson said the title of her book, *The Aquarian Conspiracy*, was taken from a statement made by the man frequently referred to as the "Father of the New Age Movement"[7]—Pierre Teilhard de Chardin. He said:

This soul can only be a conspiracy of individuals.

This Teilhard quote is found on the front page of Ferguson's book and conveys this idea that a "minority of individuals" were at work in the world and the church, quietly conspiring to introduce a "new perspective" that would "trigger a critical contagion of change." Ferguson wrote:

Teilhard prophesied the phenomenon central to this book: a conspiracy of men and women whose new perspective would trigger a critical contagion of change.[8]

The "Aquarian Conspiracy" was based on getting the world and the church to accept this core leaven, the "great heretical idea" of a "God" who is "within" everyone and everything. The "old story"— the Bible's presentation of Jesus and the true Gospel—would be replaced by a "new story"—the New Age story of the "God within." It would become the "new narrative" that would transform the world and the church. It would change history by changing *His* story—the story of how Jesus Christ died on the cross to save the world from sin. This clever "new story" was what the apostle Peter described as a "cunningly devised fable."

> For we have not followed cunningly devised fables, when we made known unto you the power and coming of our Lord Jesus Christ, but were eyewitnesses of his majesty. (2 Peter 1:16)

Marilyn Ferguson was suggesting that what the Bible described as a great heresy—"God within"—is actually a great "truth" that could save the world. People would no longer look to Jesus Christ as their Savior. They would save themselves by "awakening" to the "God within." "God within" would be the "yeast"—the leaven—the foundational centerpiece of a New Age/New Spirituality/New World Religion. Thus, the coming New World Religion would result from a "great awakening" of the world to the "great heretical idea" that God is "in" everyone and everything. And make no mistake about it, Marilyn Ferguson was taking dead aim at the Bible's explicit warning about "damnable heresies" (2 Peter 2:1) with her "great heretical idea" of the "God within."

Sadly, her "heretical" New Age teaching has pierced the walls of today's church just as surely as that North Atlantic iceberg pierced the steel hull of the *Titanic*. This small, barely detectable leaven is much like the small area that leavened the "unsinkable" *Titanic* to the bottom of the ocean. It is now an indisputable fact that it only took a little leaven—12-13 square feet—to sink the *Titanic*. And it is becoming increasingly clear that it will only take a little leaven like "God within" to shipwreck the faith of an undiscerning church.

THE GREAT "UNSINKABLE" IDEA

THE Aquarian Conspiracy is seen by many as a New Age "Bible." It is a virtual catalog of "Aquarian conspirators" who were bringing the "great heretical idea" into the 1980s and into their own particular spheres of influence—be that science, business, government, family, education, arts, entertainment, or religion. Pioneering "conspirators" were especially needed to bring this "great heretical idea" into the church. For "God within" to become acceptable to biblical Christians, they would have to be converted—en masse—to a more emergent postmodern expression of their faith that would be more compatible with the New Age/New Spirituality/New Worldview.

Just as the *Titanic* was viewed as invincible and unsinkable, the "great heretical idea" would have to be similarly seen as invincible and unsinkable within the culture at large—and within the church itself. Citing historian Theodore Roszak, Marilyn Ferguson made the point that "new ideas" like "God within" would ultimately "shake the culture."[9] However, to get the world and the church on the same page, Ferguson said that these new transformational ideas would have to be "widely communicated." She wrote:

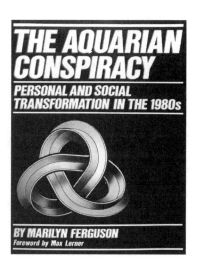

> If these discoveries of transformation are to become our common heritage for the first time in history, they must

be widely communicated. They must become our new consensus, what "everybody knows."[10]

Enter the ultimate Aquarian communicator—Oprah Winfrey. Starting in 1986, Oprah's twenty-five-year run hosting *The Oprah Winfrey Show* would eventually be viewed daily by ten million people on over 200 U.S. television stations in 150 countries around the world. As a professing Christian, the gifted communicator has consistently introduced the "great heretical idea" through the many New Age guests and New Age books she has featured and endorsed over the years. Today, more than ever, she is doing everything in her power to make the "great heretical idea"—"God within"—"our new consensus." While professing to be a Christian, she is a New Age Christian, which is to say, not a biblical Christian at all. Her New Age sympathies were in full view when she had Marilyn Ferguson on her program back in 1987.

OPRAH, FERGUSON, & THE NEW AGE

ON the 1987 *Oprah Winfrey Show* program titled "The New Age Movement," Oprah showcased Marilyn Ferguson and her book, *The Aquarian Conspiracy*. On the program, Oprah publicly endorsed Ferguson's "great heretical idea" of the "God within" when she emphatically declared—"Jesus did not come to teach how divine he was, but came to teach us that there is divinity within us."[11] Yet to this day, Oprah continues to describe herself as a Christian and denies being in any way New Age. However, on the program with Ferguson, and on so many others since, she has been in complete agreement with the "great heretical idea" that "God" is "in" everyone and everything.

OPRAH & *A COURSE IN MIRACLES*

ANOTHER defining moment of Oprah's New Age ministry occurred on a February 1992 program when she enthusiastically endorsed author Marianne Williamson's new book *A Return to Love:*

Reflections on the Principles of A Course in Miracles. Oprah stated that she believed in her "heart" that the New Age principles of *A Course in Miracles* "could change the world." She said she had "never been as moved by a book" as she was with Williamson's book about *A Course in Miracles*. She added, "If it sounds like I am trying to hype the book, I really am." She then announced that she had bought a thousand copies of Williamson's book and would be giving one to everyone in her studio audience. After Oprah's spirited endorsement, Williamson's book about *A Course in Miracles* shot to number one on the *New York Times* Best Seller list and stayed there for several months.

What Williamson and Oprah did not tell the millions of viewers watching that day was that *A Course in Miracles* was said to have been spiritually dictated by "Jesus" himself and that its teachings were founded on the "great heretical idea" of the "God within."

Oprah, while positively affirming to her viewers that the teachings of *A Course in Miracles* "could change the world," neglected to mention that its teachings contradict almost every major doctrine in the Bible. It teaches there is no sin,[12] no evil,[13] no Devil,[14] and that the "journey to the cross should be the last 'useless journey.'"[15] It also states that "A slain Christ has no meaning."[16] And there at the heart of all these false teachings is the foundational New Age leaven of the "God within." The counterfeit "Jesus" of *A Course in Miracles* teaches that we save ourselves by awakening to the "God within" and to the understanding that we are all "One," and we are all "God" because God is "in" everyone and everything.[17]

OPRAH & NEALE DONALD WALSCH

ON an *Oprah Winfrey Show* program broadcast after the 9/11 World Trade Center tragedy, Oprah featured ten "memorable thinkers." She described New Age leader Neale Donald Walsch as one of the ten most "memorable thinkers" she had ever met.[18] In his best-selling *Conversations With God* books, Walsch claimed to have had literal conversations with "God." In his post 9/11 book *The New*

Revelations, he said "God" had told him that "The era of the Single Savior is over."[19] Two years later in his book *Tomorrow's God*, Walsch wrote that "Oneness"—God "within" everyone and everything—was the "Foundational Truth" of the "New Spirituality."

Oneness is the message.

It is the Foundational Truth of the New Spirituality.

We are all One.[20]

Over the years, Oprah, as perhaps *the* chief Aquarian communicator of our times, has instantly transformed unknown authors into household names and their books into instant best-sellers. She has promoted and popularized New Age authors from Marianne Williamson, Shirley MacLaine, Eckhart Tolle, and Neale Donald Walsch to Dr. Mehmet Oz, Deepak Chopra, Gary Zukav, Wayne Dyer and many others. She has been instrumental in almost single-handedly promoting and popularizing the teachings of the New Age/New Spirituality with its "great heretical idea" of "God within" "Oneness." As one of the world's most influential communicators, she has more than fulfilled Marilyn Ferguson's prescribed role of "widely communicating" New Age ideas and making them "our new consensus, what everybody knows."

IMMANENCE & THE NEW WORLD RELIGION

OPRAH Winfrey and all of the New Age authors and teachers she has featured through the years have been simply echoing the "God within" teachings that were introduced years ago by New Age matriarchs Helena Blavatsky (1831-1891), Annie Besant (1847-1933), and Alice Bailey (1880-1949), and New Age patriarch Pierre Teilhard de Chardin (1881-1955). They have all paved the way for the New Age Christianity that Oprah would adopt and advocate years later—a New Age Christianity that uses Christian terminology to cloak its counterfeit Christ, counterfeit salvation, and counterfeit world peace. Blavatsky, Besant, and Bailey all anticipated the coming of a New Age "Christ" named Maitreya. This Maitreya allegedly arrived incognito in London in 1977 from his previously sequestered residence in the Himalayas.[21] He is said to still be secretly in the world today, waiting for humanity to call him forth.

Maitreya's messages to humanity were promoted by his chief spokesperson and advance public relations man, Benjamin Creme (1922-2016). In his 1980 book *Messages from Maitreya the Christ* channeled through Creme and published the same year as Marilyn Ferguson's *The Aquarian Conspiracy*, Maitreya presented the "great heretical idea" of the "God within." He stated:

> My friends, God is nearer to you than you can imagine. God is yourself. God is within you and all around you.[22]

In *The Reappearance of the Christ and the Masters of Wisdom*, Benjamin Creme described how Maitreya's "immanent" "God within" teaching is at the heart of the New Age/New World Religion. He wrote:

> But eventually a new world religion will be inaugurated which will be a fusion and synthesis of the approach of the East and the approach of the West. The Christ will bring together, not simply Christianity and Buddhism, but the concept of God transcendent—outside of His creation—and also the concept of God immanent in all creation—in man and all creation.[23]

As an Antichrist-type, Maitreya was fulfilling what Helena Blavatsky, Annie Besant, and Alice Bailey had written and promoted many years ago about Maitreya: How a New Age/New World Religion would be founded on the foundational teaching of the immanent "God within." In her book, *The Reappearance of the Christ*, Alice Bailey wrote:

> . . . a fresh orientation to divinity and to the acceptance of the fact of God Transcendent and of God Immanent within every form of life.
>
> These are the foundational truths upon which the world religion of the future will rest.[24]

This immanent "God within" teaching also echoed what the deceptive spirit "Julia" had told William Stead about the "immanence of the Divine"—the need for humanity to "evoke" this alleged "God within." And it was this same William Stead, whose life had been cut short on the *Titanic*, who was responsible for introducing his "good friend" Annie Besant to the theosophical teachings of Helena Blavatsky and her false Christ Maitreya.[25] And while Stead never became a theosophist himself, he was an early proponent of what would eventually become New Age Christianity—a strange blend of the occult and the misapplication of key verses from the Bible.

❧TODAY'S CHURCH❧

As cited, Marilyn Ferguson wrote in *The Aquarian Conspiracy*:

> The premonition was recorded, from time to time, that a minority of individuals would someday be yeast enough to leaven a whole society. Serving as a magnet culture, they would attract order around them, transforming the whole.[26]

It is now a sad given that the "great heretical idea" of the "God within" has entered the church through "a minority of individuals," undiscerning Christian publishing houses, Christian bookstores, and Christian television. The following is a small sampling of how this New Age leaven has crept in over the last seven decades.

New Age Leaven in the Church

Norman Vincent Peale (1952)

In his huge best-selling book *The Power of Positive Thinking*, the late Norman Vincent Peale wrote:

> God is in you.[27]

Robert Schuller (1969)

In Robert Schuller's book *Self-Love*, the late Crystal Cathedral pastor wrote:

> God lives in people.[28]

M. Scott Peck (1978)

The late, mystical, pre-emergent, "Christian" psychiatrist M. Scott Peck's best-selling book *The Road Less Traveled* was frequently sold in Christian bookstores. In it, he wrote:

> To put it plainly, our unconscious is God. God within us. We were part of God all the time.[29]

Leonard Sweet (1991)

In his book *Quantum Spirituality*, church leader Leonard Sweet states:

> Quantum Spirituality bonds us to all creation as well as to other members of the human family. . . . This entails a radical doctrine of embodiment of God in the very substance of creation.[30]

Betty Eadie (1992)

For a period of time, Betty Eadie's best-selling book, *Embraced by the Light*, was popular with Christians and sold in Christian bookstores. In it, she wrote:

> I felt God in the plant, in me, his love pouring into us. We were all one.[31]

Sue Monk Kidd (1992)

Former Christian and best-selling author Sue Monk Kidd writes in her book *The Dance of the Dissident Daughter* that "deity" and "divinity" will no longer just be "out there"; it will also be "in" everything—even "in excrement and roses alike." She says:

> It will also be right here, right now, in me, in the earth, in this river and this rock, in excrement and roses alike.[32]

Jack Canfield and Mark Victor Hansen (1993)

The original *Chicken Soup for the Soul* book has sold over eight million copies and is still being sold in some Christian bookstores. One of the stories in the book was Jack Canfield's "The Golden Buddha," in which Canfield says:

> We are all like the clay Buddha, covered with a shell of hardness created out of fear, and yet underneath each of us is a "golden Buddha," a "golden Christ" or a "golden essence," which is our real self.[33]

Eugene Peterson (1993)

In *The Message*, the late Eugene Peterson paraphrases Ephesians 4:6 to state that God is "in" everything—that He is "present in all." He writes:

> You have one Master, one faith, one baptism, one God and Father of all, who rules over all, works through all,

and is present in all. Everything you are and think and do is permeated with Oneness.[34]

Catechism of the Catholic Church (1995)
The *Catechism of the Catholic Church* states:

> For the Son of God became man so that we might become God. (#460)[35]

> Let us rejoice then and give thanks that we have become not only Christians, but Christ himself. Do you understand and grasp, brethren, God's grace toward us? Marvel and rejoice: we have become Christ. (#795)[36]

Henri Nouwen (1997)
Often quoted by Christian authors and church leaders, the late Catholic mystic Henri Nouwen states in his book *Here and Now* that God is "in" every human being. He writes:

> The God who dwells in our inner sanctuary is also the God who dwells in the inner sanctuary of every human being.[37]

Rick Warren (2002)
In his 30-million-plus best-selling book *The Purpose Driven Life*, and out of the fifteen different Bible translations he quotes from in his book, Rick Warren chose the *New Century Version* which states that God is "in" everything. Warren writes:

> Because God is with you all the time, no place is any closer to God than the place where you are right now. The Bible says, "He rules everything and is everywhere and is in everything."[38]

Robert Schuller (2003)

Consistent with his New Age leanings through the years, Robert Schuller told his November 9, 2003 international *Hour of Power* television audience that God is not only a transcendent God—"out there"—he is also an immanent God who is "in" every single human being. He stated:

> The immanence of God means here, in me, around me, in society, in the world, this God here, in the humanities, in the science, in the arts, sociology, in politics—the immanence of God. . . . Yes, God is alive and he is in every single human being![39]

Sarah Young (2004)

In her best-selling book *Jesus Calling*, Sarah Young's "Jesus" states that God is "in" everything—"in all":

> I am above all as well as in all.[40]

William Paul Young (2007)

In his best-selling book *The Shack*, William Paul Young's "Jesus" pronounces this same "God within" New Age leaven. His "Jesus" states:

> God who is the ground of all being, dwells in, around, and through all things.[41]

Glenn Beck (2011)

Influencing many professing believers, Mormon author and radio personality, Glenn Beck, openly acknowledges his New Age sympathies in his book *The Seven Wonders That Will Change Your Life*. He writes:

> If God is everything and everywhere and inside everyone, then I figured He had to be inside me, too.[42]

My father's granola-hippie New Age spirituality (which I actually really agree with) . . . [43]

Pope Francis (2016)

Speaking in Malmo, Sweden on November 1, 2016, Pope Francis stated that "new situations require new energy and a new commitment." He then proposed six new Beatitudes for modern Christians, one of them being that people are blessed by seeing "God in every person." He said:

> Blessed are those who see God in every person.[44]

Roma Downey (2018)

Catholic New Age sympathizer Roma Downey has been surprisingly well-accepted in Christian circles. In an April 2, 2018 interview, she said:

> God is everywhere, in everyone.[45]

GENTLE BUT LETHAL

AUTHOR and researcher Walter Lord wrote the following in his book *The Night Lives On*:

> Just 20 minutes short of midnight, April 14, 1912, the great new White Star Liner *Titanic*, making her maiden voyage from Southampton to New York, had a rendezvous with ice in the calm, dark waters of the North Atlantic. She brushed the berg so gently that many on board didn't notice it, but so lethally that she was instantly doomed.[46]

And so it has been with the church as it has brushed up against the false teaching of the "God within" "so gently" that most people haven't even noticed, but "so lethally" that it will shipwreck the faith of those who do not recognize it, renounce it, and flee from it.

It only took a little leaven—a small area totaling just 12-13 square feet—to completely flood and shipwreck the "unsinkable" *Titanic*. In similar fashion, it will only take a little leaven—the heretical false teaching of God "in" everything—to completely leaven and destroy an undiscerning professing church.

Ye did run well; who did hinder you that ye should not obey the truth? This persuasion cometh not of him that calleth you. A little leaven leaveneth the whole lump. (Galatians 5:7-9)

❧ 3 ❧

SMART SHIP, SMART CHURCH

The *Titanic* woke them up. Never again would they be quite so sure of themselves. In technology especially, the disaster was a terrible blow. Here was the "unsinkable ship"—perhaps man's greatest engineering achievement—going down the first time it sailed.[1]

—Walter Lord
A Night to Remember

We have the epitome of a great science . . . quantum physics . . . Everyone is God.[2]

—J. Z. Knight
New Age channeler

As I studied the theories of quantum physics, I was reminded of a prophecy given by my father, author and teacher Charles Capps, "Some things which have required faith to believe will no longer require faith, for it will be proven to be scientific fact."[3]

—Pastor Annette Capps
Quantum Faith

❧THE TITANIC❧

S ome say the Gilded Age began just after the Civil War and ended with the sinking of the *Titanic*. This period of rapid technological growth, accompanied by graft, corruption, and huge amounts of accumulated wealth, derived its name from a Mark Twain novel. His book, *The Gilded Age*, satirized a society that gilded over its serious social, economic, political, and spiritual problems with the sudden wealth that accompanied its technological boom. This new era of industrial technology produced business barons like Andrew Carnegie, John D. Rockefeller, John Jacob Astor, and J. P. Morgan. It was Morgan's International Mercantile Industrial Corporation that owned the British White Star Line that operated the *Titanic*. In fact, J. P. Morgan was to be a passenger on the ship's maiden voyage until he cancelled at the last minute.

NOT A SMART SHIP

PRIOR to the disaster, the *Irish News and Belfast Morning News* described the *Titanic* as "A Masterpiece of Irish Brains and Industry."[4] However, immediately after the disaster, author and poet Thomas Hardy referred to the *Titanic* as the "smart ship" that was not so smart. In his sardonic poem, he wrote:

> And as the smart ship grew
> In stature, grace, and hue,
> In shadowy silent distance grew the Iceberg too.[5]

Until its demise, the *Titanic* was a supreme symbol of the Gilded Age notion that man and his "smart" technology had finally outsmarted the forces of nature. Grand possibility thinking seemed to prevail throughout the land. With the rapid advances being made in technology, even the impossible seemed possible. *Titanic*, with all its sheer opulence, bold bigness, and technological superiority, stood as proof positive that man could not only dream the impossible dream, he could now make that dream come true. As far as the world was concerned, the *Titanic* was—in every conceivable way—a "Ship of Dreams."

END OF A DREAM

IN his book *Titanic: The End of a Dream*, author Wyn Craig Wade describes how the *Titanic* was the "Dream" product of the "new sciences" and "new technology" of a "new age of industrialism"[6] that would ultimately lead to "the unity of mankind" and the establishment of the "Kingdom of Heaven" here on Earth. Wade explains how the new "physical technology" was making everything possible:

> Briefly stated, the Dream held that God's laws had been more precisely defined by the new sciences—those of social Darwinism as well as physical technology. Then came a teleological step: Man's condition had been improved by the new technology so that he could better meet the more perfectly manifested laws of God. Man's purpose, therefore, was to dedicate himself to applied technology and increased materialism; then, in time, the Kingdom of Heaven would be realized on earth.[7]

Wyn Craig Wade then quoted one dream enthusiast who truly believed the new technology would fulfill "history" and lead to "the unity of all mankind":

> "We are living," he said, "at a period of most wonderful transition which tends rapidly to accomplish that great end to which indeed all history points—the realization of the unity of mankind."[8]

However, at the height of this seemingly invincible era of big money, big business, big buildings, big ships, and big dreams—the big dream went under. The *Titanic*, sailing at nearly full speed on its maiden voyage to New York City, was suddenly shipwrecked after hitting an iceberg. In less than three hours the glorious "Ship of Dreams" found itself sitting very ingloriously at the bottom of the Atlantic Ocean.

So much for *Titanic's* state-of-the-art "smart" technology. The subtitle of Wyn Craig Wade's book *Titanic* says it all—*The End of a Dream*. The "unsinkable" ship was gone, and so was the dream. The "triumph" of modern technology and the unbridled dreams of the Gilded Age had suddenly hit the wall. And now, in today's "smart" world and "smart" church, with all the "smart" everything, physical technology is morphing into a quantum technology. Accompanying this quantum technology is a "smart" new "Quantum Spirituality." However, like the "smart ship" *Titanic*, this "smart" new Quantum Spirituality is also headed for disaster.

✎TODAY'S CHURCH✌

Much like the gilded era of the *Titanic*, today's ever-evolving "smart" technology is accompanied by its own postmodern version of possibility thinking. With all the rapid technological advances from "smart cars" that drive themselves to "smart" quantum computers that drive just about everything else, the world and the church are being prepared for a quantum future, a Quantum Spirituality—and a quantum New Age Christ.

QUANTUM FUTURE

AN August 18, 2019 article in *The Washington Post* states, "The quantum revolution is coming."[9] The writer describes the "emerging field" of "quantum technology" and how it is in the process of changing life as we know it. The article is a reminder of how discoveries in the new sciences are setting the present and future pace for quantum technology by presenting new ways of approaching not only our physical life, but spiritual life as well.

Certain physicists and self-described "futurists"—both in the New Age movement and in today's church—have introduced a quantum approach for a New Spirituality. This Quantum Spirituality promises to bring an otherwise divided world into harmonic convergence and spiritual "Oneness." These quantum advocates would have us believe that humanity is about to take a "quantum leap" into a new transformational Quantum Spirituality that will unify the world and all its religions. They say this is inevitable because quantum physics will soon "prove" that God is "in" everyone and everything. And because God will seem to be "in" everyone and everything, the world will come to believe that "we are all One" and "we are all connected" because "we are all a part of God." Thus, there is nothing that humanity cannot do or undo together as "God"—including rewriting the Bible to accommodate these new alleged quantum understandings.

New Age leaders anticipate a coming "Quantum Transformation"[10] when everyone becomes part of a massive "great awakening" as they "awaken" to their scientifically "proven" quantum self—the "God within." As a result, humanity will take that "quantum leap"[11] to a New World Religion based on this Quantum Spirituality. It will be seen as "one small spiritual step for man, one quantum leap for mankind."

QUANTUM LIE

A number of New Age biologists and New Age physicists are already using quantum physics to contend that God is "in" everyone and everything. New Age physicist Fritjov Capra's 1975 best-selling book, *The Tao of Physics: An Exploration of the Parallels between Modern Physics and Eastern Mysticism*, was one of the first books to present this quantum model to a mass audience. Capra explained how he gained special spiritual insight through a mystical drug experience he had in 1969 while sitting on a beach in Santa Cruz, California. He described what happened:

> I was sitting by the ocean one late summer afternoon, watching the waves rolling in and feeling the rhythm of my breathing, when I suddenly became aware of my whole environment as being engaged in a gigantic cosmic dance. . . . As I sat on that beach my former experiences [research in high-energy physics] came to life; I "saw" cascades of energy coming down from outer space, in which particles were created and destroyed in rhythmic pulses; I "saw" the atoms of the elements and those

of my body participating in this cosmic dance of energy; I felt its rhythm and I "heard" its sound, and at that moment I knew that this was the Dance of Shiva, the Lord of Dancers worshiped by the Hindus.[12]

Toward the end of Capra's book, there is a photograph of a statue depicting Shiva Nataraja, the Hindu god of creation and destruction. Shiva Nataraja is also known as the Lord of the Dance and symbolizes the Hinduistic "life force" known as "Shakti."

Building on his experience with the Shiva-like dancing particles, Capra made his case for a New Spirituality based on quantum physics— a Quantum Spirituality of "oneness." In the twenty-fifth anniversary edition of *The Tao of Physics*, Capra states that through the union of Eastern mysticism and modern physics, a "new spirituality" of "oneness" is being developed "both within and outside the churches." He writes:

> I had come to believe that the recognition of the similarities between modern physics and Eastern mysticism is part of a much larger movement, of a fundamental change of worldviews, or paradigms, in science and society, which is now happening throughout Europe and North America and which amounts to a profound cultural transformation.[13]

> The awareness of the unity and the mutual interrelation of all things and events, the experience of all phenomena as manifestations of a basic oneness, is also the most important common characteristic of Eastern worldviews.[14]

> On the other hand, I also believe that our own spiritual traditions will have to undergo some radical changes in order to be in harmony with the values of the new paradigm. The spirituality corresponding to the new vision of reality I have been outlining here is likely to be an ecological, earth-oriented, postpatriarchal spirituality. This kind of new spirituality is now being developed by many groups and movements, both within and outside the churches.[15]

Since Fritjov Capra's presentation of this "new spirituality," others have published similar accounts that include Curtis Allen's *Quantum Christ: The Truth Beyond Science and Religion*, Dalai Lama's *The Universe in a Single Atom: The Convergence of Science and Spirituality*, Gary Zukav's *Dancing Wu Li Masters: An Overview of the New Physics*, Diarmuid O' Murchu's *Quantum Theology: The Spiritual Implications of the New Physics*, Amit Goswami's *Science and Spirituality: A Quantum Integration*, David Hoffmeister's *Quantum Forgiveness: Physics, Meet Jesus*, and Deepak Chopra's *Quantum Healing: Exploring the Frontiers of Mind Body Medicine*—along with many other books that present this New Age/New Spirituality.

What the Bleep Do We Know!? is a movie that conveyed this same quantum message as it played in movie theaters around the country in 2004. In the film, New Age channeler J. Z. Knight, channeling an alleged 35,000-year-old entity named Ramtha, also promoted this "smart" New Spirituality and proclaimed, "We have the epitome of a great science . . . quantum physics . . . Everyone is God."[16]

While this emerging "Everyone is God" Quantum Spirituality may look scientific to an unsuspecting world and church, the Bible calls it for what it is—a "lie."

> And for this cause God shall send them strong delusion, that they should believe a lie. (2 Thessalonians 2:11)

QUANTUM FAITH

SADLY, some in today's professing church are pushing the idea that quantum physics will soon "prove" our faith. In her best-selling booklet *Quantum Faith*, Annette Capps, an ordained minister and president of Capps Ministries, writes:

> As I studied the theories of quantum physics, I was reminded of a prophecy given by my father, author and teacher Charles Capps, "Some things which have required faith to believe will no longer require faith, for it will be proven to be scientific fact."[17]

Quantum Faith has sold over 100,000 copies and is also posted free on the Internet. In her introduction, before you even begin to read what she has to say, she recommends New Age leader Gary Zukav's book, *The Dancing Wu Li Masters: An Overview of the New Physics.* The title and inspiration to write this book came to him while he was attending a workshop at the New Age Esalen Institute on the Northern California coast. His book lays out a seemingly scientific groundwork for the emerging New Age/New Spirituality or Quantum Spirituality that was starting to emerge in the 1970s. Zukav, now a leading New Age figure, went deeply into the New Age after writing his book on quantum physics. Where he was ultimately heading was tipped off in a telling comment he made in *The Dancing Wu Li Masters.* He wrote:

> The Wu Li Masters know that physicists are doing more than "discovering the endless diversity of nature." They are dancing with Kali, the Divine Mother of Hindu mythology.[18]

Yet, Annette Capps, as a professing Christian, does not hesitate to recommend Zukav's *The Dancing Wu Li Masters* and to share her misguided "Quantum Faith" with the church at large. Books that attempt to blend quantum physics with biblical Christianity include Jim Groves' *Quantum Christianity,* Judy Cannato's *Quantum Grace,* Phil Mason's *Quantum Glory,* and Bethel Church's *The Physics of Heaven.* The Bethel book unashamedly promotes "quantum mysticism"[19] and would have the church believe that we are "taking back truths from the New Age." Obviously, Bethel is paving the way for a Quantum Spirituality and great deception. Thanks to their skewed interpretation of quantum physics and Scripture, churches like Bethel are no longer opposing the teachings of the New Age—they are now proclaiming these quantum New Age "truths" as their very own. *The Physics of Heaven* co-author Ellyn Davis writes:

> At that time, I could not find a single Christian leader who shared a similar interest in finding out if there were truths hidden in the New Age. Now we are beginning to hear more and more revelation that is in line with what

New Agers have been saying all along and we are hearing more and more teaching about Christians "taking back truths" from the New Age that really belong to citizens of the Kingdom of God.[20]

QUANTUM SPIRITUALITY

ONE of the most deceptive "Christian" books in this quantum area is church leader Leonard Sweet's *Quantum Spirituality: A Postmodern Apologetic*. In his book, Sweet actually praises a number of New Age leaders for being his "personal role models" and "heroes."[21] He even credits them for helping him develop his Quantum Spirituality which redefines, reinterprets, and ultimately reinvents biblical Christianity in quantum, God "in" everything, New Age terms.

As cited, New Age physicist Fritjov Capra stated in 1975 that "our own spiritual traditions will have to undergo some radical changes in order to be in harmony with the values of the new paradigm." Sixteen years later, in his 1991 book, *Quantum Spirituality*, Leonard Sweet proposed one of the "radical changes"—accepting the idea of "God within." He describes "God within" as the "radical doctrine" of the "embodiment of God in the very substance of creation." Agreeing with New Age quantum figures like Gary Zukav and Fritjov Capra, Sweet introduces the "great heretical idea" of the "God within" as the foundational "doctrine" for his "smart" new Quantum Spirituality. In his book, he states:

> Quantum spirituality bonds us to all creation as well as to other members of the human family. . . . This entails a radical doctrine of embodiment of God in the very substance of creation.[22]

Sounding more like an Aquarian conspirator than the Christian theologian he is reputed to be, Leonard Sweet says:

> The church stands on the front lines of the coming reign of God. Or as biblical scholar J. Christiaan Beker entitles his

chapter on Paul's ecclesial thought, "The Church [is] the Dawning of the New Age."[23]

To remove any possible doubt about what Leonard Sweet means by Quantum Spirituality, he describes Catholic priest Pierre Teilhard de Chardin—the "Father of the New Age movement"[24]—as "Twentieth-century Christianity's major voice."[25] Yet, Sweet vehemently, and most unconvincingly, denies being a New Age sympathizer. But even as he tries to disavow the New Age by rhyming "New Age" with "sewage," his impassioned website denial falls flat when his teachings are examined. It becomes all too evident that he is just giving his New Age "Christianity" another name—Quantum Spirituality. A rose by any other name is still a rose, and Sweet's "Christianity" by any other name is still New Age.

Jesus warned about those who serve two masters (Matthew 6:24) as they profess with their mouth, but their hearts are far from Him (Matthew 15:8). Seeming to revel in his own spiritual cleverness, Leonard Sweet speaks out of both sides of his mouth as he endorses an immanent "God" who is "in" everyone and everything. In his book *soulTsunami*—with its front cover endorsement by Rick Warren—Sweet states:

> To survive in postmodern culture, one has to learn to speak
> out of both sides of the mouth. . . . Biblical theological is not
> circular with a fixed center, but elliptical, revolving around the
> double foci of God's immanence and God's transcendence.[26]

Quantum Spirituality was one of the first quantum books to subtly penetrate today's church like an unseen iceberg. Other books, like William Paul Young's *The Shack*, also introduced this same New Age/Quantum Spirituality. Young went so far as to have his "Jesus" reference the "quantum stuff"[27] of a God who "dwells in, around, and through all things."[28] And in Sarah Young's *Jesus Calling*, her "Jesus" similarly references that he is "in all" and that readers will meet him in eternity after taking a "quantum leap." Sarah Young's "Jesus" states:

I am above all, as well as in all.[29]

When you make that quantum leap into eternity, you will find Me awaiting you in heaven.[30]

However, the "God within" "Quantum Christ" awaiting the deceived church is not the true Jesus Christ of Nazareth in the Holy Bible. Rather, he is the deceptive false Christ of the New Age movement. He is the "Christ" of a "smart" New Age/New Spirituality. He is a wolf in "scientific" sheep's clothing.

QUANTUM PARTICLE

CERN, the European Organization for Nuclear Research, is located in Geneva, Switzerland and has the largest particle physics laboratory in the world. In 2012, precisely one hundred years after the sinking of the *Titanic*, CERN announced that its Large Hadron Collider (LHC)— the world's most powerful particle accelerator—had enabled them to discover the Higgs boson—the "God particle." This "God particle" is alleged to be the foundational particle that makes up all matter and is what led to the creation of the universe. A 2015 tech article states:

> CERN want to use the LHC to find out the fundamentals of our universe and how it was created, they want to recreate the Big Bang . . . to find other dimensions and open portals to these dimensions.[31]

It may be that one day soon the world will be told that quantum physicists have "smart" indisputable "scientific proof" that literal God "energy" is the "quantum stuff" in every sub-atomic particle. This foundational "God particle" will seem to "prove" that "we are all one" because God has been discovered to be "in" every sub-atomic particle. Thus, God is "in" everyone and everything. And because quantum physics is so hard for people to understand, most people will just take the quantum physicists' "expert" word for this "new scientific understanding."

Just as science has been used to allegedly "prove" how evolution, not creation, explains the origin of the universe, so quantum physics will seem to "prove" that God is "in" everything. The false teachers of the New Age and the church will be regarded as "woke" postmodern prophets—the first ones to understand and introduce this "New Spirituality" to the world and to the church. Everything will be turned upside down. Those who warned about this coming Quantum Spirituality will be the ones who are accused of not being "woke" and the ones who are spiritually deceived.

It is worth noting that a bronze statue of the Hindu god Shiva Nataraja stands at the entrance of the CERN laboratory in Switzerland. A plaque next to the statue contains several quotes from Fritjov Capra's book *The Tao of Physics*. *The Ancient History Encyclopedia* states that "Shiva Nataraja has become perhaps the most widespread icon of Hinduism."[32]

QUANTUM DISASTER

IN 1912, as the *Titanic* departed from Southampton, England, this "unsinkable" "smart ship" was proclaimed to be an incredibly advanced state-of-the-art technological wonder. Five days later all that "smart" technology lay shipwrecked at the bottom of the Atlantic Ocean. Likewise, today's wayward world and wayward church, with all its "smart" quantum technology and its "smart" Quantum New Age/New Spirituality is another disaster just waiting to happen.

O Timothy, keep that which is committed

to thy trust, avoiding profane and vain

babblings, and oppositions of science falsely

so called: Which some professing have erred

concerning the faith. (1 Timothy 6:20-21)

❧4❧

Ship of Dreams /
Ship of God's Dreams

The ship that would never be sunk, a ship of dreams—
becomes a ship of nightmares as it is swallowed beneath
the freezing Atlantic Ocean.[1]

—Robert Plant
Titanic: Ship of Dreams

Much provision is about to be released to fulfill the
dreams of God! . . . It is now time for dreams to be fulfilled
as the Ship of Dreams heads out into the Great Sea.[2]

—Faith Marie Baczko
New Apostolic Reformation church leader

❧THE TITANIC❧

The Ship of Dreams

Described as the "Ship of Dreams," the RMS *Titanic* was operated
by the British White Star Line and was built by the Harland and
Wolff shipyards in Belfast, Ireland. When it set sail on April 10, 1912
from Southampton, England bound for New York City, it weighed
over 46,000 tons, covered the length of four city blocks (882½ feet),
was the width of a four-lane highway (92½ feet), and its nine decks
were as tall as an eleven-story office building (175 feet).[3] With its

65

spacious promenades, elegant lounge modeled after a room in the Palace of Versailles, hand-carved grand staircase, elegantly furnished staterooms, Parisian café, Turkish bath, racquetball court, swimming pool, and well-equipped gymnasium, it is no wonder the *Titanic* was described as a "floating palace" and a "Ship of Dreams."

The biggest ship, and the biggest moving object of its time, the *Titanic* was a dream come true for transatlantic travelers. Prior to boarding, and in anticipation of what lay ahead for her family, the Countess of Rothes told a *New York Herald* reporter, "I am full of joyful expectation."[4] Besides wealthy passengers like the Countess and John Jacob Astor, emigrants from many countries boarded the ship with nothing but a suitcase of basic belongings and their hope-filled dreams of a bright new future. Like the Countess, they, too, were filled with "joyful expectation."

In almost every conceivable way, the *Titanic* seemed to be a literal "Ship of Dreams." But in the end, the big ship and the big dream became a big nightmare. The luxurious and seemingly unsinkable vessel was shipwrecked five days out on its maiden voyage. Today, over a century later, the *Titanic* lies in its watery grave some 400 miles off the coast of Newfoundland. Buried at sea with the "Ship of Dreams," were the shattered dreams of over fifteen hundred men, women, and children.

ᐊᗕTODAY'S CHURCHᗒᐅ

THE SHIP OF GOD'S DREAMS

Rick Warren's 1995 book *The Purpose Driven Church*, with its subtitle *Every Church Is Big in God's Eyes*, belies Rick Warren's fascination with "bigness." Big is good. Big is desirable. Big is great. As a seminary student, Warren did a major study on what makes a church "healthy" by writing to the one hundred "largest" churches in America. His study necessarily implied that the biggest ones were also the healthiest and best.

Warren authored one of the biggest best-selling non-fiction books in the history of publishing—*The Purpose Driven Life*. And just as the *Titanic* was the biggest moving object ever, Rick Warren's Purpose Driven movement has been the biggest church movement ever. However, the *Titanic* was a prime example that biggest does not necessarily mean best.

Warren's hugely attended Saddleback Church is headquartered in Lake Forest, California, with multiple other campuses stretching from Los Angeles to Hong Kong to Buenos Aires. With some 200 ministries, over 200,000 church leaders trained in his Purpose Driven philosophy, and a pastors.com website offering pastoral guidance to church leaders around the world, Rick Warren is piloting what could easily be referred to as an evangelical "ship of state."

Warren publicly proclaimed that he had a big dream and a big plan for his big Purpose Driven movement. He calls this big dream and big plan—"God's Dream for You—And the World!"[5] However, most people in today's church have no idea that the term "God's Dream" is an overlapping New Age concept that has had its roots in Theosophy and the occult for more than a century.

It is interesting that the term "Ship of Dreams" seems to represent and idealize the hopes and dreams of many of those who were aboard *Titanic*. Similarly, thanks to both New Age and church leaders, the overlapping term "God's Dream" has come to represent and idealize the hopes and dreams of both today's world and today's church. Yet few in the church are aware of the New Age implications of the term.

"Ship of Dreams" and "God's Dreams" seem to imply a powerful sense of hopeful expectation, promise, and success. Given the lofty grandeur of these two terms, how could anything possibly go wrong? Wouldn't a "Ship of Dreams" always reach its destination? Wouldn't "God's Dream" always come true? But history records what happened to the *Titanic*, and the Bible warns "not so fast" with an unbiblical concept like "God's Dream." After all, God "shall neither slumber nor sleep" (Psalm 121:4). He does not have to dream about the world and future events. "Declaring the end from the beginning," God knows exactly what the future holds:

> Declaring the end from the beginning, and from ancient times the things that are not yet done, saying, My counsel shall stand, and I will do all my pleasure. (Isaiah 46:10)

GOD'S DREAM & THEOSOPHY

THE term "God's Dream" can be traced at least as far back as the early 1900s where it was referenced in two theosophical/occult magazines published for those interested in Theosophy and the future coming of their "Christ," Maitreya. Eight years before *Titanic's* sailing, "God's Dream" was the title of a poem that introduced an article titled "Practical Theosophy" in a 1904 issue of *New Century Path* magazine.[6] Four years after the sinking of *Titanic*, the term "God's Dream" appeared again in a February 1916 issue of *The Theosophical Path* magazine.[7]

The Encyclopedia Britannica notes that the occultism that eventually came to be known as the New Age movement in the 1970s and 1980s, had its origins in early British theosophical groups. The encyclopedia said:

> The international New Age movement of the 1970s and '80s originated among independent theosophical groups in the United Kingdom.[8]

When future *Titanic* passenger William T. Stead was editor of the British *Pall Mall Gazette*, he enlisted Annie Besant, one of his "most intimate friends,"[9] to write a review of Theosophical Society founder Helena Blavatsky's pioneering work *The Secret Doctrine* when it was first published in 1888. The New Age significance of Stead introducing Annie Besant to Theosophy through Helena Blavatsky's book was huge. Not only did Besant give *The Secret Doctrine* a favorable review, she later met Blavatsky and became the president of the Theosophical Society in 1907, sixteen years after Blavatsky's passing. She would head the Theosophical Society for over a quarter century. During this time, she became quite vocal about the coming of their "world teacher"— Maitreya. Theosophical/New Age followers, from the late 1800s to the present day, have been anticipating the coming of this false Christ figure.

GOD'S DREAM & THE NEW AGE

MOST people in today's church are not aware of the occult/New Age origin of the term "God's Dream" from the early 1900s and how it has been used by a wide variety of New Age figures ever since. Here are some of the many examples.

The Theosophical Path Magazine (1916)

The following quote is from the February 1916 issue of *The Theosophical Path* magazine:

> We shall think then that this Earth and all her bright companions in the vast space are but drops of joy solidified, and the intense wonder and beauty of God's dream.[10]

Paramahansa Yogananda (1945)

This popular Eastern guru and yogi came to America and established a spiritual center in Southern California called the Self-Realization Fellowship (SRF). His book *Autobiography of a Yogi* has been a perennial best-seller. Paramahansa Yogananda spent his last thirty years in the United States and was responsible for teaching millions of Americans how to meditate and practice Yoga. He consistently taught about the alleged unity of Eastern and Western religions and would periodically reference "God's Dream" in his talks and writings. In a 1945 talk at his Self-Realization Fellowship Temple in Hollywood, California, Yogananda stated:

> That is the philosophy the great masters of India teach— that this world, this creation, is the dream of God.[11]

Sri Chinmoy (1974)

The late United Nations resident guru, Sri Chinmoy, conducted New Age meditations at the U.N. and had close associations with Mikhail Gorbachev, Nelson Mandela, and other world leaders. He said:

> God's Dream-Boat is man. . . .
>
> When you become one with God, you see that everything in God's Dream already embodies the Reality itself.[12]

The "Jesus" of *A Course in Miracles* (1975)

Everything being taught by the counterfeit "Jesus" of *A Course in Miracles* is predicated on the New Age concept of "God's Dream." This New Age "Jesus" teaches that humanity is literally "asleep," "dreaming," and believing they are "separate" and not "one" with God. To wake a sleeping humanity from their "fearful" dream of "separation," this New Age "Jesus" says that God is now sending them his "happy dream"—"God's Dream"—to enter their own dream and "awaken" them to their oneness with God.[13]

This New Age "Jesus" who spiritually dictated *A Course in Miracles* to Helen Schucman, channeled the *Course* to allegedly clarify concepts like "God's Dream" and "oneness" to enable humanity to save themselves and save the planet by "awakening" to the "God within." The "Jesus" of *A Course in Miracles* teaches that God has sent his dream of "oneness" to replace humanity's fearful dream of "separation." He says:

> Accept the dream He gave instead of yours. It is not difficult to change a dream when once the dreamer has been recognized. Rest in the Holy Spirit, and allow His gentle dreams to take the place of those you dreamed in terror and in fear of death.[14]

In a talk with the Schulleresque title—"God Will Redeem His Dream"—New Apostolic Reformation (NAR) "apostle" Dutch

Sheets sounds just like the counterfeit "Jesus" of *A Course in Miracles* regarding "God's Dream" when he says:

> That's the way God works. He gives you a dream but he hides a dream of his in your dream.[15]

Unbelievably, New Age *A Course in Miracles* study groups, led by a Robert Schuller staff member, met in classrooms at Schuller's Crystal Cathedral in the mid-1980s.[16] During this same time that they were meeting, pastors and church leaders from the U.S. and around the world were attending Schuller's Institute for Successful Church Leadership on the same cathedral grounds. But those attending didn't seem too concerned about Schuller's obvious New Age sympathies. They were too busy studying Schuller's "dare to dream" "God's Dream" success strategies on how to make their churches bigger and better and more successful.

Sun Myung Moon (1978)

Claiming to be the second coming of Christ, the late Sun Myung Moon was the false Christ leader of the "Moonies" and their worldwide Unification Church. His description of "God's Dream" is very similar to references in both the New Age movement and the NAR of today's professing church. In a 1978 talk, he stated:

> God's dream still remains unfulfilled. It was not fulfilled 2,000 years ago, or in the home of any religious leader or any American home, and today the Unification Church is here to pledge to fulfill that dream. We don't want to confine that fulfillment to our Church, but to expand it all over the world. Wouldn't that be the Kingdom of God on earth?[17]

Maitreya (1980)

As cited, Maitreya claims to be here in our world waiting for humanity to call him forth. In his 1980 channeled book, *Messages from Maitreya the Christ*, he reinforced the 1916 *The Theosophical Path* magazine article referencing "God's Dream." He stated:

> I am with you as God's Representative, as the Spokesman for that Divine Being Whose dreams we are.[18]

Wayne Dyer (1989)

The late best-selling author and psychologist, Wayne Dyer, was a familiar figure on Public Television (PBS) as he presented his New Age take on things. In his 1989 book *You'll See It When You Believe It*, he stated:

> Who is the ultimate dreamer? Call it as you will: God, higher consciousness, Krishna, Spirit, whatever pleases you. . . .
>
> One dream, one dreamer, billions of embodied characters setting out that one dream . . . Your true essence is that you are part and parcel of the one big dream.
>
> You the dreamer . . . God the dreamer.[19]

Neale Donald Walsch (2008)

This New Age author has had a series of best-selling books and writings based on his alleged "conversations with God" on a variety of subjects, including "God's Dream." In a 2008 online message, he wrote:

> God's "dream," if you please, is that we will all one day be completely realized [as "God"].[20]

Oprah Winfrey (2016)

At a 2006 "Live Your Best Life" seminar, Oprah used the term "God's Dream." She said:

I live inside God's dream for me. . . . God can dream a
bigger dream for you than you can dream for yourself.[21]

She also talked about "God's Dream" at the 2016 Essence Festival
in New Orleans. She asked those gathered:

What is God's Dream for you? . . . The key, the secret, the
magic is to surrender to God's Dream for you.[22]

When "God's Dream" is searched on the Internet, there are also
countless Christian references to this key New Age phrase. Pastors,
church leaders, evangelists, authors, bloggers, musicians, politicians,
and everyday believers regularly cite this New Age term as if it has
some sound scriptural basis. But it does not. It is never—not even
once—ever brought up in Scripture. What becomes apparent is
that this century-old New Age concept has become an overlapping
term to unify the world and the church through a mutually shared
dream—"God's Dream."

GOD'S DREAM & THE CHURCH

THE New Age concept of "God's Dream" was brought into the
church as early as 1974 by the late Robert Schuller. It was rein-
troduced, reinforced, and highly popularized by Pastor Rick Warren in 2003—and on up to the present. Thanks to Schuller and
Warren, "God's Dream" has become a go-to metaphor in today's
church. The following is just a small sampling of how this overlapping term has entered the church and continues to be a falsely
unifying metaphor.

Robert Schuller (1974)
The late Robert Schuller introduced the term "God's Dream" in
his 1974 book *Your Church Has Real Possibilities*. He wrote:

> Now pray the prayer of surrender. . . . Then ask the Holy
> Spirit to fill your mind with God's dream for your life.[23]

He used the term "God's Dream" in his 1978 book *Discover Your Possibilities*:

> Pray, seek God's guidance and what's going to happen? You'll
> get a dream to pursue. . . . Find a dream. Once you've got
> that dream and you know it's God's dream for your life, then
> be daring. Dare to say it. Let the redeemed of the Lord say
> so. Announce to the whole world that it's going to happen.[24]

Schuller continued to lay the groundwork for "God's Dream" by elaborating on the concept in his 1982 book *Self-Esteem: The New Reformation*. He used the term in a number of different contexts. He wrote:

> When God's dream is accepted, we must be prepared to pay
> a high price.[25]

> I am not fully forgiven until I allow God to write his new
> dream for my life on the blackboard of my mind, and I dare
> to believe "I am; therefore, I can. I am a child of God. I am
> somebody. God has a great plan to redeem society. He needs
> me and wants to use me."[26]

> Tremendous human energy is needed to walk God's walk,
> work God's work, fulfill God's will, and complete his dream
> for our self-esteem.[27]

Robert Schuller continued to use and popularize the term "God's Dream" up to the time of his death in 2015. In fact, the last book he wrote was titled *Don't Throw Away Tomorrow: Living God's Dream for Your Life*.

Rick Warren (2003)

In an October 27, 2003 e-mail to his church titled "God's Dream for You—And the World!," Rick Warren introduced "God's Dream" as being at the heart of his "New Reformation" Global Peace Plan. Some two decades after Robert Schuller introduced "God's Dream" as being at the heart of *his* "New Reformation" plan to "redeem society," Rick Warren effectively re-presented a more detailed version of Schuller's original plan.

Following Schuller's 1978 instruction to "Announce to the whole world" that "God's Dream" is "going to happen," Rick Warren did just that. He presented "God's Dream" for the church and the world and used Schuller's own words to reaffirm that "God's Dream" "is going to happen." He also said that his "God's Dream" "Global P.E.A.C.E. Plan" would "bring worldwide revival"[28] and "change history." In this 2003 e-mail to his church to be shared with the world, Rick Warren headlined it with "God's Dream" and wrote the following:

GOD'S DREAM FOR YOU—AND THE WORLD!

THIS WEEKEND, I'll begin a series of five messages on God's dream to use you globally—to literally use YOU to help change the world! I'll unveil our Global P.E.A.C.E. plan, and how God has uniquely prepared you for this moment of destiny. . . .

God is going to use you, and all of us together at Saddleback, to change history! . . .

The Global Peace Plan IS GOING TO HAPPEN.[29]

Over the years, Rick Warren has continued to popularize this overlapping New Age concept of "God's Dream." It is found in a number of his sermons, writings, radio programs, and videos. In the process, he has passed the concept of "God Dream" on to countless pastors and church leaders who trust him and look to him for leadership.

In 2016, Rick Warren issued a six-part sermon series on DVD titled *God's Dream for Your Life*. The title is the exact subtitle of Robert Schuller's 2014 book *Don't Throw Away Tomorrow: God's Dream for Your Life*. A Rick Warren article titled, "How You Can Realize God's

Dream for Your Life" was also published in a 2016 issue of *Charisma* magazine.[30] In a 2016 *Daily Hope* devotional piece titled "Dream Big," Rick Warren used Robert Schuller's 1978 "dare to dream God's Dream" concept, teaching that in order to receive God's blessing, you "must dare to ask," "God, what's your dream for my life?" He went so far as to suggest that one's faith is dependent on "choosing and believing God's dream for your life." In that devotional piece, he wrote:

> If you want God's blessing on your life this year, you must dare to ask for it. You must say, "God, what's your dream for my life?"[31]

> Faith is choosing and believing God's dream for your life. Nothing starts happening in your life until you start dreaming.[32]

Beginning in February 2020, Rick Warren initiated a 40-day "spiritual growth campaign" titled "Time to Dream" that again focused on the concept of "God's Dream." In a sermon titled "Dreaming the Future God Wants for You," Warren stated:

> If you don't dream you are sinning.[33]

The accompanying sermon notes said:

> After your relationship with Jesus, knowing God's dream for your life is the second-most important thing you will ever discover.[34]

Bruce Wilkinson (2003)

In October 2003, one of Rick Warren's self-described "best friends in the whole world," Bruce Wilkinson,[35] came to Saddleback to preach for a whole week about various aspects of "God's Dream." His messages, along with his new book *The Dream Giver*, were perfectly timed and designed to set the stage for Rick Warren's announcement about "God's Dream"—his Global P.E.A.C.E. Plan for the church and the world. In *The Dream Giver*, Wilkinson writes:

> You have been handcrafted by God to accomplish a part of His Big Dream for the world.[36]

Sarah Young (2004)

Jesus Calling author Sarah Young claims to have received messages from "Jesus." She writes them down and has turned these messages into numerous best-selling "Christian" books. In 2004 in *Jesus Calling*, her "Jesus" says:

> I may infuse within you a dream that seems far beyond your reach.[37]

The concept of "God's Dream" was also included in her 2010 book for children titled *Jesus Calling: 365 Devotions for Kids*. Her "Jesus" states:

> Dream your biggest, most incredible dream—and then know that I am able to do far more than that, far more than you can ever ask or imagine. Allow Me to fill your mind with My dreams for you.[38]

Brian McLaren (2006)

In his 2006 book *The Secret Message of Jesus*, emergent church leader and former pastor Brian McLaren writes:

> The call to faith is the call to trust God and God's dreams enough to realign our dreams with God's, to dream our little dreams within God's big dream.[39]

McLaren juxtaposes the concept of "God's Dream" with Martin Luther King's famous "I have a dream" speech—even though King never used the term "God's Dream" in his writings. McLaren writes:

> For all these reasons, "the dream of God" strikes me as a beautiful way to translate the message of the kingdom of God for hearers today. It is, of course, the language evoked by Dr. Martin Luther King Jr. as he stood on the steps of the Lincoln Memorial on August 28, 1963. His dream was God's dream, and that accounted for its amazing power.[40]

Shane Claiborne (2008)

In his 2008 book *Jesus for President*, this emergent author and social activist states:

> The end of war begins with people who believe that another world is possible and that another empire has already interrupted time and space and is taking over this earth with the dreams of God.[41]

Ravi Zacharias (2008)

The late Ravi Zacharias highlighted his 2008 National Day of Prayer keynote address in Washington DC by referring to "God's Dream," stating:

> You're the dream of God. He fashions you into his dream.[42]

Ten years later in 2018, speaking to 300 pastors and church leaders at a National Day of Prayer event honoring them, Zacharias again stressed the concept of "God's Dream" when he said:

> Prayer is what takes place when God is making you His dream. I think to me God was unfolding His dream in my life as He was unfolding it for a whole nation.[43]

Jim Wallis (2016)

In 2016, social-justice activist Jim Wallis stated that "God's dream" will "shape the end of human history." He wrote:

> We are still very much in the midst of the fulfillment of God's dream, but it is deeply satisfying that, even in the face of our pain and struggle, we have seen that dream and believe it will shape the end of human history.[44]

Joel Osteen (2017)

On a March 11, 2017 YouTube video, Houston Lakewood Church pastor Joel Osteen delivered a sermon titled "God's Dream for Your Life Is to Be Blessed and Be a Blessing to Others." It was not the first or last time that Osteen sounded like Robert Schuller and Rick Warren. In a July 2014 daily devotional titled "God's Dream for Your Life," Osteen stated:

> God's dream for your life is much bigger than your own.[45]

Pope Francis (2018)

Pope Francis frequently uses the term "God's Dream." He has stated:

> God's "dream" is his people.[46]

> God wants us to be able to dream like he does and, with him as we journey, to be quite attentive to reality—dreaming of a different world.[47]

> We are the dream of God who, truly in love, wants to change our life through love.[48]

Dr. Alan Keyes (2020)

In a June 9, 2020 article posted at ChurchMilitant.com and titled "God's Dream Is Better for Us," conservative Catholic political reformer, Alan Keyes, expressed his thoughts about the death of George Floyd and the massive protests that ensued. Equating "God's Dream" with Martin Luther King's "dream," Keyes presented "God's dream" as the positive antidote for America's social, political, and racial unrest. Joining the chorus of voices that are all invoking "God's Dream," Keyes wrote:

> Like MLK, America has a dream. These deluded self-made gods have only a nightmare. Whatever our faults, Americans must never forget: God's dream for us is better. Let us open our eyes to Him and let it be.[49]

The term "God's Dream" has also been used by Chip Ingram,[50] Mark Batterson,[51] James Robison,[52] Sally Lloyd-Jones,[53] Kenneth Copeland[54] and many other church leaders. Because the concept of "God's Dream" has been so heavily championed by Robert Schuller

A photo taken in front of an Assemblies of God church in Northern California

and Rick Warren over the years, this overlapping New Age term is now deeply embedded in today's professing church. It is becoming a more recognized part of our common language and may soon be a commonly accepted meme. It has come a long way from those obscure references in New Age theosophical magazines over a century ago.

GOD'S DREAM & REVIVAL

A question that necessarily arises is: Why are so many Christian leaders using a term like "God's Dream" that has no biblical precedent or scriptural justification? The answer is because they have unwittingly adopted an overlapping New Age term brought into the church and popularized by Robert Schuller and Rick Warren. "God's Dream" is now being used to characterize, encourage, and bring to fruition a "great awakening," a "great worldwide revival." The following are some of the ways this "God's Dream" "revival" is being presented by today's church leaders and how it will allegedly change and fulfill "history."

Leonard Sweet (1999)

Leonard Sweet described this future world "revival" as the fulfillment of "God's Dream." In his 1999 book *soulTsunami*, he says it is "a race to the future" and that we all have to "save God's Dream":

> There is a race to the future. Who will get there first? Will the Christian church? The time to save God's Dream is now. The people to save God's Dream are you. . . .
>
> God is birthing the greatest spiritual awakening in the history of the church. God is calling you to midwife that birth. Are you going to show up?[55]

Rick Warren (2003)

As previously cited, Saddleback pastor Rick Warren introduced his Global Peace Plan in 2003 as "God's Dream for You—And the World!" and how it would "change history." One of his former chief apologists stated that one of Warren's purposes regarding his "God's Dream" Peace Plan is to "bring worldwide revival."[56]

Bill Johnson (2006)

In his 2006 book *Dreaming With God*, NAR Bethel Church pastor Bill Johnson writes:

> Learning the dreams of God for this world is our beginning place.[57]

> I write that His Church would rise to her potential and change the course of world history.[58]

Lou Engle (2008)

In 2008, NAR leader Lou Engle called for the "dreamers of God's dream" to be "history-makers." A video once posted on Engle's website showed a stadium full of young people with a Scripture marked on their foreheads. One article noted:

> A highly disturbing video posted at The Call's website describes the extreme nature of this youth movement, and states that "those who come will be marked forever and they will be history-makers and dreamers of God's dream.[59]

The day-to-day heading on revivalist Lou Engle's 2020 website features the concept of "God's Dream." It states:

> When God created you, he had a dream and wrapped a body around that dream to fulfill it.[60]

Right below this is the big bold statement: "HISTORY IN THE MAKING."[61]

Lou Engle was featured with Bill Johnson, Rodney Howard-Browne, Benny Hinn, Todd White, Francis Chan, and other church figures in a

2019 "The Send" Conference led by NAR leaders to give further impetus to their much heralded "God's Dream" revival—their "Great Spiritual Awakening." More "revival" events have been planned for the future.

Sean Feucht (2020)

Echoing Lou Engle, Sean Feucht, a "revivalist" with a recent history as a worship leader at Bill Johnson's Bethel Church, writes:

> [A] company of people exists in almost every city. . . . They are the dreamers. They are the history makers.[62]

Feucht, having been greatly influenced by Lou Engle, is the founder of Burn 24/7, a "revival" movement in which its "heartbeat" is rooted in the concept of "God's Dream"—"to see the Father's dream for this generation realized."[63] On Feucht's Burn 24/7 website, under core values, it states:

> We can become the dream of God.[64]

THE SHIP OF DREAMS CHURCH

NAR "prophetess" Faith Marie Baczko uses some ironic metaphors as she puts this coming "revival" into ominous perspective. By combining the *Titanic*'s "Ship of Dreams" label with the overlapping New Age term of "God's Dream," Baczko describes the church as a "Ship of Dreams" heading out to sea to fulfill "the dreams of God." However, choosing the *Titanic*'s "Ship of Dreams" label linked with the New Age concept of "God's Dream" does not bode well for her gospel ship—or for the coming "revival." In fact, it has all the makings of both a metaphoric and literal shipwreck. She writes:

> Much provision is about to be released to fulfill the dreams of God! . . . It is now time for dreams to be fulfilled as the Ship of Dreams heads out into the Great Sea.[65]

As this *Titanic* "Ship of Dreams" namesake departs, lost in the rush for revival are the Bible's warnings about the danger that awaits them out there in the "Great Sea"—a "beast" and a beast system that will "rise up out of the sea" like an unforeseen iceberg, to turn their "Ship of Dreams" into a total nightmare:

> And I stood upon the sand of the sea, and saw a beast rise up out of the sea, having seven heads and ten horns, and upon his horns ten crowns, and upon his heads the name of blasphemy. (Revelation 13:1)

The New Age concept of "God's Dream" has been in the world for well over a century. But God doesn't dream, daydream, or pipedream when it comes to the future. God already knows the future and what it holds. Thankfully, He has warned us about it ahead of time in Scripture. Instead of a coming great revival, He has warned about a coming great deception. He says this deception will come through false Christs, false prophets, false teachers, false signs and wonders, and a false peace that is orchestrated by our Spiritual Adversary. And He specifically warns us to beware of "filthy dreamers" (Jude 1:8) and "dreamer[s] of dreams" (Deuteronomy 13:1-3) who prophesy "false dreams" like "God's Dream," that have nothing to do with Him.

Behold, I am against them that prophesy false dreams, saith the LORD, and do tell them, and cause my people to err by their lies, and by their lightness; yet I sent them not, nor commanded them: therefore they shall not profit this people at all, saith the LORD. (Jeremiah 23:32)

℘5℘

THE LAUNCH

After taking a little over two years to construct, and the efforts of as many as 3,000 shipyard workers, the *Titanic* ship launched to great fanfare, attended by a throng of spectators and members of the world's press.[1]

—titanicfacts.net

I thank God for what He is doing throughout the earth today. I thank Him for the fire that broke out in Toronto and spread around the globe. . . . He will make you ready, and then—at the appropriate time—He will launch you.[2]

—Randy Clark
Lighting Fires

℘THE TITANIC℘

On May 31, 1911, over 100,000 people, including ninety newspaper representatives from around the world, gathered at Belfast, Ireland's Harland and Wolff shipyard and along the banks of the River Lagan to watch the public launch of the RMS *Titanic* from land into water. Present for this historic occasion were J. P. Morgan, the president of the International Mercantile Marine Company and owner of the White Star Line; J. Bruce Ismay, chairman and managing director of the White Star Line; Lord William James Pirrie, the chairman of Harland and Wolff; the mayor of Belfast; and a host of other dignitaries.

The anticipation and excitement of the crowd was tangible. After two years of construction and the dedicated commitment of three thousand workers, the largest moving object in the world—the "Ship of Dreams"—was about to slide into the Victoria Channel. With a rocket exploding in the sky overhead, the hydraulic triggers restraining the ship were released at slip number three. Twenty-two tons of tallow, soft soap, and train oil enabled the massive ship to slide along 772-foot-long platforms and into the water in a short but breathtaking sixty-two seconds. One of the ship workers was overheard saying, "We just builds 'em and shove 'em in."

Once the ship slid completely into the water, six anchor chains and two piles of drag chains that weighed eighty tons apiece secured it. Five tugboats then towed it to a nearby berth where the next phase of work took place with the ship machinery being installed and all the lavish interior and exterior finishing work meticulously completed.[3]

PREMONITIONS

AMIDST all the positive fanfare at the launch, who in attendance would have ever imagined they had just witnessed the launch of a future disaster? George Behe, founder of the Titanic Historical Society, discovered that at least 899 people claimed they had "premonitions of disaster."[4] They either did not proceed to book passage as planned, or they cancelled their existing reservations because of their uneasiness about the ship.

Behe described how Mr. B. O. Shepherd from Hemingford, Nebraska finished his business in England and made a reservation well in advance to return home on the *Titanic*. However, he cancelled it when his wife had a "frightening" dream that the *Titanic* would sink. Behe wrote:

> Back home in Hemingford, his wife had a frightening dream
> in which she saw *Titanic* sinking. So shaken was she that she

immediately wrote a letter to her husband, asking him not to take *Titanic* home. Deciding that her letter was not enough, she then sent him a cable repeating her plea. Upon reading these missives from his wife, Mr. Shepherd was so impressed that he did cancel his reservation on *Titanic* and transferred to another White Star steamship.[5]

Several days after the disaster, the *Denver Post* described how Cleveland's J. C. Middleton, president of the Canton and Akron Railroad, had a "terrible" recurring dream before sailing that he shared with his wife and two friends. At the urging of his wife, he canceled his reservations. The two friends signed affidavits affirming that he had told them of his dream "prior to the tragedy." Mr. Middleton stated:

> I was to have sailed on the *Titanic,* having booked my passage on March 23. On the night of April 3 I experienced this terrible dream. I saw the *Titanic* go down in midocean and hundreds of people struggling frantically in the water. The

next night I had the same dream. When I told my wife she immediately importuned me to cancel our passage and I did so after ascertaining that business in America did not necessitate my return at this time.[6]

In another case, Mrs. Edward Bill from Philadelphia convinced her husband to cancel their reservations after experiencing feelings of fearful foreboding regarding the *Titanic*. Booking passage on another ship, they never boarded the doomed vessel. Her husband recounted what happened:

I had our rooms all picked out on the *Titanic*, and I told my wife that it would be interesting to be on the greatest ship in the world on her maiden trip. Mrs. Bill was not very enthusiastic, and when I started for the White Star office to get the tickets, she begged me not to go. She said that she couldn't tell why, but said she didn't want to go on the *Titanic*. I had never known her to object to any plan of travel I suggested before, but this time she was immovably firm, and I yielded to her wishes reluctantly.[7]

The "Ship of Dreams" may have seemed unsinkable to many people, but not to Mrs. B. O. Shepherd, Mr. J. C. Middleton, Mrs. Edward Bill, and many others. Something about the highly heralded ship just didn't seem right. And so it would be with the celebrated launch of an alleged revival some eighty-two years later in Toronto, Canada.

Massive numbers of people would converge on the Toronto Airport Vineyard Fellowship. They believed that the so-called "Toronto Blessing" was the launch of a great modern-day revival. However, to many others—the Shepherds, the Middletons, and the Bills of the church—the launch of the Toronto Blessing felt more like the launch of the *Titanic*. Something about it felt very wrong and dangerous.

❧TODAY'S CHURCH☙

Toronto Blessing

On January 20, 1994, the Toronto Blessing—an alleged outpouring of the Holy Spirit—was launched when hyper-charismatic pastor Randy Clark spoke at the Toronto Airport Vineyard Fellowship in Toronto, Canada. Local pastor John Arnott had invited the St. Louis pastor to be the guest speaker. Clark described how a phenomenon that became known as "holy laughter" totally transformed his life and ministry. After his giving witness to this alleged move of the Holy Spirit, various manifestations erupted among those gathered—most particularly "holy laughter." With people laughing and falling to the floor, it seemed to most of those gathered that God was bringing much-needed "joy" and "revival" to the church.

But were any of those getting "hit" with "holy laughter" praying for God's "wisdom" (James 1:5) regarding what was happening? Was anyone "testing the spirits" (1 John 4:1-3) or "searching the Scriptures" (Acts 17:11) to see if these manifestations were really from God? Most people just went with the flow. They took for granted that what they were experiencing was a touch from God and the launch of a great revival.

Because of the "joy" and "laughter" generated by Pastor Clark's presence, he was asked to stay on and hold daily meetings at the Toronto church. For the next six weeks as he preached and testified, "holy laughter" continued to manifest as news of the Toronto Blessing spread like wildfire. The word was out: God was doing "a new thing" in Toronto, and more than 2300 pastors flew in from around the world. No one wanted to miss out on what was happening.

Within a year of the "holy laughter" launch, this fast-growing Vineyard church that could only seat four to five hundred people, moved to a new location that could seat five thousand. Within five years, over two million people had traveled to Toronto to experience the "revival." Canadian journalist Robert Hough's article in *Toronto Life* magazine provided readers with some of what he witnessed regarding "holy laughter" and the so-called revival. He wrote:

> The man sitting beside me, Dwayne from California, roared like a wounded lion. The woman beside Dwayne started jerking so badly her hands struck her face. People fell like dominoes, collapsing chairs as they plunged to the carpeting. They howled like wolves, brayed like donkeys and—in the case of a young man standing near the sound board—started clucking like a feral chicken.[8]

HOLY GHOST BARTENDER

HOWEVER, the man behind all the laughter—the one who was actually responsible for launching the Toronto Blessing and all the "holy laughter"—was not Randy Clark but rather a transplanted South African evangelist named Rodney Howard-Browne. Previous to his appearance at the Toronto church, Clark said he had received his "anointing" from Howard-Browne at a large conference in Tulsa, Oklahoma. Clark recounted how Rodney Howard-Browne "slapped" him gently on the head, and down he went. When he tried to get up, he couldn't move. He felt like he was "stuck to the floor." It was there he had his "first indication" that something "totally new" was taking place. Not really knowing "what was going on," he just assumed that what he was experiencing was from God. Recounting the incident, Clark explained:

> That's the first indication I had that God was doing something totally new on earth today. I lay on the floor for forty-five minutes while the evangelist walked around the auditorium, proclaiming, "Fill! Fill! Fill!" I didn't understand what was going on. I just thought, This is my last chance, and lay there until God was finished doing whatever it was that He was doing that I didn't understand.[9]

Later when he could finally stand up, he got in line again and had another encounter with Howard-Browne. Clark described the incident:

> When he came to me, Rodney Howard-Browne said, "You don't get drunk on a sip!" He slapped me on the head again, and again down I went. This time I was up and in another line before I knew it, and for a third time he slapped me as he prayed, "Fill! Fill! Fill!" This time I remember thinking, Oh no! I'm in trouble now! Down I went for a third time.[10]

Howard-Browne later commented in an interview about the impartation and "anointing" Clark received from him at that conference:

> All I know is that a guy by the name of Randy Clark came to the meeting, and God fell on him and he came forward. I remember him coming to me with his hands ablaze and said, "My hands are burning." I said, "Yeah, that's the anointing. You know what it's for?" I said, "Go back to your church and lay hands on everything that moves." And he went back to his church, laid hands on everything that moved, the next week he went to Toronto and the rest is history.[11]

At church gatherings like the one in Tulsa, Rodney Howard-Browne would exhort people like Randy Clark to "take a drink" as he called down "fire from heaven" and "imparted" the spirit of "holy laughter" and "joy" through his preaching, his laying on of hands, and by his very presence. Laughing hysterically and uncontrollably, people fell to the floor—some for hours—doing what came to be known as "carpet time." It was this highly transferrable "impartation" from Rodney Howard-Browne that Pastor Clark had brought to the Toronto Airport Vineyard Fellowship in 1994. This Vineyard Fellowship was subsequently renamed the Toronto Airport Christian Fellowship (TACF) in 1996 and was renamed again in 2010 as Catch the Fire Toronto.

The Toronto Blessing was the "mother ship"—if you will—for other alleged revivals that have broken out since. Countless present-day ministries, like that of Bethel's Bill Johnson, can be traced back to Toronto and the influence of Rodney Howard-Browne. Reflecting on the Toronto Blessing, TBN television host Sid Roth described his frequent guest, Rodney Howard-Browne, as a catalyst who "brought the move of the Holy Spirit for the three greatest revivals in modern-day history."[12] Roth called Howard-Browne a "fire starter" and how those touched by him become "fire starters" too.[13]

Yet as Rodney Howard-Browne's popularity increased, so did many questions about the self-described "Holy Ghost Bartender." Was the "drunken" "holy laughter" and "holy ghost fire" he called down from Heaven really from God? Or was it the "strange fire" warned about in the Bible that was not from God (Leviticus 10:1-10)? One thing was for sure, like the Israelites dancing around the golden calf, Rodney Howard-Browne's uproarious meetings seemed more like a bacchanalian revolt than anything resembling legitimate revival.

WHEN REVIVAL IS REVOLTING

MANY people were not impressed by "holy laughter" and the Toronto Blessing. The "revival" was seen as a sure "fire" sign-of-the-times. The hysterical laughter, loss of self-control, mental confusion, and falling to the floor, sometimes for hours, seemed to bear no resemblance to true revivals—revivals where holy sorrow and deep repentance took precedence. But "holy laughter" advocates like Sid Roth equated what happened in Toronto with historic revivals of the past. And those who searched the Scriptures and tested the spirits regarding "holy laughter" were immediately branded as modern-day "Pharisees"—the "frozen chosen." They were disdainfully described as "quenching the spirit" and being "totally blind" to what "God was doing."

So while "holy laughter" convinced countless Christians that God was doing a "new thing" and sending a great end-days revival, others believed that God was allowing a great end-days deception—that the "laughing revival" was a "strong delusion" and founded on "all power and signs and lying wonders" that were not from Him (2 Thessalonians 2:9-11).

Many believed that Rodney Howard-Browne was deceived and deceiving others (2 Timothy 3:13). They were convinced the power displayed in his meetings was not from God and the "drinks" the "Holy Ghost Bartender" was dispensing were spiked with "another spirit" (2 Corinthians 11:4). Many thought that Howard-Browne may have gotten his own wish when he said he would rather have the Devil "manifesting" in his meetings than to have no manifestations at all. In *The Coming Revival*, Howard-Browne wrote:

> But I'd rather be in a church where the devil and the flesh are manifesting than in a church where nothing is happening because people are too afraid to manifest anything. . . .
>
> And if a devil manifests, don't worry about that, either. Rejoice, because at least something is happening.[14]

MY WILL BE DONE

THE major concern regarding Rodney Howard-Browne is how he received his alleged "anointing" in the first place. On Sid Roth's television program *It's Supernatural*, Howard-Browne told the TBN host that he received his "fire," "laughter," and "tongues," after "shouting" at God for "about 20 minutes" at "the top" of his voice. He said he told God to either "come down" and "touch" him with His "fire" or he would go "up there" to "touch" Him. "Shouting" his insistent demands, he said:

> "Lord, I want your fire." And I was shouting at the top of my voice, and I did this for about 20 minutes. . . . And I was crying out, I said, "Lord, either you come down and touch me or I'm coming up there to touch you." And I meant it. "I've got to have your touch." And it was like suddenly somebody

poured like it was warm oil or honey, or however you want to describe it. I sometimes say like gasoline and then took a match, I mean just set me on fire. From the top of my head to my feet. It was like electricity was running through me. . . . This was glorious. . . . It was like a river was flowing out of me. I was laughing, I was crying, and I was speaking in tongues all at the same time. I was beside myself.[15]

Rodney Howard-Browne's presumptuous "my will be done" prayer was hardly biblical or godly. In fact, his threat to go up and "touch" God if his own needs were not met, sounded more like Satan's "I will ascend into heaven" (Isaiah 14:13) than the humble request of a man who fears and reveres the Most High God. Jesus was very clear. We are to pray, "Lord, thy will be done" (Matthew 6:10), not I want what I want—"my will be done." Howard-Browne's actions are reminiscent of the Bible's account of Simon the Sorcerer—yet even more extreme. After Simon the Sorcerer "believed" and "was baptized," he wanted the disciples to lay hands on him so that he, too, could receive the Holy Ghost power he had been witnessing in them. He wanted it so he could lay hands on people and impart this same power. But his request was denied because his heart was "not right in the sight of God" (Acts 8:9-24). Many people believe that Rodney Howard-Browne's demands were similarly denied—that his "my will be done" heart was "not right in the sight of God."

There is no doubt that Rodney Howard-Browne received "power"—but what kind of power did he receive, and who did he receive it from? And what did this "power" do to his soul and to the souls of those he touched? God doesn't send His Holy Spirit to people on demand. In fact, the Bible warns that in the latter days, God will be sending "strong delusion" to those who do not have a love of the truth—whose hearts, like Simon the Sorcerer—are not right with God (2 Thessalonians 2:11). Sometimes, God will *seem* to give people their request but will send "leanness into their soul" instead.

And he gave them their request; but sent leanness into their soul. (Psalm 106:15)

No Laughing Matter

THOSE concerned about Rodney Howard-Browne and "holy laughter" were immediately countered by the high praise heaped upon him by the 700 Club, TBN, *Charisma* magazine, pastors, church leaders, talk-show hosts, and other professing believers. The launch of the Toronto Blessing, along with other "revival" gatherings over the last twenty-five years or so, have convinced many in today's church that God is about to bring a "great spiritual revival" to the world and the church. Toronto pastor John Arnott stated that the church needs to prepare "for the greatest harvest of souls the world has ever seen." He said:

> I think God is up to something big. I believe we're headed for the greatest harvest of souls the world has ever seen, and we want to be prepared.[16]

Steve Schultz, founder and publisher of the NAR's "Elijah List," quoted revivalist Faith Marie Baczko regarding the shift into "a new season" as people "graduated from preparation to being launched out":

> We have shifted into a new season and have graduated from preparation to being launched out as an apostolic people with assignments to establish the government and rule of God in our communities, cities and even some nations—with signs and miracles.[17]

Other voices, not just the hyper-charismatics, have also been preaching about the coming of a historic revival. Today's church is being told to overlook denominational differences for the sake of this "revival"—that we must come together in "unity" for the purpose of this "great awakening." However, the late researcher and author Tamara Hartzell warned that spiritual deception and spiritual disaster arise when truth is sacrificed on the "altar of unity."[18] This is especially so when some of what are being called "minor" differences among church people are actually "major" differences—most notably when the "fire" driving the "revival" is a "strange fire" (Leviticus 10:1) and the "spirit" behind the "revival" is "another spirit" (2 Corinthians 11:4).

HOLY LAUGHTER APOLOGIST

LONGTIME church figure Dr. Michael Brown wrote a 1995 book after the launch of the Toronto Blessing. It was titled *From Holy Laughter to Holy Fire: America on the Edge of Revival.* He alleged that the "holy laughter" phenomenon helped launch what would become an "international awakening" of "huge"—"titanic" if you will—proportions. He wrote:

> There is no question but that we are at the beginning of an international awakening of huge proportions.[19]

However, the Bible makes no mention of a great "international awakening" at the end of time. Church figures like Rodney Howard-Browne, Randy Clark, and Michael Brown may affirm it—but Scripture does not. It is worth noting that the deceptive spirit "Julia"—who was channeled through *Titanic* passenger William T. Stead—also pointed to an international awakening. "Julia" described it as a future "great spiritual awakening among the nations." "Julia" said this international "awakening" would be founded on the doctrine of "the immanence of the Divine"—God "in" everything. As previously cited, "Julia" had channeled the following through Stead:

> What they tell me on all sides, and especially my dear guides, is that the time is come when there is to be a great spiritual awakening among the nations, and that the agency which is to bring this about is the sudden and conclusive demonstration, in every individual case which seeks for it, of the reality of the spirit, of the permanence of the soul, and the immanence of the Divine.[20]

NEW AGE PLANETARY PENTECOST

TODAY'S New Age leaders—along with many church figures like John Arnott and Dr. Michael Brown—are similarly heralding a future "great awakening" like the one described by "Julia" well over a century ago. The New Age leaders are describing this coming worldwide "revival" as a "Planetary Pentecost."[21] Many of today's church leaders similarly describe this coming "revival" as a "Second Pentecost."[22] Sounding much akin to "holy laughter," the New Age Planetary Pentecost is also referred to as the "Planetary Smile."[23] Also sounding like "holy laughter," the false New Age Christ has made it known that in his coming Planetary Pentecost "all sensitive persons" will experience "the joy of the force, flooding their systems with love and attraction" and "uncontrollable joy." He says:

> An uncontrollable joy will ripple through the thinking layer of the Earth. The co-creative systems, which are lying psychologically dormant in humanity will be activated. From within, all sensitive persons will feel the joy of the force, flooding their systems with love and attraction.[24]

Twisting passages from the Bible's Book of Joel in an attempt to prove that this Planetary Pentecost is prophesied in Scripture, the New Age Christ states that when humanity recognizes its "oneness" with everyone and everything, God's Spirit will be poured out on all flesh.[25]

The false Christ Maitreya's channel and spokesman, the late Benjamin Creme, promised that this coming world "revival" will be "a Pentecostal experience for all"—"even the fundamentalists."[26]

One must wonder if the "holy laughter" experienced by many in today's church has actually been a deceptive dress rehearsal for the coming New Age Christ and his Planetary Pentecost. And it is more than curious that the counterfeit "Jesus" of the New Age *A Course in Miracles* states that when all humanity "awakens" to "God's

Dream" of "unity" and "oneness," history will be fulfilled and "the world will end in laughter."[27]

Channeling through New Age leader Barbara Marx Hubbard in her book *The Revelation*, the false New Age Christ also states that his Planetary Pentecost—his "Planetary Smile"—with its "joy of the force" and "uncontrollable joy," will produce an irreversible shift of human consciousness. It will be a "Quantum Transformation" felt and experienced around the world.[28] This Quantum Transformation will be for all those who surrender themselves to the "joy of the force"—to this "Pentecostal experience for all."

The New Age Christ describes how people who submit themselves to this "uncontrollable joy" will find themselves making a "quantum leap"[29] to the next level of their spiritual growth. He proclaims it will be a born again "Planetary Birth Experience"[30] for the whole human race—a "collective awakening"[31] to a joyful "Oneness" with the world through the shared experience of the "God within."

Even though this Planetary Pentecost sounds almost identical to the "Second Pentecost" being heralded by many of today's church leaders, hardly anyone wants to talk of the obvious similarities between the two groups. However, definite questions need to be asked. For instance, will the coming "international awakening" described by Dr. Michael Brown and other church leaders merge with this "great spiritual awakening" heralded by William Stead's "Julia," today's New Age leaders, and their false New Age Christ? Will Leonard Sweet's Quantum Spirituality morph and merge with the New Age/New Spirituality and their Quantum Transformation? Is all this "revival" activity paving the way for all humanity—including a deceived professing church—to make a "Quantum leap" in a "Quantum instant"[32] to a Quantum New Age Christ? And are all the present calls for revival—in the world *and* in the church—preparing the way for Jesus Christ *or* Antichrist? These and other questions are not being addressed as today's professing church launches out on its own "Ship of Dreams" that bears far too much resemblance to that 1912 "Ship of Dreams" that never reached its appointed destination.

There is a curious footnote to these New Age teachings on the "joy of the force" and the Quantum Transformation. While visiting a friend in Florida, I happened to catch Rodney Howard-Browne on cable television. Pacing around as he so often does, he said, something to the effect of, "You can gain the whole world and lose your family." He mentioned he was about to become a grandfather. Almost out of nowhere he suggested that maybe the grandchild would be named "Q"—or maybe the child would be named "Quantum."

CHURCH AS A SHIP OF DREAMS

NEW Apostolic Reformation "prophetess" Faith Marie Baczko discussed her involvement with the 1994 Toronto Blessing and how she believes the "dreams of God" have been furthered by the wide reach of the Toronto movement. As cited, she likens the church to a "Ship of Dreams" that symbolizes and represents a last great revival movement she believes is yet to come:

> The move of the Holy Spirit in 1994, known as the Toronto Blessing I believe is a key to understanding of the present times. God suddenly showed up in Canada in 1994 in one of the most powerful moves of the Holy Spirit, a move that has touched millions of lives globally . . . the question that arises is, was this a random act of mercy, or was it unto something much greater in God's end-time campaign?

> At the height of the renewal, I was there at every opportunity, sometimes three or four times per week. . . . Since 1994, I have also heard thousands of testimonies of pastors, leaders, ministries and individuals who, having been mightily touched by God in Toronto, went on to birth the awesome and wonderful dreams of God that have greatly impacted the church and the world![33]

I believe The Toronto Blessing was the initial Move of the Spirit in a "Short Work" of preparation for the last great outpouring of glory! THE ARMIES OF HEAVEN ARE PREPARING TO INVADE PLANET EARTH IN THE LAST GREAT INVASION to fulfill the plan of God! The long great journey of His-story is on its last leg. . . . In God's END GAME He is strategically preparing "LANDING CITIES" for an invasion of His Heavenly Hosts all over the earth, positioned for revival.[34]

Much provision is about to be released to fulfill the dreams of God! . . . It is now time for dreams to be fulfilled as the Ship of Dreams heads out into the Great Sea.[35]

The *Titanic*'s White Star Line management was very proud of their "Ship of Dreams." Today's New Apostolic Reformation church leaders seem to be equally proud of their "Ship of Dreams." Having launched their "Ship of Dreams," NAR leaders like Faith Marie Baczko are urging today's greater church to climb aboard. Claiming to speak for God, she says it is time for the "dreams of God" to be fulfilled as the church's "Ship of Dreams" heads out into the "Great Sea" for a "great revival." The "Ship of Dreams" *Titanic* and the "Ship of Dreams" professing church: Two seemingly unsinkable ships with seemingly unsinkable dreams. The former being a long-ago shipwreck. The latter being a shipwreck that is in progress today.

Behold, they shall surely gather together,

but not by me. (Isaiah 54:15)

❧6❧

Ark of Safety/Ark of Oneness

Titanic was not labelled the "unsinkable" ship purely by chance. She possessed a number of cutting edge and well thought out safety features that made those involved in her construction supremely confident that she would never founder.[1]

—ultimatetitanic.com

Humanity's spiritual Ark is being built by many groups as the platform of the new world religion (Emerging One Church). Although it gives the appearance of being "Christian," or "following Christ," it is a New Age Ark of Oneness. The builders of this Ark are offering the peace and safety of Oneness with God and with each other to all who are spiritual enough to get on board.[2]

—Tamara Hartzell
"New Age Ark of Oneness"

It's time to build new arks.[3]

—Leonard Sweet
soulTsunami

❧THE TITANIC❧

As the *Titanic* set sail on April 10, 1912 from Southampton, England bound for New York City, nearly everyone believed the huge ship to be invincible. Like Noah's Ark, it was considered to be an unsinkable ark of safety—a lifeboat in and of itself. A 1911 issue of *Shipbuilder* magazine described the *Titanic* as being "practically unsinkable."[4] When Mrs. Albert Caldwell was boarding the *Titanic* in Southampton, she asked a crew member if it was true the ship was unsinkable. He told her—"Yes, lady, God himself could not sink this ship."[5]

With its sixteen compact watertight bulkhead compartments, *Titanic* could remain afloat even if any two of these compartments were breached—even four of the first five. But it did not occur to anyone that more than two of these compartments would ever be penetrated—much less the five that were. It was generally assumed that even a head-on collision with another ship or iceberg would only pierce two of the watertight compartments at most.

Seven months before *Titanic's* maiden voyage, her sister ship, the *Olympic*, with the same Captain Edward Smith at the helm, had a serious accident when the Royal Navy cruiser HMS *Hawke* was inadvertently drawn into *Olympic's* powerful wake. A collision ensued, but even with a huge hole in *Olympic's* steel hull, only two of the ship's safety compartments were breached. As a result, the injured vessel stayed completely afloat as passengers were transferred to a nearby rescue ship by *Olympic's* existing lifeboats. And while there were not enough lifeboats for every passenger, there were sufficient lifeboats to ferry everyone to the safety of the rescue ship. The damaged *Olympic* was then towed back to the Belfast shipyard for necessary repairs.

This *Olympic* incident served to reinforce the already established assumption that *Titanic* would similarly stay afloat after any type of accident. Because of this belief, there was no real concern that its twenty lifeboats could only accommodate half of those on board. *Titanic* management considered the lifeboats they had to be more than adequate to ferry people to a nearby rescue ship in case of an accident. In fact, they were proud of the fact that their ship carried four more lifeboats than the minimum sixteen required by law. Captain Smith stated a number of times prior to *Titanic's* sailing that the ship was, for all intents and purposes, unsinkable. He said that even if the ship were cut in half, "each half would remain afloat indefinitely."[6]

Incredibly, the existing British shipping regulations did not require a lifeboat seat for every passenger. The outdated regulations had not anticipated the huge ships that were about to be built. The number of required lifeboats had been calculated for ships up to 10,000 tons, not for the bigger and more recently built ships like *Titanic* that weighed 40,000 tons or more. Also, the British Board of Trade agency responsible for lifeboat regulations was largely comprised of shipowners who had a vested interest in economy. They were more concerned about luxurious deck space for passenger comfort than for seemingly unnecessary lifeboats.

UNSINKABLE NEW AGE ARK

THE Bible records that "Noah found grace in the eyes of the LORD" and was told by God to prepare an Ark that would be a safe refuge from the massive flood He was about to send upon the Earth (Genesis 6:8-22). Because of Noah's obedience to God, the Ark became an Ark of Safety from God's judgment upon a world gone wrong—a world that was "corrupt before God" and "filled with violence." Because Noah was faithful (Hebrews 11:7) and obedient (Genesis 6:22), he "found grace in the eyes of the Lord" (Genesis 6:8), thus, he and his family were spared.

The New Age "Jesus" teaches that "God's Dream" is based on the New Age idea of "Oneness"—"Oneness" being the shared universal divinity of all mankind. Using Noah's Ark as a metaphoric lifeboat for all humanity, he states that "God's Dream" will be fulfilled and humanity saved when everyone acknowledges their shared divinity by boarding his "Ark of Oneness." The New Age ark is said to be a guaranteed "ark" of "peace and safety" for all who come aboard. But humanity must first accept "God's Dream" of "Oneness" in order to board his New Age ark; and to accept "God's Dream" of "Oneness," everyone must first "awaken"—be "woke"—to the universal "God within."

By accepting "God's Dream" of unity and "Oneness" and not their own self-deluded dream of "separation," people would be acknowledging that all creation is "One" because God is "in" everyone and everything. This realization—this "great awakening"—is said to be humanity's ticket to peace and safety and ultimate salvation. The false New Age Christ, through his many channeled books and New Age spokespersons, teaches it is only by "awakening" to the "God within" and their "Oneness" with "God" that the members of humanity can save themselves and save the world.

The false New Age "Jesus" assures everyone that by affirming their God "in" everything "Oneness," they will be safely delivered through troubled waters and troubled times. To avoid danger and destruction, all they need to do is accept "God's Dream" and climb aboard his "Ship of God's Dreams"—his "ark of peace"—his "ark of safety"—his "unsinkable" "Ark of Oneness." The counterfeit New Age "Jesus" lays it all out:

> The recognition of God is the recognition of yourself.[7]

> God's Oneness and ours are not separate, because His Oneness encompasses ours.[8]

> The oneness of the Creator and the creation is your wholeness, your sanity and your limitless power.[9]

> Creation is the holy Son of God. . . . Its oneness is forever guaranteed inviolate.[10]

> The ark of peace is entered two by two, yet the beginning of another world goes with them.[11]

> The world will wash away and yet this house will stand forever, for its strength lies not within itself alone. It is an ark of safety.[12]

ONENESS: THE ARK OF HUMANITY

NEW Age matriarch Helena Blavatsky referred to this spiritual "Ark of Oneness" as the "new ark called Humanity."[13] New Age leader Deepak Chopra, echoing Blavatsky and other occult/New Age sources, refers to it as an "Ark of Hope" for a "New Humanity."[14] What the New Age "God" and "Christ" have been saying through their designated spokespersons is cunningly clear: Their "Gospel of Oneness" will save the world. It is said to be an "unsinkable" "ark of peace and safety" for all who climb aboard and enter in.

This "Ark of Oneness" is being presented to a troubled world as the way out of our planetary predicament. To save ourselves and save our planet, we must accept "God's Dream" and board his "unsinkable" "Ark of Oneness"—his "ark of peace and safety." Yet the Bible specifically warns about the future sudden destruction that will follow a time of "peace and safety," which, by way of analogy, brings to mind the "peace and safety" that prevailed on the *Titanic* before its sudden destruction.

> For when they shall say, Peace and safety; then sudden destruction cometh upon them, as travail upon a woman with child; and they shall not escape. (1 Thessalonians 5:3)

BOARD THE NEW AGE ARK OR DIE

IN Tamara Hartzell's monograph "New Age Ark of Oneness," she warned:

> Boarding this Ark of Oneness denies that the Lord Jesus Christ is the truth and declares that all religions have their own truth included.[15]

> Sooner than we think, people will be given the choice to either get on board the Ark of Oneness or remain in the great sea of separateness and get "swallowed up" in the coming storm of judgment.[16]

Channeled through numerous New Age leaders, the New Age Christ makes it clear that a choice looms before humanity if it wants to survive. Offering free passage on his "Ark of Oneness," this false Christ nevertheless warns that those who refuse to board his "Ark" will die just as surely as those who were not aboard Noah's Ark. He says those who reject "God's Dream" of "peace and safety" through "Oneness" are free to do that. However, their insistence on remaining "separate," and their refusal to see God "in" everything, will necessarily hinder the flow of divinity in the body of humanity—which is said to be the body of "God" and "Christ." Those who refuse to subscribe to "God's Dream" and to the "God within" are said to disrupt and short-circuit the flow of "God energy" in humanity's body. These "resisters" are regarded as "self-centered" and "separate." These "nay-sayers" are seen as "cancer cells" and must be healed or eliminated. The New Age Christ warns:

> [T]he fundamental regression is self-centeredness, or the illusion that you are separate from God. I "make war" on self-centeredness.[17]

> At the co-creative stage of evolution, one self-centered soul is like a lethal cancer cell in a body: deadly to itself and to the whole.[18]

> The surgeon dare leave no cancer in the body when he closes up the wound after a delicate operation. We dare leave no self-centeredness on Earth after the selection process.[19]

> The selection process will exclude all who are exclusive. The selection process assures that only the loving will evolve to the stage of co-creator.[20]

> All that hinders the manifestation of man's divinity must be driven from our planet.[21]

In other words: Get on board the New Age "Ark of Oneness" or physically die. Yet the Bible warns that if you get on this deceptive ark of "peace and safety," this deceptive "Ship of Dreams," you will *spiritually* die. To get on board the New Age "Ark of Oneness" would be the equivalent of boarding a postmodern *Titanic*. This New Age "Ship of God's Dreams" is not unsinkable. It *will* go down.

✖TODAY'S CHURCH✖

NEW AGE ARK OF ONENESS

In her "New Age Ark of Oneness" monograph, Tamara Hartzell describes her extreme disappointment in revisiting the Noah's Ark exhibit she remembered so fondly from her childhood in Fresno, California. She wrote:

> As a child growing up in Fresno, my favorite attraction was Roeding Park with its Zoo and Storyland. As its name implies, Storyland is a play area for kids featuring explorative displays and audio recordings of different children's stories, such as The Three Little Pigs, Goldilocks, and various others. A Noah's Ark display has also been included that featured a walk-through Ark made into a Christian Chapel, complete with stained glass windows and pews.
>
> This past spring I had the opportunity to revisit Roeding Park. At first, the Noah's Ark display appeared unchanged. It still seemed to be the same Christian Chapel. However, as I entered the Ark/Chapel I stood stunned and in disbelief. Neatly painted on the back of the pews were messages from different religions. As I stood there in dismay, I knew that I should not be surprised at the change. Yet despite having watched and warned about the New Spirituality's relativism sweeping through the world and churches, I still found myself taken aback by the transformation to this attraction for young kids.[22]

Hartzell said it was with "polished subtlety" that "deceptive interfaith messages" from Buddhism, Islam, Confucianism, Judaism, and Zoroastrianism were written on the various pews along with the Christian sayings.[23] She further observed how the transformation of her childhood Christian ark was symbolic of what is happening in the church today:

> These changes to the ark exemplify what is happening in Christianity today. The universal faith of the Emerging One Church is becoming so dominant in our sleeping churches and world that many people will look at the above messages and wonder what, if anything, is wrong with them. Even worse, many people won't even care, little realizing that not understanding the answer could end up costing them their very soul. As is happening in today's Christianity, this Christian ark has been successfully transformed into a New Age Ark of Oneness, yet many people would look at it and believe that it is still completely Christian. After all, aren't the messages just positive goodwill messages about truth, peace, love, and brotherhood? How could this possibly cost anyone their soul?[24]

GOSPEL OF ONENESS

AS mentioned, the "Gospel of Oneness" teaching that God is "in" everyone and everything has already breached the walls of the church. This leeched-in leaven has entered the church through multiple best-selling "Christian" books and undiscerning church leaders.

The late Eugene Peterson invoked the New Age concept of "Oneness" in his *Message* paraphrase of Ephesians 4:6 when he stated that God was "present in all." However, the apostle Paul's words were specifically addressed to believers in the Lord Jesus Christ. His "you" in the Scripture specifically referred to "the saints which are at Ephesus" and "the faithful in Christ Jesus," not to humanity in general. Yet Peterson chose to universalize this passage, making it totally compatible and "One" with New Age teachings about the "God within" and universal "Oneness." Compare Ephesians 4:6 as rendered in *The Message* with the *King James Version*:

One God and Father of all, who is above all, and through all, and in you all. *(KJV)*

. . . one God and Father of all, who rules over all, works through all, and is present in all. Everything you are and think and do is permeated with Oneness. *(MSG)*

In a more indirect and tangential way, Peterson presented this same New Age reference to "Oneness" in his *Message* paraphrase of the Lord's Prayer. Instead of the standard phrase "in earth as it is in heaven," Peterson rendered it "as above, so below." Unbeknownst to most believers, "as above, so below" is a several thousand-year-old occult term that refers to the immanent "God within"—the "God" who is "in" everyone and everything. This occult maxim is well known in New Age circles. It is said to be the key to all magic and mystery. In their book *As Above, So Below*, the editors of the *New Age Journal* describe how this occult concept signifies the unifying and fundamental truth of the universe—"Oneness":

This maxim implies that the transcendent God beyond the physical universe and the immanent God within ourselves are one. Heaven and Earth, spirit and matter, the invisible and the visible worlds form a unity to which we are intimately linked.[25]

NEW AGE IN THE CHURCH

LEONARD Sweet is one of the more prominent church figures to have introduced the "great heretical idea" of "God within" and its attendant "Oneness" into the church. In his 1999 book *AquaChurch: Essential Leadership Arts for Piloting Your Church in Today's Fluid Culture*, Sweet purports to advise the church on how to make its way through the world's troubled waters. However, Sweet's book advising the church on how to successfully navigate through today's "fluid culture" is like *Titanic* Captain Edward Smith writing a book on "How to Avoid Colliding with Icebergs as You Travel Through the North Atlantic Ocean."

As cited, Leonard Sweet revealed his New Age sympathies in his 1991 book *Quantum Spirituality: A Postmodern Apologetic*, when he described the "Father" of the New Age movement, Pierre Teilhard de Chardin, as "Twentieth-century Christianity's major voice."[26] However, to the unsuspecting Christian reader, Sweet's *AquaChurch* might appear to be totally biblical. Especially when the word "piloting" in the subtitle of his book is presumably drawn from the beloved church hymn "Jesus, Savior, Pilot Me." He quotes the whole first stanza in his book:

Jesus, Savior, pilot me
Over life's tempestuous sea;
Unknown waves before me roll,
Hiding rock and treacherous shoal;
Chart and compass come from Thee:
Jesus, Savior, pilot me.[27]

Yet in the very next paragraph, immediately after quoting those lines from the Christian hymn, he enthusiastically quotes Pierre Teilhard de Chardin. Leonard Sweet, by juxtaposing the lines from "Jesus Savior, Pilot Me" with the "Father" of the New Age movement, obscures the New Age implications of what he is doing. Throwing church martyrs, church forefathers, and most Bible-believing Christians under the proverbial bus, Sweet implies that Teilhard—and other enlightened leaders like Sweet himself—see "Christ" in a "much more magnificent way" than those who have had a more fundamental biblical view throughout history. Right after quoting those lines from "Jesus Savior, Pilot Me," note how Sweet quotes Pierre Teilhard de Chardin's rather smug New Age proclamation:

Christ is in the Church in the same way as the sun is before our eyes. We see the same sun as our fathers saw, and yet we understand it in a much more magnificent way.[28]

By linking the words of a traditional Christian hymn with the words from the "Father" of the New Age movement, Leonard Sweet is clearly speaking out of both sides of his mouth again. As previously cited, he uses this "double-tongued" practice to seemingly assert that God is being seen in a much more magnificent way because He is not only transcendent ("out" there), but also immanent ("in" everyone and everything). He writes:

> To survive in postmodern culture, one has to learn to speak out of both sides of the mouth. It should not be hard, since Christianity has always insisted on having things both ways. Isn't it based on the impossible possibility of Jesus being "beyond us, yet ourselves" (poet Wallace Stevens)? Biblical theological is not circular with a fixed center, but elliptical, revolving around the double foci of God's immanence and God's transcendence.[29]

As also previously cited, Sweet had already defined what he meant by "immanence" in his book *Quantum Spirituality*. He stated that God is embodied "in the very substance of creation":

> Quantum spirituality bonds us to all creation as well as to other members of the human family. . . . This entails a radical doctrine of embodiment of God in the very substance of creation. . . . But a spirituality that is not in some way entheistic (whether pan- or trans-), that does not extend to the spirit-matter of the cosmos, is not Christian.[30]

Also in *Quantum Spirituality*, Sweet makes his case for worldwide "unity" and "Oneness" by quoting Catholic mystic and New Age sympathizer, Thomas Merton:

> We are already one. But we imagine that we are not. And what we have to recover is our original unity.[31]

Thus, it is quite telling when Leonard Sweet describes himself as "dangerously Christian." In *soulTsunami*, he states:

> I tell people I am "dangerously Christian." I proclaim a "shock gospel." I confess to being an "out-of-control disciple."[32]

I believe what Sweet is really saying is that he is a professing Christian who is "dangerously" New Age: That he is an "out-of-control disciple" who is so hidden in plain sight that his "shocking" New Age gospel doesn't seem so shocking to an undiscerning and unsuspecting church.

SWEET & WARREN TOGETHER

IN a recorded 1995 audio presentation titled *The Tides of Change: Riding the Next Wave of Ministry*, Leonard Sweet and Rick Warren have a "quantum" conversation as they favorably discuss "quantum metaphors" and the New Spirituality they see "being birthed" around them. Among other things, they talk of "waves of revival," "waves of renewal," and "waves of receptivity in the church." Sweet tells Warren:

> Yeah, this is a wave period. I really love that metaphor of the wave and the wavelength. First of all, it is a quantum metaphor. It brings us out of the Newtonian world into this new science [quantum physics]. The other way I like about it so much, is that it brings us into the language of resonance. Wavelength. [33]

Waves, wavelengths, quantum metaphors—all leading to a New Spirituality based on false New Age teachings and a spiritual perversion of quantum physics. It is not hard to see why the man who wrote *Quantum Spirituality* chose a hymn that had the line "unknown waves before me roll" just prior to his introducing Pierre Teilhard de Chardin's New Age take on postmodern Christianity.

Rick Warren and Leonard Sweet's audio presentation was part of an ongoing tape series called "Choice Voices for Church Leadership," distributed by Abington Press. The title may very well have been taken from one of Teilhard's most famous quotes. Teilhard wrote:

> The day will come when, after harnessing the ether, the winds, the tides, gravitation, we shall harness for God the energies of love. And, on that day, for the second time in the history of the world, man will have discovered fire.[34]

Not surprisingly, Teilhard's passage is quoted in *The Aquarian Conspiracy* and in other New Age books and writings. It refers to the consuming fire of the New Age Christ and how his allegedly enlightened New Age Spirituality will change the world and change the "tides" of history. *The Tides of Change: Riding the Next Wave of Ministry* title seems to perfectly frame Leonard Sweet and Rick Warren's talk about waves, wavelengths, quantum metaphors—and changing church tides.

Teilhard's rediscovered "fire"—the "strange fire" of "God within" "Oneness"—will probably be presented as scientific "quantum" fact in the future. As such, it will put people under the "strong delusion" that they are understanding "Christ" in a newly enlightened and "much more magnificent way."

QUANTUM TITANIC

IN reflecting on the subtitle of *AquaChurch* about "piloting your church in today's fluid culture," one marvels at Leonard Sweet's attempts to "enlighten" the church with his New Age ideas. In *A "Wonderful" Deception*, I noted how Sweet—much like *Titanic's* Captain Edward Smith—was racing the church into some very dangerous waters. I wrote:

> Highly intellectual and well-read, Leonard Sweet almost dares you to keep up with him as he charges through the spiritual marketplace. Operating at lightning speed and quoting from countless books and articles, he will impress many readers with his quick wit and spiritual insights. However, as he treacherously dives into New Age waters and challenges his readers to go

there with him, serious problems arise within his "postmodern apologetic."[35]

In 2008, Rick Warren conducted two small-group workshops with Leonard Sweet in California and Georgia. When Sweet's New Age sympathies and his open alignment with Warren were brought to public light in 2009, Warren's chief apologist at the time quickly defended Sweet:

> Doctrinally/theologically, Leonard Sweet is about as Christian as anyone can get.[36]

But the truth is that Leonard Sweet's Quantum Spirituality is about as dangerously New Age as any Christian can get. It disarms unsuspecting believers by seeming to present the true Gospel while simultaneously introducing the Quantum/New Age/New Spirituality gospel of "Oneness." The much respected pastor Harry Ironside specifically warned about false teachings that combine truth and error. He stated:

> Error is like leaven, of which we read, "A little leaven leaveneth the whole lump." Truth mixed with error is equivalent to all error, except that it is more innocent looking and, therefore, more dangerous. God hates such a mixture! Any error, or any truth-and-error mixture, calls for definite exposure and repudiation. To condone such is to be unfaithful to God and His Word and treacherous to imperiled souls for whom Christ died.[37]

Leonard Sweet introduces the idea of building new arks. However, his new arks dovetail with the New Age "Ark of Oneness." Meanwhile, his reference to the *Titanic* in his book *soulTsunami* falls flat as he bids the church to "save God's Dream" by climbing aboard a "new ark"—a seemingly unsinkable Ark of Oneness that is, in reality, just another *Titanic*—a quantum *Titanic*. Sweet writes:

> Like the *Titanic*, the modern world has taken on water and is sinking fast.[38]

It's time to build new arks.[39]

The time to save God's Dream is now. The people to save God's Dream are you.[40]

God is birthing the greatest spiritual awakening in the history of the church. God is calling you to midwife that birth. Are you going to show up?[41]

Again, almost as an "All aboard" call for this "new ark"—his quantum "Ark of Oneness," Sweet quotes Thomas Merton:

We are already one. But we imagine that we are not. And what we have to recover is our original unity.[42]

Leonard Sweet, Rick Warren, and other church figures allude to the need for a "New Reformation" in today's church—a "wave revival" that will be the greatest "spiritual awakening" in the "history" of the church. However, the "Ship of God's Dreams" they are "piloting" through our "fluid culture" bears more resemblance to the New Age "Ark of Oneness" and the *Titanic* than it does any true Gospel ship.

In Genesis 11:6-9, regarding the Tower of Babel, the Lord is not pleased with those who are into worldly "Oneness":

Behold, the people is one, and they have all one language; and this they begin to do: and now nothing will be restrained from them, which they have imagined to do. Go to, let us go down, and there confound their language, that they may not understand one another's speech. So the LORD scattered them abroad from thence upon the face of all the earth: and they left off to build the city.

It is also important to note that the way of "Oneness" is an all-inclusive "broad" way. By subscribing to New Age Oneness, the world and a deceived church will be on the broad way that leads to "destruction"—the broad way that the biblical Jesus said "many" would go down. He warned that the way to "life" is not broad but "narrow," and "few" actually find it.

> Enter ye in at the strait gate: for wide is the gate, and broad is the way, that leadeth to destruction, and many there be which go in thereat: Because strait is the gate, and narrow is the way, which leadeth unto life, and few there be that find it. (Matthew 7:13-14)

The apostle Paul warned the church "night and day with tears" that after his departing "grievous wolves" would "enter in" "not sparing the flock" as they spoke "perverse things." (Acts 20:29-31). Jude warned of certain "ungodly men" who "crept in unawares" (Jude 1:4). Jesus Himself warned us to beware of these "false prophets" who come "in sheep's clothing, but inwardly they are ravening wolves" (Matthew 7:15). In similar manner, Peter warned about these same "false prophets" and "false teachers" whose "damnable heresies"—like the "God within"—will bring "destruction" upon themselves and to those who choose to follow them.

But there were false prophets also among the people,

even as there shall be false teachers among you,

who privily shall bring in damnable heresies, even

denying the Lord that bought them, and bring

upon themselves swift destruction. (2 Peter 2:1)

❧7❧

FALSE CONFIDENCE, COMPLACENCY, & DENIAL

When anyone asks how I can best describe my experience in nearly forty years at sea, I merely say, uneventful. . . . I never saw a wreck and never have been wrecked, nor was I ever in any predicament that threatened to end in disaster of any sort.[1]

—*Titanic* Captain Edward Smith (1907)
Five years prior to *Titanic's* sinking

It helps to know that Satan is entirely predictable.[2]

—Rick Warren
The Purpose Driven Life

❧THE TITANIC❧

In his classic book about the *Titanic*—*A Night to Remember*—author Walter Lord wrote that the sinking of the *Titanic* "marked the end of a general feeling of confidence."[3] The shipwreck sent shockwaves throughout the world as confidence in modern technology took a direct hit. The "unsinkable" ship had done the unthinkable. It had suddenly shipwrecked and was now at the bottom of the North Atlantic Ocean.

On April 18, 1912, just three days after the *Titanic* sank, the *Denver Post* reported that Captain Smith had told an American friend prior to the ship's sailing that the *Titanic* was unsinkable, and the ship would "mark a high point of safety and comfort in the evolution of ocean travel." The article was boldly captioned: "*TITANIC* CAN'T SINK, SMITH TOLD FRIEND."[4] It described a dinner conversation Captain Smith had in Flushing, Long Island with Mr. and Mrs. W. P. Willis, the night before he sailed to Europe to assume captaining the *Titanic*. Mr. Willis said that Captain Smith was "enthusiastic" about his new command and that he and the ship's designers had the "utmost confidence" in the ship's capability. Smith told him that "it was impossible for her to sink." It was the same bravura Captain Smith had expressed in a 1907 interview published in New York papers after successfully bringing another White Star Liner, the *Adriatic*, across the ocean on its maiden voyage. He said:

> When anyone asks how I can best describe my experience in nearly forty years at sea, I merely say, uneventful . . . I have never been in any accident of any sort worth speaking about. . . . I never saw a wreck and never have been wrecked, nor was I ever in any predicament that threatened to end in disaster of any sort. You see, I am not very good material for a story. I cannot imagine any condition which would cause a ship to founder. I cannot conceive of any vital disaster happening to this vessel. Modern shipbuilding has gone beyond that.[5]

It was the same false confidence expressed by the *Titanic* deck hand who told Mrs. Albert Caldwell that "God himself could not sink this ship." Even after the boat sank, *Titanic* officials were still declaring the ship to be unsinkable. When news of the disaster started to reach New York on April 15th, Philip Franklin, vice president of the White Star Line tried to pacify the public by assuring them that the *Titanic* couldn't have sunk because it was unsinkable. He told them:

> We place absolute confidence in the *Titanic*. We believe that the boat is unsinkable.[6]

After receiving further reports, Franklin had to correct his previous statement. Openly distraught, he said:

> I thought her unsinkable, and I based my opinion on the best expert advice. I do not understand it.[7]

THE HYMN-SING

FALSE confidence in the ship had been expressed by many people in many ways. Surviving passenger Lawrence Beesley recounted that several hours before the fatal collision, Reverend Ernest C. Carter of the Church of England and a hundred or so passengers had gathered together that last Sunday evening for a "hymn-sing." Beesley recalled that many of the hymns people sang had to do with "dangers at sea." He said he noticed "the hushed tone" when everyone sang "For Those in Peril on the Sea." In closing the evening hymn-sing, Beesley remembered Reverend Carter giving thanks for the "safety" of the voyage thus far and affirming "the great confidence" they all had in the "steadiness" and "size" of the ship and the "happy outlook" they all had. Beesley wrote:

> Mr. Carter brought the evening to a close by a few words of thanks to the purser for the use of the saloon, a short sketch of the happiness and safety of the voyage hitherto, the great confidence all felt on board this great liner with her steadiness and her size, and the happy outlook of landing in a few hours in New York at the close of a delightful voyage; and all the time he spoke, a few miles ahead of us lay the "peril on the sea" that was to sink this same great liner with many of those on board who listened with gratitude to his simple, heartfelt words. So much for the frailty of human hopes and for the confidence reposed in material human designs.[8]

Reverend Carter added an ironic note as he closed the evening hymn-sing. He said:

> It is the first time that there have been hymns sung on this boat on a Sunday evening, but we trust and pray it won't be the last.[9]

NOT ENOUGH LIFEBOATS

IT is well known that the *Titanic* was tragically deficient in the number of lifeboats available for passengers and crew, even though there was enough deck space for a sufficient number of lifeboats. Ironically, the ship's twenty lifeboats were four more than the sixteen that were only required by the grossly outdated British shipping regulations. There were fourteen main wooden lifeboats with a seating capacity for 65 people in each. There were two emergency sea boats with a seating capacity for 40 people in each. In addition, there were four Englehardt collapsible boats with a capacity for 47 people in each. However, these 20 lifeboats could only accommodate 1178 of the over 2200 people on board, and that was only if all of the lifeboats were filled to capacity—which they were not. It's estimated that just over 700 people made it into the lifeboats and survived. Over 1500 people died.

Because Captain Smith knew there were not enough lifeboats for everyone, he ordered that women and children be given preference in the lifeboats. Several men would be allowed on to serve as oarsmen. If women and children were unwilling or unavailable at the time of a particular lifeboat loading, discretionary seating for male passengers was permitted on the starboard side of the ship by First Officer William Murdoch. However, Second Officer Charles Lightoller, strictly maintained the women and children only rule on the port side. He did not allow any additional men on his lifeboats even if seats were available. Due to a variety of misunderstandings, misinformation, and insufficient training, the lifeboats were sent out to sea with over 470 empty seats. For instance, lifeboat #7 with a capacity for 65 people was sent out with just 28 on board and lifeboat #1 with a capacity for 40 people was sent out with just 12 on board.

False Confidence in a Sinking Ship

ANOTHER big reason for the empty lifeboat seats was that many passengers had more confidence in the doomed vessel than in what would prove to be the sure safety of the lifeboats. Years later, surviving passenger Alice Cleaver Williams recalled people's false confidence in the sinking ship. She said:

> [T]here was plenty of room in the lifeboats, because people refused to leave thinking it was safer on the ship.[10]

Typical of many passengers who could have boarded a lifeboat but chose to stay on the *Titanic*, Harry Widener told fellow traveler William Carter:

> I think I'll stick to the big ship, Billy, and take a chance.[11]

Lack of Preparedness

TITANIC was woefully unprepared for disaster; while the most obvious deficiency was in not having enough lifeboats for everyone, there were other factors too. For instance, the lack of thorough sea trials was one of the most serious shortcomings. Walter Lord described *Titanic's* half day of sea trials as "amazingly perfunctory" when contrasted with the six weeks of sea trials undertaken by the ocean liner *United States*.[12] He explained:

> Certainly the *Titanic's* trials could not have been very helpful. They took up only half a day in Belfast Lough. During this time she never went at full speed. First, she spent several hours making twists and turns, then four more hours on a straight run down the Lough and back. She made only one test to see how fast she could stop.[13]

Titanic Sea Trials, April 2, 1912

It has also been well documented that the _Titanic_ crew was unfamiliar with the new ship. The practice of properly uncovering the lifeboats, loading them, and then lowering them to the sea below had been very brief. Also, as cited, the scheduled boat drill on Sunday, the day of the collision, had been cancelled by Captain Smith.

Other factors signified a general unpreparedness: If those watertight compartments had been built just one deck higher, the ship would not have flooded so quickly and rescue ships like the _Carpathia_ could have arrived in time to save everyone. Also, the binoculars assigned to the crow's nest lookouts were missing and thus not available for use. In addition, the telegraph operators were not White Star Line employees, and their communication with the officer's bridge was less than ideal. The telegraph itself was relatively new and regarded more as a vehicle for sending passenger messages than in communicating with other ships to assure ship safety.

Responding to the suddenness and overall unpreparedness of the _Titanic_ tragedy, Salvation Army General William Booth sent a telegram to American president William Howard Taft. He said that the _Titanic_ disaster shows us the necessity of spiritually preparing for the world to come. He wrote that it "speaks to the multitudes of the reality and nearness of the world to come, and of the urgency and overwhelming necessity of preparing for it."[14]

GREED

NOVELIST Joseph Conrad, author of the literary classics *Lord Jim* and *The Heart of Darkness*, had been at sea much of his life. After the *Titanic* disaster, he cynically noted how safety had been compromised in the building of big luxurious ships like the *Titanic*. He wrote:

> For my part I could much sooner believe in an unsinkable ship of 3,000 tons than in one of 40,000 tons. In reading the reports, the first reflection which occurs to one is that, if that luckless ship had been a couple of hundred feet shorter, she would probably have gone clear of the danger. But then, perhaps, she could not have had a swimming bath and a French café. That, of course, is a serious consideration.[15]

Conrad's sarcastic remarks were indicative of many people who were seeing how luxury and greed had played their part in the disaster. For example, deck space that should have accommodated sufficient lifeboats was left open to make it more appealing for passengers to take casual walks and relax in deck chairs. It was clear that *Titanic* management made luxury, not safety, their first priority. What had been a floating palace became a sinking deathtrap.

Stanley Bowdle, a marine engineer, was quoted after the disaster stating that the many lives lost had been sacrificed to luxury. He said that big extravagant ships like the *Titanic* were "degenerate in size, foolish in enjoyment, and criminal in speed."[16] And *The Washington Post* quoted Navy Admiral George Dewey stating:

> I think that every passenger who crosses the North Atlantic takes his life in his hands every time. . . . For myself, I would rather go around the world in a well-equipped man-of-war than make a trip across the North Atlantic in a transatlantic vessel. The greed for money-making is so great that it is with the sincerest regret that I observe that human lives are never taken into consideration.[17]

No Fear of God

BENJAMIN Hart booked passage on the *Philadelphia* for himself, his wife Esther, and their young daughter Eva. They would relocate to Canada after arriving in New York City and visiting with Benjamin's sister. However, Esther was uncharacteristically anxious about their forthcoming trip. She was temporarily relieved when a miner's strike kept the *Philadelphia* from sailing. Her husband quickly booked second-class tickets on another ship bound for New York. When Esther heard the name of the ship—*Titanic*—she understood the reason for her fear and anxiety. She told her husband:

> Because this is the ship that they say is unsinkable, and that is flying in the face of the Almighty. That ship will never reach the other side.[18]

She tried to talk her husband out of traveling altogether, but to no avail. Upon boarding the *Titanic* in Southampton, she told him that while aboard the ship, she would not allow herself to sleep at night. She would only sleep during the day. She later recounted that for the first few days of the trip, it seemed like "a large, black eagle" was perched on her shoulder, and she couldn't get it off.[19] While she wasn't taken seriously about any of her expressed fears, being up at the time of the late night collision probably saved her life and that of her daughter. Unfortunately, her husband died in the disaster.

❧TODAY'S CHURCH❧

*T*itanic passengers who were able to leave the sinking ship in lifeboats were wise to do so—it saved their lives. Professing believers would be similarly wise to depart from churches that are putting their trusting congregants in spiritual danger through their complacency, pride, and lack of spiritual discernment. A "see no evil, hear no evil, speak no evil" attitude does not protect anyone from spiritual error that can come in the form of false doctrines, signs and lying wonders, and false revivals that are "flying in the face of the Almighty."

REVIVAL OR DECEPTION?

LOOKING for spiritual experiences while hurrying toward "revival" without identifying, confronting, and repenting of the false teachings, false teachers, and spiritual danger in our midst, makes no sense at all. Rather, it is symptomatic of the same false confidence and complacency the crew of the *Titanic* exhibited as they underestimated the physical danger in their midst. The Bible describes a great last-days deception, *not* a great last-days revival. Yet we are hearing almost nothing about spiritual deception from today's church leaders—a sure sign that they and those they lead are being deceived one way or another (1 Corinthians 14:8).

Meanwhile, "revival" has become almost a magical word in the church. It is held up as a practically "unsinkable" church concept. What could possibly be wrong with revival? This kind of thinking parallels those who doubted that anything could go wrong with the *Titanic*. However, for the church to have revivals without repenting of the sin and deception entrenched in it does not make for a true revival.

Somehow Christian leaders and the church at large have been deceived into believing they can't be deceived. However, all the New Testament warnings about spiritual deception, signs and lying wonders, and people falling away from the faith in the last days are issued to believers. Today's professing church is falsely confident, strangely indifferent, and unabashedly unrepentant for all its idols, false gods, false teachers, and false teachings as the spiritual deception only grows stronger. How can legitimate revival ever take place in a church where Quantum Spirituality, "God's Dream," talking with the "dead," "holy laughter," Yoga, contemplative prayer, the Enneagram, channeled devotionals, grave-sucking, watered-down

Bible translations, and books like *Jesus Calling* and *The Shack* are given a general pass as they all point the way to the false "God within"—the false God nobody seems to notice or talk about—much less repent of?

Yet, there continues to be a frantic spiritual thrust from church leaders to disregard all this as they push for a new "Jesus Revolution," a "New Reformation," a "God's Dream Peace Plan," and a "great revival" that will allegedly change the world and change history. In the meantime, spiritual discernment is at an all-time low as the professing church moves further and further toward false revival—the ultimate spiritual trap.

CHRISTIAN GREED

WITH unbiblical books, devotionals, and spiritual experiences to please, placate, and distract people from the truth (2 Timothy 4:4), who wants to hear that the world and a deceived church are being prepared for Antichrist and a New World Religion? Especially when Christian publishers and bookstores are reaping huge profits from some of these products that are leading people into spiritual deception.

With truth being sacrificed for profit, the destructive result is a famine for the hearing of the Word of God (Amos 8:11). This is especially the case when new Bible translations and best-selling books have New Age implications that lead people further and further away from the truth. A perfect example is *The Voice* translation released on April 10, 2012—one hundred years to the day from when the *Titanic* set sail from Southampton, England on its fatal voyage. Contributors to this new translation include Leonard Sweet and Brian McLaren. A side by side comparison of a verse from the *King James Version* and *The Voice* says it all as *The Voice* drops the word Christ from Jesus' title while heralding the coming of the New Age:

2 PETER 3:18

But grow in grace, and in the knowledge of our Lord and Saviour Jesus Christ. To him be glory both now and for ever. Amen. (*KJV*)

Instead, grow in grace and in the *true* knowledge of our Lord and Savior Jesus, the Anointed, to whom be glory, now and until the coming of the new age. Amen. (*The Voice*)

BLIND GUIDES

AT his popular Institute for Successful Church Leadership, the late Robert Schuller taught many of today's pastors and church leaders his seemingly positive but wayward approach to modern Christianity. His "possibility thinking" teachings, emphasizing church growth at the cost of spiritual discernment, influenced thousands of pastors as they studied at his Institute. In his book *Discover Your Possibilities*, Schuller wrote:

> Concentrate on the positive. If you accept Jesus Christ as your Savior and take Him in your life, you'll never have to worry about the devil.[20]

Twenty-five years later, exuding Schuller's same false confidence, complacency, and denial regarding the wiles of the Devil, Robert H. Schuller Institute "graduate" Rick Warren[21] offers similar counsel to his millions of *Purpose Driven Life* readers when he writes:

> It helps to know that Satan is entirely predictable.[22]

Declaring this is like a shepherd telling his sheep—"It helps to know that wolves are entirely predictable." For church leaders like Schuller and Warren to make these statements is as falsely confident and empty as Captain Smith telling his Long Island friends that the *Titanic* was unsinkable. Robert Schuller and Rick Warren played right into the spiritual deception by ignoring the subject of spiritual deception. And by doing so, they were completely discounting the Bible's explicit warnings to be "sober" and "vigilant," and not to be "ignorant" of Satan's "devices":

> Be sober, be vigilant; because your adversary the devil, as a roaring lion, walketh about, seeking whom he may devour. (1 Peter 5:8)

> Lest Satan should get an advantage of us: for we are not ignorant of his devices. (2 Corinthians 2:11)

> Put on the whole armour of God, that ye may be able to stand against the wiles of the devil. . . . that ye may be able to withstand in the evil day, and having done all to stand. (Ephesians 6:11, 13)

The Bible warns that Satan is anything *but* predictable and often comes as a deceptive "angel of light" and his ministers as "ministers of righteousness" (2 Corinthians 11:14-15). To teach that Satan is "entirely predictable" is a far cry from putting on the "whole armor of God" and standing fast against "the wiles of the devil" so we "may be able to stand in the evil day."

PROPHECY IS NONE OF OUR BUSINESS?

SOME church leaders like Rick Warren go so far as to actively discourage the study of prophecy—especially in regard to the coming of Christ. Most people are not aware that Rick Warren's statements about prophecy and Christ's coming are very similar to those made by New Age matriarch Alice A. Bailey back in 1948. And while Rick Warren was purportedly talking about Jesus Christ, Bailey was talking about her occult/New Age Christ—Maitreya. She wrote:

> If our work is rightly done, He will come at the set and appointed time. How, where or when He will come is none

of our concern. Our work is to do our utmost and on as large a scale as possible to bring about right human relations, for His coming depends upon our work.[23]

Fifty-four years later, in his best-selling book *The Purpose Driven Life*, Rick Warren echoes Alice A. Bailey's words by telling his readers that the details and signs preceding Christ's return are "none of your business" and that "fulfilling your mission" will bring Jesus "back sooner." He writes:

> When the disciples wanted to talk about prophecy, Jesus quickly switched the conversation to evangelism. He wanted them to concentrate on their mission in the world. He said in essence, "The details of my return are none of your business. What *is* your business is the mission I've given you. Focus on that!"
>
> If you want Jesus to come back sooner, focus on fulfilling your mission, not figuring out prophecy.[24]

Controversial church figure Brian McLaren, using the same over-lapping language, similarly teaches the church that prophecy and the historic details of Jesus' return are "none of their business." Sounding like Alice Bailey and Rick Warren, McLaren says that Jesus tells His disciples not to focus on prophecy but on their "mission." He writes:

> Instead, he tells them it's none of their business to speculate about how God plans to work out history, and then he gives them a mission to accomplish.[25]

My experience coming out of the New Age movement taught me just the opposite of what Alice Bailey, Rick Warren, and Brian McLaren are teaching. In *Deceived on Purpose: The New Age Implications of the Purpose Driven Church*, I describe how the prophetic details of Jesus' return had enabled me to see how deceived I had been in following a false New Age Christ. My understanding of these details had been instrumental in my salvation. I explained:

> Coming out of New Age teachings, I had learned in a very personal way that the details of Jesus' return are definitely our business. Understanding the events surrounding His return was critical to understanding how badly I had been deceived by my New Age teachings. I had learned from reading the Bible that there is a false Christ on the horizon and that for a number of years I had unknowingly been one of his followers. Because the Bible's clear authoritative teachings about the real Jesus and His true return had been brought to my attention, I was able to see how deceived I was. By understanding that there is a false Christ trying to counterfeit the true Christ's return, I was able to renounce the false Christ I had been following and commit my life to the true Jesus Christ.[26]

NOT PROTECTING THE FLOCK

THE unbiblical discouragement of prophecy and discernment by many of today's church leaders is a sure sign of the times and a harbinger of real disaster. If Jesus didn't want us to know any of the details and circumstances surrounding His return, He would not have given us the many details and warnings He did. In Matthew 24 alone, He lays out many specific details regarding His return. He warns of false prophets, false Christs, false teachings, false peace, false signs and wonders, and the coming of Antichrist.

If church leaders want to talk about mission, the overriding mission of any shepherd is to protect their flock from any and all spiritual danger—just as it is the responsibility and duty of every ship captain to protect his passengers from any and all physical danger. This was not done on the *Titanic,* and it is not being done in much of today's church.

JIM JONES & THE PEOPLES TEMPLE

HAVING grown up in Redwood Valley, California, it would seem that Rick Warren would be one of the first people to warn about the spiritual deception and false teachers in our midst. Why? Because not everyone has grown up with the infamous Jim Jones and his Peoples Temple based in their own hometown.

In 1965, one of history's chief cult leaders and antichrist-type figures—the "Reverend" Jim Jones—moved his Peoples Temple from its urban Indianapolis, Indiana headquarters to the small Northern California town of Redwood Valley—Saddleback pastor Rick Warren's hometown. Somewhere Jones had read that Redwood Valley would be the safest physical place to be during a possible nuclear fallout. But Redwood Valley definitely wasn't the safest spiritual place to be for the local townspeople once Jones moved there. Many locals ended up being seduced into Jones' abusive church.

While Rick Warren was growing up in Redwood Valley, Jim Jones and his Peoples Temple were less than two miles from Rick Warren's family home. The Peoples Temple was one of the few churches in town. In a September 3, 2006 article, the *Orange County Register* reported that the "Reverend" Jones had taught at Rick Warren's high school and that "dozens" of Warren's classmates had died in the jungles of Guyana. The article stated:

> Jim Jones, the suicidal Pied Piper of Jonestown, housed his Peoples Temple less than two miles from Warren's house, and taught at Warren's high school. In 1978, dozens of Redwood Valley's residents—including some of Warren's classmates— were among the 914 cult members who followed Jones to Guyana and to a metal bucket full of purple, cyanide-spiked Flavor Aid.[27]

Jim Jones and his Peoples Temple were an extreme example of how a seemingly Christian church can be so spiritually dangerous and go so terribly wrong. Throughout the years that Peoples Temple was based in Redwood Valley (1965-1974), and then later in San Francisco and Guyana, "Reverend" Jones was an ordained Christian minister in the nationally accredited Disciples of Christ denomination.

To highlight how completely Jim Jones pulled the wool over people's eyes, he had the support and confidence of a number of California politicians, including Senator Willie Brown, San Francisco Mayor George Moscone, and Supervisor Harvey Milk. One year before ordering the mass murder/suicides of over 900 people in Guyana, Jones was presented with the prestigious Martin Luther King Jr. Humanitarian Award by one of San Francisco's most celebrated ministers, the Reverend Cecil Williams, at his popular Glide Memorial Church.[28] "Reverend" Jim Jones, the man who seemed to fool everyone wherever he went, had been anything but "predictable."

Believers who have come out of cult backgrounds or lived in the midst of communities where cult organizations were based, are often the first to warn about them. It would seem that as Rick Warren looks back at what happened in his own "backyard," he would want to warn the church from his own experience about deceptive false Christ figures like Jones who come in the name of Christ but actually oppose Christ.

TRUE CONFIDENCE

AS we learned from the *Titanic*, our safety, strength, refuge, and "strong confidence" come not from big men, big ships, and big churches that can ultimately "founder and sink" but through our reverential fear of the Lord and His Holy Word.

In the fear of the LORD is strong confidence: and his children shall have a place of refuge. (Proverbs 14:26)

❧8❧

WASTED WARNINGS

Never again would men fling a ship into an ice field, heedless of warnings, putting their whole trust in a few thousand tons of steel and rivets. From then on Atlantic liners took ice messages seriously, steered clear, or slowed down. Nobody believed in the "unsinkable ship."[1]

—Walter Lord
A Night to Remember (1955)

This is not only the story of a shocking catastrophe. The *Titanic* and all of its intricacies embody a wake-up call to the body of Christ.[2]

—Pastor Casey Sabella
Titanic Warning (1994)

❧THE TITANIC❧

The April presence of icebergs and ice fields in North Atlantic waters was no surprise to Captain Edward Smith and his *Titanic* officers. Iceberg awareness was an important part of their job and training. In fact, a 1909 book, *United States Pilot (East Coast), Part 1*, referred to by the British Admiralty's Hydrographic Office, warned large ships like the *Titanic* about the increased danger of icebergs and ice fields in April—the very month the huge vessel was sailing. It said:

> To these vessels, one of the chief dangers in crossing the Atlantic lies in the probability of encountering masses of ice, both in the form of bergs and of extensive fields of solid compact ice, released at the breaking up of winter in the Arctic regions, and drifted down by the Labrador Current across their direct route. Ice is more likely to be encountered too in this route between April and August, both months inclusive, than at other times.[3]

So what happened? When Captain Smith and his crew set out in April, they were aware that ice could be a problem. In the warm spring of 1912, the Labrador Current had brought especially large ice-flows down from Greenland and into the North Atlantic shipping lanes where many ocean liners traveled. In addition to this knowledge, *Titanic* received a number of warnings en route about the dangerous ice that lay before them. Yet, despite the warnings, Captain Smith had the ship sailing at almost full speed as he neared the treacherous iceberg that fatal April night. The vessel's high speed has been generally regarded as a main cause of the shipwreck. In an April 18, 1912 letter sent to the *New York Evening Post*, Admiral F. E. Chadwick stated:

> The *Titanic* was lost by unwise navigation, by running at full speed, though so amply forewarned, into the dangerous situation, which might easily have been avoided. This is the fundamental sad, and one important fact. It accounts for everything.[4]

However, running at such a high rate of speed—even amidst treacherous ice—was common practice with most ship captains at that time. They were confident they could spot any approaching ship, iceberg, or ice field well in advance. But things didn't work out that way for the *Titanic*.

The iceberg believed to have been hit by *Titanic*

On April 12, 1912, the third day of its maiden voyage, the *Titanic* received a warning message from the captain of the French liner, *La Touraine*. He warned that icebergs were in *Titanic's* path.[5] On April 13th when the ocean liner *Rappahannock* was in close proximity to *Titanic*, it warned by blinker of an ice field ahead. *Titanic* blinked back its acknowledgment and continued on its way.[6] Then on April 14th, the day of the collision, *Titanic* received six specific warnings about the dangerous ice fields that lay before them. The following are those warnings:[7]

SIX "LAST DAY" WARNINGS TO THE *TITANIC*

1) *Caronia* to *Titanic* (9 a.m.)—The *Caronia*, traveling eastbound from New York to Liverpool: "Captain, *Titanic*—West-bound steamers report bergs, growlers and field ice in 42° N, from 49° to 51° W, April 12. Compliments, Barr."

Response: The message was delivered to Captain Smith.

2) *Baltic* **to** *Titanic* **(1:42 p.m.)**—Eastbound from New York to Liverpool: "Greek steamer *Athinai* reports passing icebergs and large quantities of field ice today in latitude 41° 5' N, longitude 49° 52' W . . . Wish you and *Titanic* all success. Commander."

Response: Captain Smith was handed a copy of the *Baltic* warning. But rather than immediately posting it on the command bridge, he gave it to the managing director of the shipping lines, J. Bruce Ismay, who promptly put it in his pocket. At one point in the afternoon, Ismay pulled the message out and showed the warning to two female passengers. He mentioned the ice to them as if it was some tourist attraction they were passing along the way—rather than the potential danger that it was. Ismay had the message for over five hours before Captain Smith requested it back at 7:15 p.m. and finally posted it in the chart room.

3) Hydrographic office in Washington DC (1:45 p.m.)—

Message to all ships: "*Amerika* passed two large icebergs in 41° 27' N, 50° 8' W on April 14."

Response: This general warning should have been reported to the officers bridge because it related to ship navigation. But it was not. It was apparently set aside by *Titanic* wireless operator Harold Bride. None of the *Titanic* officers ever saw this warning.

Note: The Hydrographic office later reported that even though Captain Smith slightly altered *Titanic*'s course in an attempt to avoid the hazardous ice field, the ship still traveled north of the southern perimeter of the ice reported by the *Caronia* and the *Baltic*.

4) *Californian* **to** *Antillian* **(7:30 p.m.)**—Message from the *Californian* to the *Antillian* and overheard by *Titanic*: "To Captain, *Antillian*: . . . Latitude 42° 3' N, longitude 49° 9' W. Three large bergs 5 miles to southward of us. Regards. Lord."

Response: *Titanic* wireless operator Harold Bride overheard this warning to the *Antillian* and took it to one of the officers on the bridge.

He could not recount which officer he gave it to. Captain Smith was not personally informed of this warning as he was attending a private dinner party hosted by Mr. and Mrs. George D. Widener.

5) *Mesaba* to *Titanic* (9:40 p.m.)—Message received by *Titanic* wireless operator Jack Phillips: "From *Mesaba* to *Titanic*. In latitude 42° N to 41° 25' N, longitude 49° W to longitude 50° 30' W, saw much heavy pack ice and great number large icebergs, also field ice, weather good, clear."

Response: This message was received and set aside by Jack Phillips so that a backlog of passenger messages could be sent to friends and family. The messages had accumulated from the previous day when their radio had broken down and was out of commission for seven or so hours. *Mesaba*'s warning was never delivered to the bridge and was never read by any of the ship's officers. The message warned of large icebergs that were directly in *Titanic*'s path.

6) *Californian* to *Titanic* (10:55 p.m.)—With the *Californian* stopped for the night because of heavy ice, Captain Stanley Lord directed his radio man, Cyril Evans, to notify the *Titanic* of the heavy existing ice and their particular situation. Evans started his message, "Say, old man, we are stopped and surrounded by ice" when he was abruptly interrupted by *Titanic* wireless operator Jack Phillips.

Response: This last warning from the *Californian* came just 45 minutes before *Titanic* collided with the iceberg. Jack Phillips was still catching up on the backlog of passenger messages to be sent and hastily told Evans, "Shut up! Shut up! I'm busy. I'm working Cape Race."[8] (Cape Race was the Newfoundland wireless relay station where he was sending the passenger messages).

While all six warnings were received by the *Titanic* wireless operators, not all of them reached Captain Smith and the command bridge. Telegraph operator Jack Phillips' abrupt dismissal of that last warning from the *Californian* proved to be especially critical. The message he rebuffed warned of the very ice *Titanic* would soon be encountering.

These six critical warnings did not cause *Titanic* to slow down in the least. The ship continued traveling at nearly full speed toward the massive ice field. At the most, only three of the six warnings from other ships actually reached ship officers on the command bridge. No one will ever know what might have happened if the *Californian's* 10:55 p.m. iceberg warning had been properly conveyed to Captain Smith and acted upon before the collision forty-five minutes later. Would this crucial warning have prompted the captain to slow the ship, post extra lookouts, and take other necessary precautions—perhaps even stopping for the night like the *Californian*?

One thing is certain. The *Titanic* officers did not seem to understand the importance of the newly installed telegraph system in providing a continual 24/7 source of navigational assistance in safely piloting the ship. The telegraph operators also did not seem to grasp the full importance of what they were doing.

ᔐTODAY'S CHURCHᔑ

In the end, the six lightly regarded, disregarded, and missed messages—particularly the rejected warning from the *Californian*—raised many questions regarding the shipwreck. And so it is with today's church. Serious warnings about spiritual deception—particularly New Age deception—have been lightly regarded, disregarded, or completely missed by most of today's church leaders. While these warnings from concerned individuals and various discernment ministries have been largely overlooked, it does not seem to matter that many of the warnings were backed up by the Bible itself. Nevertheless, much of today's church continues to sail full speed ahead into the very danger of which they have been fully warned.

Titanic received six serious last-day warnings about present and impending physical danger. Today's church has received many serious last-days warnings about present and impending spiritual danger. Early warnings were issued in pioneering books in the 1970s and 1980s that described how Eastern/New Age teachings were flooding into the world and starting to trickle into the church. The following are six early warnings that, in most respects, are still applicable today.

SIX "LAST DAYS" WARNINGS TO THE CHURCH

1) *Death of a Guru* by Rabindranath R. Maharaj with Dave Hunt (1977)—This is the testimonial warning of a young man born in India who was destined to be an important and influential guru. However, he abandoned his ordained Hindu path to follow Jesus Christ. His was a very early and clear warning about the dangers of Eastern mysticism, contemplative prayer, transcendental meditation, Yoga, and all that would soon be called New Age. In his important testimony, Rabi Maharaj describes the beginning of his realization that he would have to warn everyone, particularly those in the West and the church, about this massive spiritual deception:

> I discovered that young people by the thousands were not just dropping out to turn on with drugs, they were taking up transcendental meditation and various other forms of Yoga. Their whole way of thinking became clouded by Eastern mysticism. . . . Slowly and with a growing sense of alarm I became convinced that Satan was masterminding an invasion of the West with Eastern mysticism. I could see that few Christians really understood his plan and were prepared to combat it. Could it be that God was preparing me, an ex-Hindu, to sound a warning alarm to the millions in the West who were falling for an Eastern philosophy that I knew was false?[9]

Rabi Maharaj was later featured in an important 1985 documentary, *Gods of the New Age*. It warned of the invasion of Eastern mysticism into Western society. At the end of this film that can be viewed free online, Maharaj powerfully presents the Bible's scriptural warnings about false Christs, lying signs and wonders, and the urgent need to accept and follow Jesus Christ (Matthew 24, John 14:6).

2) *The Beautiful Side of Evil* **by Johanna Michaelsen (1982)—** This was an early warning to the world and church of how a dark and evil spirit world can appear to be "beautiful." Johanna recounts her experiences as a young undiscerning Christian and how she became involved with occult practices that included Yoga, Silva Mind Control, and working with a psychic surgeon in Mexico City. She describes how she had her own spirit guides, including one that masqueraded as Jesus Christ. Her book was a strong warning about spiritual deception (Matthew 24:3-5), seducing spirits (1 Timothy 4:1), and rightly dividing the Word of God (2 Timothy 2:15). It was also a severe warning how the world and a deceived church were being "carefully groomed" for the coming of Antichrist. Michaelsen wrote:

> The world is being carefully groomed for the arrival of the one whom Scripture calls "the man of lawlessness . . . the son of destruction" (2 Thessalonians 2:3), "that is, the one whose coming is in accord with the activity of Satan, with all power and signs and false wonders," (2 Thessalonians 2:9)—the Antichrist. I believe this man is in the world today and Satan is working overtime to prepare mankind to hail the satanic signs and miracles he will perform (Revelation 13:13) as being wonders from the hand of God Himself.[10]

For my wife, Joy, and I, it was Michaelsen's book, *The Beautiful Side of Evil*, that opened our eyes to Jesus' victory on the cross of Calvary and initiated our departure from the New Age movement into a saving relationship with the true Jesus Christ.

3) *The Hidden Dangers of the Rainbow: The New Age Movement and Our Coming Age of Barbarism* **by Constance Cumbey (1983)—** This book exposed the New Age movement as a deceptive and dangerous threat to the world and the church. The author, a practicing attorney, further warned how this movement was preparing the way for the coming of Antichrist. While many church leaders resisted her book and what it revealed, Constance Cumbey clearly documented how the Bible's description of a dangerous last-days deception was unfolding right before everyone's eyes. She wrote:

> It is the contention of this writer that for the first time in history there is a viable movement—the New Age Movement—that truly meets all the scriptural requirements for the antichrist and the political movement that will bring him on the world scene.
>
> It is further the position of the writer that this most likely is the great apostasy or "falling away" spoken of by the Apostle Paul and that antichrist's appearance could be a very real event in our immediate future.[11]

Many church leaders tried to downplay, disparage, and discredit Cumbey's well-researched warnings. Despite the attempts to undermine the author and her book, many believers knew and appreciated that her book was a serious warning about spiritual deception and the times in which we live.

4) *The Seduction of Christianity: Spiritual Discernment in the Last Days* by Dave Hunt and T.A. McMahon (1985)—This book created quite a stir as it exposed false teachers and false teachings that had crept into the church. The book's intention was not to cause division but to simply warn the church about the many ways it was getting seduced and deceived. The authors wrote:

> It should be profoundly disturbing to Christians that growing numbers of pastors and Christian leaders are teaching that humans are destined to be gods. The fact that this belief is spreading within the church at the same time that it is being embraced by increasing millions in virtually every area of secular society as part of the growing New Age movement can hardly be coincidence.[12]

> There can be little doubt that we are in the midst of an unprecedented revival of sorcery worldwide that is deeply affecting not only every level and sector of modern society, but the church as well. Known as the New Age, Holistic, Human Potential, or Consciousness movements, at its heart is what anthropologists now call shamanism, which is simply the old occultism made to sound native, natural, earthy, and thus wholesome. It is also made to sound Christian. We have attempted to present an understanding of the various ways under which the same delusion that is preparing the world for the Antichrist is now seducing Christianity itself.[13]

While this book opened many people's eyes, three years after the book's well-publicized warnings, the problems they described in their book had grown significantly worse rather than better.

5) *Gods of the New Age* by Caryl Matrisciana (1985)—Republished in 2008 under the title *Out of India*, this book was another strong personal testimony from someone who came out of the New Age movement and warned about its incredible deception. Among other things, Caryl described how Benjamin Creme—the spokesman for the false Christ Maitreya—was presenting the spiritual framework for a New World Religion. Creme stated that it was the dawning of a New Age and that Maitreya, as "the Christ," would fulfill the prescribed expectations of each of the world's major religions. She quoted Creme regarding the false Christ Maitreya and his New Age/New World Religion. Creme said:

> It is a truism today to say that we are at the dawn of a New Age—the Age of Aquarius. And it is important to remember that all of the great religions await the coming of a leader. The Christians are awaiting the return of the Christ. The Muslims await the Imam Mahdi. At the same time the Buddhists await the coming of another Buddha. The Hindus

await the return of Krishna. And the Jews, as always, await the coming of the Messiah. I am speaking today about the return of such a teacher.[14]

6) *Inside the New Age Nightmare: A Former Top New Age Leader Takes You on a Dramatic Journey* by **Randall N. Baer (1989)**—This former New Ager's strong personal warning was the first published testimony of a major New Age leader and best-selling author coming to a saving relationship with Jesus Christ. Sadly, he died in a tragic car accident just as his book was being released to the public. Baer warned:

> In effect, the New Age is one of several major gateways for the adversary to unleash his plans and forces for global domination. The Antichrist comes bearing an innovative orthodox science in one hand and a Universal Oneness (neo-New Age) philosophy in the other, seated on a politico-economic throne of worldly power. A One-World Order, headed by the ultimate wolf in sheep's clothing, offers a desperate world many miracles, gifts, and wonders in the name of peace, love, planetary healing and universal brotherhood.[15]

CHURCH RELUCTANCE

IN my book *False Christ Coming: Does Anybody Care?*, I describe the strange reluctance of the church to heed the Bible's warnings about spiritual deception in the latter days. In the book, I state:

> Somehow, Christians don't seem to grasp Jesus' warnings about the tremendous deception that characterizes the time of the end. Perhaps deceived into thinking that we can't be deceived, we don't take seriously enough His warnings that a Hitler-like Antichrist figure will one day rise to rule the world—and that many people calling themselves "Christians" will support this spiritual counterfeit who will actually come in the name of Christ. Our adversary wants us to believe that

these warnings are for another people at another time. Yet through Scripture, and in our heart of hearts, the Spirit of God tells us that they are not. As we study the Bible, and as we watch and pray and observe the events all around us, we come to understand that these future times described by Jesus are now suddenly and undeniably upon us.[16]

But as the warnings to the church grow ever more serious, so does its resistance to these warnings. Disregarding, ignoring, and denying the many warnings being issued, today's church appears to be almost totally oblivious to the whole issue of spiritual deception.

It seems that in today's church, if you try to "sound the alarm" in Zion (Joel 2:1)—you are an "alarmist!" If you "critique false teachers" within the church (Ephesians 5:11-13)—you have a "critical spirit!" If you expose heresy (Titus 3:10)—you are a "heresy hunter!" If you "rightly divide" the Word of God (2 Timothy 2:15) and "mark them which cause divisions and offences contrary to the doctrine which ye have learned" (Romans 16:17)—you are the one who is "divisive" and causing "divisions!" If you warn about latter-days deception and the Antichrist (Matthew 24)—you are a "doomsday deceiver!" Needless to say, those trying to warn the church are lightly regarded and poorly heeded by most of today's professing Christians.

CHURCH LEADERS TO CRITICS: "SHUT UP! SHUT UP!"

A controversial church talk by Francis Chan was posted on YouTube in 2018. In it, Chan tried to use 1 Corinthians 3:16-17 to falsely teach that any Christian who critiques another believer's teachings is "taking a sledge hammer" and "destroying" the "temple of God" and, by so doing, is being "divisive" and is in danger of being killed by God.[17]

To try and make his futile case, he references the biblical account of Ananias and Sapphira. Those being targeted by Chan would include sincere apologists, legitimate discernment ministries, and anyone daring to question church leadership on *anything* they are saying or doing. But what Chan is teaching completely contradicts the apostle

Paul commending the Bereans who "searched the scriptures daily" to see if the things being presented were really "so" (Acts 17:11). Paul said it is "a shame" we have to expose certain things, but they must be "made manifest" and brought into the "light" (Ephesians 5:12-13).

Frances Chan said God had given this warning to him and that he was issuing it to the church on God's behalf. In other words, for the sake of alleged "unity" and future "revival"—don't say anything that might seem critical about another believer's teachings. But what if that pastor, church leader, author, or fellow believer is talking with the dead or endorsing this forbidden practice? What if they are teaching that prophecy is "none of your business"? What if they are saying that "Satan is entirely predictable"? What if they are teaching that God is "in" everything? What if they are calling New Age leaders their "role models" and "heroes"? What if they are teaching overlapping New Age concepts like "God's Dream"? What if they insist that "holy laughter" is a sure sign from God? In other words, how do these things get legitimately critiqued and discussed? Yet Frances Chan was adamant: Don't openly critique any believer or church leader about anything, or God might strike you down. You must listen to your appointed Christian leaders and do whatever they say.

However, Francis Chan's attempt to shield himself and other Christian leaders from reasonable inquiry is a far cry from disciples like Paul and John exposing false teachers and naming names such as Hermogenes, Hymenaeus, Philetus, Phygellus, Alexander the Coppersmith, and Diotrephes (1 Timothy 1:20; 2 Timothy 1:15; and 3 John 1:9).

What becomes evident as one surveys today's church scene is that Chan's alleged threat from God serves to protect false teachers, not the flock. In fact, what Chan and other church leaders are generally saying to those trying to warn of spiritual danger is what the *Titanic* wireless operator told the *Californian* wireless operator when being warned of physical danger—"Shut up! Shut up!" Today's professing church does not seem to have any interest or desire to receive spiritual warnings.

Look Up, but Look Out!

SADLY, the warnings issued by those of us who came out of the New Age have been as casually and complacently disregarded as the iceberg warnings given to the *Titanic* before it collided with the iceberg. As church leaders minimized and marginalized our warnings about the New Age, they were simultaneously injecting New Age concepts, teachings, and language into their sermons, talks, and writings. And when absolutely forced to deal with the subjects of the New Age and spiritual deception, many of these leaders would quickly dismiss New Age teachings as being "silly," "stupid," or as Rick Warren put it—"a bunch of baloney!"[18] As a result, the New Age has been allowed to flow into the church just as surely as that North Atlantic sea water flowed into the *Titanic*.

Jesus told us to "look up" (Luke 21:28), but He also told us to "look out" (Matthew 24:3-5). After His strong warning in the Olivet Discourse to "Take heed that no man deceive you" (Matthew 24:4), He warned about false prophets, false Christs (Matthew 24:24)—and the coming of Antichrist (Matthew 24:15).

The *Titanic* had lookouts, and ships today have lookouts. These lookouts are the "eyes of the ship." They are there to spot danger and warn about it ahead of time. The church also needs lookouts. These lookouts are watchmen on the wall. They are the "eyes" of the church. They are there to spot danger and warn about it ahead of time. And, actually, *any* believer who spots danger has a responsibility to warn those around him.

Titanic had been warned by other ships of the danger that lay before them, but they were complacent. They did not take the warnings seriously. They believed they were on an unsinkable "Ship of Dreams" as they raced toward New York City. They did not slow down. They did not post extra lookouts. Disaster resulted.

In similar fashion, today's professing church has been warned about the spiritual danger before them, but they have been complacent. They have not taken the warnings seriously. They believe they are on an unsinkable "Ship of God's Dreams" as they race toward an "international awakening"—a great "worldwide revival." They have not slowed down. They have not posted any extra lookouts. In fact, they have not posted any discernable lookouts at all. Nor have they bothered to listen to the lookouts that were sent to them from outside their usual church leadership circles. The lookouts were sent because most church leaders have abandoned their God-given responsibility to spiritually protect the church.

Today's church leaders are like the head saying to the body that it has no need of eyes. And because they have no need of eyes, they do not have the eyes to see what is before them and already in their midst. Rather than having their eyes "wide open," their eyes are "wide shut." Like the *Titanic* to the *Californian*, they tell those trying to warn them of danger to "Shut up! Shut up!" Somehow, in the rush of today's world, church leaders have forgotten the importance of having lookouts to serve as watchmen for the body—to be the eyes of the church. But this is not so with our United States Navy.

The Navy has a *Lookout Training Handbook*. The utter and absolute necessity of having lookouts—even with today's sophisticated computer technology—is stressed in the handbook's introduction. It reads:

> In the United States Navy, with its nuclear-powered warships, computerized guidance systems, and the most accurate search radars in the world, you, the lookout, play a critical role in safe ship operations. Your trained human eye is far superior to the most sophisticated equipment. As a lookout, you are the eyes and ears of the ship, and your alertness and skill ensures the safety of the ship. In the naval service there is probably no Rule of the Road more conscientiously observed than Rule 5 of the *Navigation Rules*, Commandant Instruction M16672.2, which states:

> "Every vessel shall at all times maintain a proper look-out by sight and sound as well as by all available means appropriate in the prevailing circumstances and conditions so as to make a full appraisal of the situation and of the risk of collision."[19]

When the rescue ship *Carpathia* headed into the dangerous ice field to rescue the *Titanic* survivors adrift in lifeboats, Captain Arthur Rostron doubled his lookouts. As today's church moves into an even more dangerous future, it seems to have no lookouts at all.

Titanic lookout George Symons, who was on duty with Archie Jewell just prior to Frederick Fleet and Reginald Lee's infamous last shift, said he could "smell" ice as early as 9 p.m.—more than two and a half hours before the *Titanic* struck the iceberg. At the British Inquiry, he said, "As a rule you can smell the ice before you get to it."[20]

Similarly, many of us who were formerly involved in the New Age movement can sense—"smell"—New Age teachings as they enter the church. However, like those six "last-day" warnings to the *Titanic*, our "last-days" warnings have been similarly disregarded and mostly dismissed. Today's professing church is so focused and distracted by "revival," it is overlooking the Bible's prophetic description about spiritual deception in the latter days. In *False Christ Coming: Does Anybody Care?* under the subtitle "Where is the Church Heading?" I wrote:

> Expecting only revival and the return of the true Christ, will people calling themselves Christians be deceived by the one who will come in the name of Christ and pretend to be Him? Caught unawares, will they mistake the counterfeit Christ's "Planetary Pentecost" for the great "move of God" they had been told to expect? Is this all a set up for the great delusion described in the Bible? Is there any good reason to not at least consider this possibility?[21]

And for this cause God shall send

them strong delusion, that they should

believe a lie. (2 Thessalonians 2:11)

❧ 9 ❧

RACING TOWARD DISASTER

Citizens were still bewildered over why an experienced
seaman like Captain E.J. Smith had driven his ship at full
speed into a danger of which he had been fully warned.[1]

—Wyn Craig Wade
The Titanic: End of a Dream

There is a race to the future. Who will get there first?[2]

—Leonard Sweet
soulTsunami

We are in a race. It's a race between what is and what could be.[3]

—Pastor Bill Johnson
Dreaming With God

❧THE TITANIC❧

The United States Senate Subcommittee Hearing on the *Titanic*
began just four days after the disaster on April 19, 1912. It was
held at the Waldorf Astoria Hotel in New York City. The chairman
of the hearing was Michigan Senator William Alden Smith. After
everyone had spoken, and all the evidence weighed, the subcommittee unanimously concluded that one of the chief factors causing the

disaster was the ship's excessive speed—especially when they had been repeatedly warned of the dangerous ice fields that lay before them. The report read:

> No general discussion took place among the officers; no conference was called to consider these warnings; no heed was given to them. The speed was not relaxed, the lookout was not increased, and the only vigilance displayed by the officer of the watch was by instructions to the lookouts to keep "a sharp lookout for ice."[4]

> The speed of the *Titanic* was gradually increased after leaving Queenstown. The first day's run was 464 miles, the second day's run was 519 miles, the third day's run was 546 miles. Just prior to the collision the ship was making her maximum speed of the voyage.[5]

Twelve days after the disaster, an article in *Scientific American* directly attributed the shipwreck to Captain Smith's "high speed" at night in the midst of heavy ice fields. The April 27, 1912 article stated:

> How such [an] experienced commander as Captain Smith should have driven his ship at high speed, and in the night, when he knew he was in the proximity of heavy ice fields is a mystery, which may never be cleared up. . . . Whatever the motive, it seems to be well established that the ship was not slowed down; and to this fact and no other must the loss of the *Titanic* be set down.[6]

TRYING TO MAKE RECORD TIME?

TITANIC researchers John P. Eaton and Charles A. Haas recounted what passengers were feeling that last full day:

> In the saloons and smoking rooms there were rumours of a record crossing. Many passengers and, indeed, some crew

believed the company wished to display its new liner in a most favourable light by bringing her across to New York with a new speed record.[7]

Surviving *Titanic* fireman John Thompson from Liverpool, England, told the *New York World* newspaper that the ship was racing "to beat all records" when it hit the iceberg. On April 22, 1912, the paper reported:

> From Queenstown out, he said, all the firemen had been talking of the orders we had to fire her up as hard as we possibly could. We were to make as quick a passage as possible, the orders ran, and we were to beat all records on our maiden trip.[8]

Titanic survivor, Mrs. Elizabeth Lines, recounted a conversation she overheard between Captain Smith and White Star Line managing director J. Bruce Ismay on April 13th—the day before the collision. Seated near them in the ship lounge, her interest was piqued when she happened to hear how many miles the ship had traveled each day so far. She recalled Ismay remarking:

> "Well, we did better today than we did yesterday, we made a better run today than we did yesterday, we will make a better run tomorrow. Things are working smoothly, the machinery is bearing the test, the boilers are working well." They went on discussing it, and then I heard him make the statement: "We will beat the *Olympic* and get into New York on Tuesday."[9]

J. Bruce Ismay

Mrs. Lines explained that Ismay was drawing a comparison between the *Titanic* and *Olympic*. She said:

> It was comparison, and that the *Titanic* was doing equally well, and they seemed to think a little more pressure could be put on the boilers and the speed increased so that the maiden trip of the *Titanic* would exceed the maiden trip of the *Olympic* in speed.[10]

J. Bruce Ismay denied having that specific conversation, but his credibility was suspect for several reasons. His company's liability was on the line, he had stepped onto one of the last lifeboats when women and children were still on the ship, and he was the one chiefly responsible for denying the ship architect's original request to have the ship carry twice as many lifeboats. With his mistaken belief that *Titanic* was unsinkable, why carry unnecessary lifeboats? As the head of the shipping line responsible for *Titanic* and the safety of its passengers, Ismay was widely disparaged for being both personally and commercially self-serving.

The Devil's Hole

Captain Edward Smith

THE last evening, Sunday April 14th, as *Titanic* neared the fatal ice field, Captain Edward Smith attended a private dinner party in his honor. It was hosted by the George Widener family. After thirty-eight years of service with the White Star Line, Captain Smith would be retiring after *Titanic*'s maiden voyage. Known as the "millionaire's captain" for the many millionaires who chose to sail with him, the congenial captain was well-liked and well-respected by passengers and crew alike. While he was socializing and enjoying what turned out to be a long and leisurely gathering, *Titanic* continued at almost full speed toward the perilous ice field. After dinner, the captain visited the officer's bridge before retiring for the night. He told the officer in charge to call him at the least sign of trouble.

That same evening, Mrs. Charlotte Collyer recalled a ship stewardess telling her that they were heading into a "dangerous part of the ocean" known as the "Devil's Hole." Rather than being frightened, Mrs. Collyer said she felt reassured knowing the crew was aware of the danger and would obviously be taking all necessary precautions to ensure their safety. Mrs. Collyer recounted what the stewardess had told her:

> "Do you know where we are" she said pleasantly, "we are in what is called the Devil's Hole." "What does that mean?" I asked. "That is a dangerous part of the ocean," she answered. "Many accidents have happened near there. They say that icebergs drift down as far as this. It's getting to be very cold on deck so perhaps there is ice around us now." She left the cabin and I soon dropped off to sleep, her talk about icebergs had not frightened me, but it shows that the crew were awake to the danger.[11]

Feeling reassured, Mrs. Collyer fell asleep in her cozy cabin. However, in a few short hours she would be shivering in a lifeboat, watching the ship where she felt so safe, sink right in front of her. Later, after being rescued, she said that as far as she could recall—even in the "Devil's Hole"—"we had not slackened our speed in the least."[12]

THE COLLISION

AFTER the testimonies were given at the senate hearing, this is how the ship reportedly went down: At 11:40 p.m., as the *Titanic* raced across the Atlantic nearly full speed ahead at 22 ½ knots (almost 26 mph), lookout Frederick Fleet suddenly spied what he described as a "black mass" some 500 feet in front of them. With any appreciable moonlight, the iceberg could have been spotted much sooner. With even a little wind, small waves would have been seen lapping up against the berg and exposing its presence. Normally, with even minimal moonlight and any kind of breeze, icebergs could be detected up to a half mile away. But on this moonless, windless night, the ocean was as smooth as glass. Because it was "darker than dark," lookout Fleet did not see the iceberg until it was a moment too late. He rang the crow's nest alarm bell three times. Then, picking up the ship phone, he gave the urgent message that was relayed to First Officer William Murdoch, who was on bridge duty at the time—"Iceberg right ahead!"

Murdoch quickly issued a "Stop!" order to quartermaster Robert Hichens at the wheel, in a desperate effort to avoid colliding with the iceberg. Murdoch's "Stop!" order was immediately telegraphed to the engine room and all engine activity immediately ceased. He then ordered Hichens to steer the ship "hard-a-starboard." As the ship slowly swung out, it successfully avoided a head-on collision with the ice, only suffering what seemed to be a slight glancing blow as the ship side-swiped the iceberg along the starboard side of the ship's hull.

From Fleet's first observance of the iceberg to the ship's contact with it, was a short but fraught-filled thirty-seven seconds. What was not known in the moment was that five of the sixteen watertight bulkhead compartments had been fatally pierced, and the ship was already sinking. Ironically, if the ship had hit the iceberg straight on, probably no more than two of the watertight compartments would have been compromised. That being the case, the ship would not have sunk and most of the passengers would have survived.

Titanic **Lookout and survivor, Frederick Fleet**

A Glancing Blow

PASSENGERS who were still up at the time of the collision saw the seventy-five to hundred-foot iceberg as it passed by. Much like a phantom punch in a boxing match that suddenly floors the seemingly unbeatable opponent, the iceberg's subtle blow fatally damaged the "unsinkable" ship. Yet, at first, the incident seemed almost inconsequential to many of the passengers.

Mrs. Stuart White said, "It was just as though we went over about a thousand marbles. There was nothing terrifying about it at all."[13] Lady Cosimo Duff described it "as though someone had drawn a giant finger all along the side of the boat."[14] Mrs. Walter B. Stephenson said what she felt wasn't as bad as "the first ominous jolt" she experienced in the 1906 San Francisco earthquake.[15] English schoolmaster Lawrence Beesley said he only "felt a slight jar."[16] He stated that some men playing cards had barely taken notice, and they quickly resumed playing "without any thought of disaster."[17] As the ship took on water and the tragedy unfolded, it was like Jesus' warning that the latter days would be "as in the days of Noah." People would just continue doing whatever they were doing, like "eating and drinking"—and playing cards—"until the flood came, and took them all away" (Matthew 24:37-39).

WE THOUGHT IT WAS FUN!

PEOPLE'S false confidence in the "unsinkable" ship left them unprepared for what was happening. However, third-class steerage passengers in the bowels of the ship saw the incoming water and immediately knew something was wrong. But that was not the case with many of the other passengers. In fact, some of the first-class and second-class passengers thought the iceberg incident was rather amusing. In an interview with the British Broadcasting Corporation (BBC), first-class passenger Edith Russell, later Edith Rosenbaum, described her initial encounter with the iceberg as "fun":

> And as I got out on the promenade deck, I saw a large grey, what it looked to me like a building floating by, good big grey thing. But that building kept bumping along the rail, and as it bumped it sliced off bits of ice and ice fell all over the deck. And I, and a great many of our foolish fellow passengers,

we just picked up the ice and started playing snowballs. We thought it was fun![18]

In a similar vein, young Jack Thayer told his parents that he was "going out to see the fun."[19] Mrs. Natalie Wick noticed that passengers were picking up pieces of the ice and "playfully throwing chunks at each other."[20] Major Arthur Godfrey Peuchen reported meeting a friend on the stairway "who laughingly said that we had struck an iceberg."[21] Lawrence Beesley recalled how snowballing matches were planned for the next morning:

> To illustrate further how little danger was apprehended—when it was discovered on the first-class deck that the forward lower deck was covered with small ice, snowballing matches were arranged for the following morning, and some passengers even went down to the deck and brought back small pieces of ice which were handed round.[22]

Totally unaware of the perilous plight they were in, many of the passengers and crew continued to make light of what was happening. A man in the second-class smoking room asked if he might get some ice for his highball.[23] Mrs. Frank M. Warren said her husband returned to their cabin with a piece of ice that someone had given him as a "souvenir."[24] A ship steward told Mr. and Mrs. Dickinson Bishop, "We have only struck a little piece of ice and passed it."[25] After checking out what happened, Harvey Collyer returned to his cabin and told his wife, "We have struck an iceberg, a big one, but there is no danger—an officer just told me so."[26] William T. Stead, after asking fellow passenger Frank Millet what happened, was told "Icebergs." Yet, even with his own published stories about perilous icebergs, fatal shipwrecks, and ships carrying insufficient lifeboats, Stead told Millet—"I guess it's nothing serious; I'm going back to my cabin to read."[27]

SAFE ON A SINKING SHIP?

WHEN Major Peuchen noticed the ship was tilting and shared his dismay with fellow passenger Charles M. Hays, Hays' confident reply was that the ship was unsinkable:

> As he [Major Peuchen] stood with Mr. Hays at the forward end of A Deck, looking down at the steerage passengers playing soccer with the loose ice, he sensed a very slight tilt in the deck. "Why, she is listing!" he cried to Hays. "She should not do that! The water is perfectly calm and the boat has stopped."
>
> "Oh, I don't know," Mr. Hays replied placidly, "you cannot sink this boat."[28]

Passengers like Mr. Hays, despite being confronted with clear evidence that something was wrong, continued to believe that the ship was unsinkable, and they were not in harm's way. Even as the situation became more apparent, the denial of any real danger persisted for many. When Captain Smith ordered women and children into the lifeboats, many passengers still believed they were safer on the ship than they would be in one of the lifeboats. Walter Lord underlined the irony of people feeling safer on the sinking *Titanic* than on one of the lifeboats that could have saved their lives:

> The response was anything but enthusiastic. Why trade the bright decks of the *Titanic* for a few dark hours in a rowboat? Even John Jacob Astor ridiculed the idea: "We are safer here than in that little boat."[29]

IN RETROSPECT

IN the end, most people agreed that Captain Smith had the *Titanic* traveling way too fast in those dangerous waters. In an interview with a journalist many years later, ninety-two-year-old survivor Marjorie Newell Robb recounted how she felt in lifeboat number six on the morning of April 15, 1912, as she waited at daybreak to be rescued. Seeing massive icebergs all around her, she said she understood how "irresponsible" Captain Smith had been, sailing so fast through the treacherous ice fields.[30] In his book *The Loss of the S.S. Titanic*, survivor Lawrence Beesley said he believed Captain Smith was ultimately responsible for the high speed and the loss of the ship:

> I suppose, that the direct responsibility for the loss of the *Titanic* and so many lives must be laid on her captain. He was responsible for setting the course, day by day and hour by hour, for the speed she was travelling; and he alone would have the power to decide whether or not speed must be slackened with icebergs ahead.[31]

At the United States Senate Subcommittee Hearing, people defending Captain Smith argued that traveling at nearly full speed through iceberg areas was customary for ships at that time. It was assumed ship lookouts would see the icebergs before they came upon them. But business as usual didn't work for the *Titanic*. And it won't work for the church either as we move into an increasingly challenging future.

✎TODAY'S CHURCH✌

Charlotte Collyer trusted that everything was all right because she believed the *Titanic* officers were looking out for their safety. She was not aware that Captain Smith was apparently more focused on reaching New York City in record time than in taking the precautions that would insure everyone's safety and well-being. Similarly, most of today's church assumes its leaders are looking out for them as these leaders race the church toward a world "revival" that will fulfill "God's Dream" and "change history." However, no one seems to see how the church's "Second Pentecost" might one day merge with the New Age Planetary Pentecost. The following section shows how some church leaders are presenting this recurring theme of how "revival" and the fulfillment of "God's Dream," will "change history."

RACING TOWARD HISTORY

Leonard Sweet

As previously cited, church leader Leonard Sweet states it is "a race to the future." He says the church is needed to save the future. He implores the church to build "new arks" as they "race" to "save God's Dream" and experience the "greatest spiritual awakening in the history of the church." He writes:

> It's time to build new arks.[32]

> There is a race to the future. Who will get there first? Will the Christian church? The time to save God's Dream is now. The people to save God's Dream are you. . . .

> God is birthing the greatest spiritual awakening in the history of the church. God is calling you to midwife that birth. Are you going to show up?[33]

In *Quantum Spirituality*, Sweet says that to birth this "greatest spiritual awakening" the church needs "New Light" "revivalists" because "Old Light" "revivalists" are the "fundamentalists" who "put a freeze on history" with their "Back to the Bible" approach to life. Mocking "Old Light," "Back to the Bible," "fundamentalists," he states:

> Old Lights are revivalists of the old. . . . Old Lights include the resurgent fundamentalists in every religion who put a freeze on history and fortify their adherents against the "new dark age" in which they are forced to live. "Back to the Bible," Old Lights shout. . . . But not everything Old Lights say is wrong. Much is right. Even a stopped clock is right twice a day, the old adage reminds us.[34]

However, Leonard Sweet's plea for "New Light" leadership and "New Light" revivalists appears to come right out of Marilyn Ferguson's book *The Aquarian Conspiracy*. Eleven years before Leonard Sweet's book *Quantum Spirituality*, Ferguson had already written about quantum physics and "old light" resistance to this new mystical "frontier science." What she subsequently described as needed "new light" leadership was totally equated with "New Age" leadership. She wrote:

> As controversy grows, the traditionalists or "nativists," those who have most at stake in the old culture or who are most rigid in their beliefs, try to summon the people back to the "old lights." . . .
>
> Someone is always trying to summon us back to a dead allegiance: Back to God, the simple-minded religion of an earlier day.[35]

Bruce Wilkinson

This best-selling Christian author came to Rick Warren's Saddleback Church in October of 2003 for a full week of preaching to prepare everyone for the "God's Dream" "Peace Plan" Warren would be introducing the next Sunday. Repeatedly extolling and expounding upon the theme of "God's Dream," Wilkinson told everyone to "prepare for the Dream that is coming"—how "history" was being "made" through the fulfillment of "God's Dream." In one of his sessions, he prayed:

> Father in heaven, how we love to live in history. History's being made right now. . . .
>
> We ask you, Holy Spirit, that your full and complete Dream for this church and every person in this audience, that this will be the greatest living illustration in the history of the church.[36]

Rick Warren

In an October 27, 2003 e-mail after Bruce Wilkinson's week-long build-up, Rick Warren promoted his forthcoming series on his "Global Peace Plan." He described it as "God's Dream for You— And the World!" Proclaiming that "God's Dream" would "change the world" and "change history," Warren said:

> You could sense that God is preparing our church for a great dream to change the world! . . .
>
> God is going to use you, and all of us together at Saddleback to change history![37]

Brian McLaren

In his book *Everything Must Change*, Brian McLaren also focused on "God's dreams" and how "history" was allegedly being made through their fulfillment." He wrote:

> We considered how this message of the kingdom—contrary to popular belief—was not focused on how to escape this world and its problems by going to heaven after death, but instead was focused on how God's will could be done on earth, in history, during this life. We described God's kingdom in terms of God's dreams coming true for this earth, of God's justice and peace replacing earth's injustice and disharmony.[38]

Lou Engle

As previously cited, in 2008, New Apostolic Reformation leader and "revivalist" Lou Engle posted a video on his website that has since been removed. It featured a stadium filled with young people who had a Scripture written on their foreheads as they celebrated "God's Dream" en masse. The video narrator heralded those who come to these "revivals" as "history-makers" and "dreamers of God's dream"—who will be "marked forever." He stated:

> [T]hose who come will be marked forever and they will be history-makers and dreamers of God's dream.[39]

Twelve years later, the same "God's dream" and "history making" themes continue to be featured on his 2020 "Lou Engle Ministries" website. The very first statements posted on the home page are about fulfilling "God's dream" and "history" being made. They read:

> When God created you, he had a dream and wrapped a body around that dream to fulfill it.[40]

Under this is written: "HISTORY IN THE MAKING"

Sean Feucht

Regarding "revival," former Bethel worship leader Sean Feucht writes:

> I personally believe that if we recover this one thing [selflessness], we will stumble into the greatest revival in history.[41]

> We can become the dream of God.[42]

Bill Johnson

In his book, *Dreaming With God*, Bethel Church pastor and "revivalist" Bill Johnson writes:

> We've been given the capacity to dream and, more importantly, to dream with God.[43]

> I write that His Church would rise to her potential and change the course of world history.[44]

Jim Wallis

This self-described evangelical and social-justice activist, similarly states that "God's dream" is in the process of being fulfilled and that it "will shape the end of human history." He writes:

> We are still very much in the midst of the fulfillment of God's dream, but it is deeply satisfying that, even in the face of our pain and struggle, we have seen that dream and believe it will shape the end of human history.[45]

Faith Marie Baczko

As previously cited, president of Headstone International Ministries and Headstone Academy, NAR "revivalist" Faith Marie Baczko ironically describes today's church as a "Ship of Dreams." She states that this "Ship of Dreams" is setting out on its maiden voyage to fulfill "the dreams of God" as it "heads out into the "Great Sea" in the "Church's greatest hour in its History" and is positioned for "revival." She writes:

> Much provision is about to be released to fulfill the dreams of God! . . . It is now time for dreams to be fulfilled as the Ship of Dreams heads out into the Great Sea.[46]

> The long great journey of His-story is on its last leg. . . . He is strategically preparing "LANDING CITIES" for an invasion of His Heavenly Hosts all over the earth, positioned for revival.[47]

> I believe all that has taken place in the Body of Christ up to this point has been training and preparation for the Church's greatest hour in its History![48]

That other "Ship of Dreams"—the RMS *Titanic*—also headed out to sea in 1912 on its maiden journey, but it never reached its destination. Something rose up out of the "sea" to keep it from fulfilling its dreams.

In like manner, the Bible warns that the church's "Ship of Dreams" and its "God's Dream" for worldwide "revival" will also be upended by something that rises up out of the sea. And what seems like a "world revival" that will "change history," will actually be a worldwide deception that will try to "change His Story."

DREAMERS & HISTORY-MAKERS

COUNTLESS leaders, both in the New Age and in the church, are presenting this notion that God has a dream. And if the dream is "fulfilled," the world will be saved, and "history" will be made. This perfectly conforms to what Marilyn Ferguson wrote in *The Aquarian Conspiracy*. She said that for a "paradigm shift" to occur across the board, New Age concepts like "God's Dream," "God within," and "Oneness" have to become part of "our common heritage" and "history" by being "widely communicated." They have to become our "new consensus," what "everybody knows." As cited, Ferguson wrote:

> If these discoveries of transformation are to become our common heritage for the first time in history, they must be widely communicated. They must become our new consensus, what "everybody knows."[49]

It should be noted that the false Christ Maitreya presented these same concepts, in the context of "God's Dream," as part of his overall Plan to change "history":

> I am with you as God's Representative, as the Spokesman for that Divine Being Whose dreams we are.[50]

> Humanity today is living at a unique time in its history. . . . We are at the end of a civilization, and therefore at the beginning of a new one: if we would have it so, this can be the most brilliant in our long history.[51]

DISREGARDING DANGER

AFTER *Titanic* collided with the iceberg, and with water flooding into the bowels of the vessel, some of the passengers frolicked in an almost party-like atmosphere around the estimated two tons of ice that had spilled out onto the foredeck of the already sinking ship. Several hours later, some of those involved in the merrymaking would be fighting for their lives in the freezing Atlantic Ocean.

So-called modern-day "revivals," like the Toronto Blessing with its "holy laughter" and party-like atmosphere, are reminiscent of the *Titanic* passengers who, unaware of the disaster unfolding around them, wanted to join in all "the fun." *Charisma* magazine, reporting on the Toronto Blessing back in August 1994, wrote about those who went to Toronto to "join the fun."

> When the services were broadcast on the radio, more curiosity seekers showed up to join the fun.[52]

PARTYING WITH GOD?

Randy Clark
Pastor Randy Clark, in describing the Toronto Blessing, said that sometimes there was "so much laughter" going on in services that it seemed to be "more of a party than church":

> Sometimes there was so much laughter as we ministered that what we were doing seemed to resemble more of a party than church.[53]

Clark recounted how one participant described the Toronto "revival" as "one big party." The man had said:

> It's like someone's throwing one big party![54]

Brian McLaren

In *The Secret Message of Jesus*, after referencing "God's Dream," emergent church leader Brian McLaren wrote how "God is inviting" everyone to "a party."

> Today we could say that God is inviting people to leave their gang fights and come to a party, to leave their workaholism and rat race and come to a party, to leave their loneliness and isolation and join the party . . . to stop fighting or complaining or hating or competing and instead start partying and celebrating the goodness and love of God.[55]

Rick Warren

In a January 29, 2020 church e-mail framed with the heading "Time to Dream" and titled "The Power and Purpose of Parties!," Rick Warren was acknowledging Saddleback's 40th anniversary party that had just been held at their church. It had also been a celebration for Warren's forty years of ministry.

Warren used his e-mail to present a mini-Bible study on "The Power and Purpose of Parties!" He said that Jesus was so into partying that today's "Pharisees" would call Jesus "a party animal." Rick Warren's effort to present Jesus as a big "party" person seemed more than strange. But not to Rodney Howard-Browne, Randy Clark, Brian McLaren, and other church leaders who also portray "Jesus" as a last days "party" person.

SPIRITUAL DISTANCING

GIVEN all this, two questions beg to be asked: Are future revivals going to be spiritual offshoots of the Toronto Blessing—like someone is throwing a big party? And are we to believe that the someone throwing the big party is going to be Jesus Himself because he is so into "partying"? For those who have a love of the truth and a love of the true Jesus Christ, we are not told to work out our salvation with complacency, shallow repentance, and "holy laughter"-type partying." We are told to work out our salvation with "fear and trembling" (Philippians 2:12). Scripture is very clear about the last days. We are to watch (Matthew 24:42). We are to be sober and vigilant (1 Peter 5:8). We are to stand fast (2 Thessalonians 2:15). We are not to let our faith get shipwrecked by false teachings (1 Timothy 1:19). We are not to fall away from our faith (1 Timothy 4:1).

In short, we are not to be deceived and to take part in spiritual "revivals" that have "another Jesus"—a "party Jesus" who is not the true Jesus Christ. We are not to take part in "revivals" that have "another spirit"—a "party spirit"—that will merge one day with the Planetary Pentecost of the New Age and its false "God within."

TRUE REVIVAL

LEONARD Sweet said, "This is an extraordinary moment in history"[56] because "God is birthing the greatest spiritual awakening in the history of the church."[57] Dr. Michael Brown has defended "holy laughter" and has written that we are on the edge of a major revival—an "international awakening"[58] that is preparing the way for the coming of Jesus Christ. But the false New Age Christ has also spoken of an international awakening—a Planetary Pentecost—where "God's Dream," laughter, partying, and "changing history" all play a part in preparing the way for this false Christ's ultimate coming.

Prior to sinking, *Titanic* was seen as invincible and unsinkable and was viewed with widespread positive regard. Revival is regarded in much the same way. It brings up similar notions of invincibility, unsinkability, and positive regard. What could possibly be wrong with revival? Who doesn't want true revival—a revival filled with heartfelt repentance and powerfully met with God's mercy and amazing grace? But the word *true* is key. True revival must be authoritative and God-given, inspired only by God's true Holy Spirit and in accordance with His Word.

Run With Patience & Self-Control

SCRIPTURE declares that "the prize" at the end of the race—the "incorruptible" crown—is won by those who are temperate and bring their bodies and spiritual lives "into subjection" to the Lord:

> Know ye not that they which run in a race run all, but one receiveth the prize? So run, that ye may obtain. And every man that striveth for the mastery is temperate in all things. . . . I keep under my body, and bring it into subjection: lest that by any means, when I have preached to others, I myself should be a castaway. (1 Corinthians 9:24-27)

This is not a race to the future. This is not a race to "fulfill God's Dream." This is not a race to "change the world" and to "change history." In *Titanic's* race to "set a record," the warnings of danger in their midst were, for all intents and purposes, missed or dismissed. As a result, the *Titanic* shipwrecked and never reached its appointed destination. The only record *Titanic* set was in the number of lives lost due to complacency, haste, and recklessness. The Bible makes it clear that the race is not to the swift (Ecclesiastes 9:11) but to those who "run with patience the race that is set before us."

Wherefore seeing we also are compassed about

with so great a cloud of witnesses, let us lay

aside every weight, and the sin which doth so

easily beset us, and let us run with patience the

race that is set before us. (Hebrews 12:1)

∽10∾

THE ICEBERG &
THE ANTICHRIST

In the years ahead, the New Age will be escalating into a major worldwide force to be reckoned with as Satan uses it as a tool to give rise to the Antichrist forces. Stay tuned. By keeping up with current trends in the New Age, many of these forces' movements and strategies lay exposed, and Christians may be forewarned and forearmed regarding the lurking dangers of tomorrow's impending titanic world events.[1]

—Randall Baer
Inside the New Age Nightmare

The question we should be asking regarding Maitreya is—"What can we learn from this perennial false Christ figure? And why have most Christian leaders paid almost no attention to this deceptive Christ who has been around for so many years? Because his teachings are so completely in sync with those of the New Age and with what has been coming into the church, it is important for the church to become more familiar with Maitreya and what he teaches.[2]

—Warren B. Smith

❧THE TITANIC❧

CONVERGENCE WITH THE ICEBERG

As cited, right after the *Titanic* disaster, author/poet Thomas Hardy wrote a stark poem about the "smart ship" that was not so smart, titled "The Convergence of the Twain."[3] "Convergence" has been commonly defined as the "oneness" that results from "two or more things coming together, joining together or evolving into one."[4] And it was this disastrous "convergence" with the iceberg—this tragic oneness—that resulted in *Titanic's* demise and gave title to Hardy's poem. Describing the inevitable and fateful "convergence" of the ship and the iceberg, the poet wrote:

> And as the smart ship grew
> In stature, grace, and hue
> In shadowy silent distance grew the Iceberg too.

Hardy's epic poem was a stinging indictment of the times. It described the hedonistic "Pride of Life" that "planned" the "smart ship" which suddenly converged with the fatal iceberg. The poet wrote that their "convergence" was the "consummation" of "twin halves" of an "event" that "jars two hemispheres." And how "history" would forever bear record of their deadly wedded oneness—the "intimate welding" of the "smart ship" with its "sinister Mate."

This 1912 poem about the convergence of the *Titanic* and the iceberg serves as a harrowing harbinger of the prophesied "convergence" of the world with its fateful "sinister Mate"—Antichrist. It illustrates how this future "beast" and beast system will "rise up out of the sea"—like a treacherous iceberg—to deceive and destroy (Revelation 13), and it vividly portrays how the Bible testifies that a not-so-smart world and a not-so-smart church are being prepared for an "intimate welding"—a wedded oneness and ultimate "consummation" with this promised evil ruler. If Thomas Hardy had written about this prophesied convergence of a deceived church with the Antichrist and Antichrist system of Revelation, he might have penned these lines:

> And as the smart church grew
> In stature, grace, and hue
> In shadowy silent distance grew the Antichrist too.

CONVERGENCE WITH ANTICHRIST

PIERRE Teilhard de Chardin, the "Father" of the New Age movement, used this same word "convergence" to falsely allege that "the only possible conversion of the world" to "a religion of the future" would require a "general convergence" of the world's religions "upon a universal Christ." He wrote:

> A general convergence of religions upon a universal Christ who fundamentally satisfies them all: that seems to me the only possible conversion of the world, and the only form in which a religion of the future can be conceived.[5]

Yet, church leader Leonard Sweet would have today's church believe that Teilhard was "Twentieth-century Christianity's major voice."[6] In his book *soulTsunami,* with its front cover endorsement by Rick Warren,[7] Sweet states that today's smart church needs to "build new arks"[8] and submit to the smart leadership of men like Rick Warren and himself. Why? Because they claim to have the "essential leadership arts for piloting your church in today's fluid culture."[9] However, their modern-day "ark"—their "Ship of God's Dreams"—bears an all too uncanny resemblance to that 1912 "Ship of Dreams" that ended up at the bottom of the ocean.

Icebergs have often been described as having a wondrous yet treacherous beauty. Arthur Rostron, the heroic captain of the rescue ship *Carpathia,* described how, in the early morning post-disaster aftermath, the ominous icebergs from the night before appeared as "pearly pink ice mountains glorified into celestial beauty."[10] He recounted one survivor's description of the icebergs surrounding them:

> Terrible as was the disaster one of them had caused, there was an awful beauty about them which could not be overlooked.[11]

Captain Rostron also recalled how one of the survivors, a young American girl, had been "awed by the dazzling twenty-one-mile span of pack ice" and how it "glistened like a never-ending meadow covered with new fallen snow." He remembered her saying:

> Those same white mountains, marvelous in their purity, had made of the just ended night one of the blackest the sea has ever known.[12]

While icebergs may be "dazzling" and "marvelous" to behold, it should be kept in mind that most of their physical mass is hidden beneath the surface of the sea. In similar fashion, deceptive spirits may also appear to have a "dazzling" beauty and "marvelous" presence when they come hidden as "angels of light." The Bible warns:

> And no marvel; for Satan himself is transformed into an angel of light. Therefore it is no great thing if his ministers also be transformed as the ministers of righteousness. (2 Corinthians 11:14-15)

The dazzling and deceptive beauty of Satan and his "ministers of righteousness" is what former occultist Johanna Michaelsen has described as the "beautiful side of evil." Referring to the night of *Titanic*'s collision with the iceberg, *Titanic* researcher and author Tim Maltin contends in his book *A Very Deceiving Night* that the unique atmospheric conditions on that beautiful but treacherous night created a dazzling but deadly refraction of light that may have kept the *Titanic* lookouts from seeing the iceberg sooner and from seeing the Morse lamps that were signaling them from the nearby ship *Californian*.[13]

The Iceberg & The Antichrist \ 173

Tragically, Captain Smith and his *Titanic* officers did not successfully "pilot" their ship through the much-warned-about ice-laden waters. And contrary to Leonard Sweet's *AquaChurch* assertions, he and other church leaders are not successfully "piloting" the church through "today's fluid culture." Sadly, the trap has been set. The trigger has been pulled. Antichrist—the ultimate spiritual iceberg—draws closer and closer as his antichrist system moves firmly into place.

ᔓTODAY'S CHURCHᔓ

ANTICHRIST RIGHT AHEAD!

A moment too late, *Titanic* lookout Frederick Fleet discerned the perilous iceberg—"a black mass"[14] that was "darker than the darkness."[15] And "darker than the darkness" is an apt description of the ultimate deceiver, who presents himself as an "angel of light" but is the epitome of darkness itself. The one prophesied in the Bible to "rise up out of the sea"—like an iceberg—to deceive and destroy (Revelation 13:1).

In a 2006 online "Update" to my 2002 book *Reinventing Jesus Christ: The New Gospel*—later republished as *False Christ Coming: Does Anybody Care?*—I describe how most of today's professing church has grossly underestimated our Spiritual Adversary. I explain how the church is disregarding the Bible's prophetic detail concerning what lies before them and how the church is strangely reminiscent of the *Titanic* as it continues to "plow full speed ahead into certain disaster."[16]

When the disciples asked Jesus about the sign of His coming and the end of the world, He immediately warned about spiritual deception (Matthew 24:3-5). He followed that with a warning about the Antichrist—the "abomination of desolation" (Matthew 24:15). Jesus further warned that "false christs" and "false prophets," showing "great signs and wonders," would be preparing the way for this future world ruler (Matthew 24:11, 24). In fact, Scripture is replete with "iceberg warnings" about the deception, betrayal, and disaster that will occur in the latter days. But today's church leaders—much like the *Titanic* ship officers—remain strangely complacent about the spiritual danger around them.

This complacency has been especially evident as church leaders continue to overlook a prominent false Christ figure who claims to be in the world today. While many false Christs have come and gone over the years, this false Christ figure has allegedly been in the modern world since 1977. His presence was publicly announced in 1982, and he is said to still be here today as he patiently waits for humanity to call him forth. This false Christ is named—Maitreya.

MAITREYA

ON April 25, 1982, major newspapers around the world carried a prominent full-page ad announcing that "the Christ is now here."[17] However, the ad stated that his name was Maitreya "the Christ"—not Jesus Christ. They said that Maitreya was here to simultaneously fulfill the prophecies of all the world's religions: He was the Universal Christ who would meet all their expectations and needs. The headline read:

THE CHRIST IS NOW HERE.

HOW WILL WE RECOGNIZE HIM?

The announcement stated:

> Look for a modern man concerned with modern problems—political, economic, and social. Since July 1977, the Christ has been emerging as a spokesman for a group or community in a well-known modern country. He is not a religious leader, but an educator in the broadest sense of the word—pointing the way out of our present crisis. We will recognize Him by His extraordinary spiritual potency, the universality of His viewpoint, and His love for all humanity. He comes not to judge, but to aid and inspire.

The full-page announcement then asked and answered the following question:

WHO IS THE CHRIST?

> Throughout history, humanity's evolution has been guided by
> a group of enlightened men, the Masters of Wisdom. They
> have remained largely in the remote desert and mountain
> places of earth, working mainly through their disciples
> who live openly in the world. This message of the Christ's
> reappearance has been given primarily by such a disciple
> trained for his task for over 20 years [Benjamin Creme]. At
> the center of this "Spiritual Hierarchy" stands the World
> Teacher, Lord Maitreya known by Christians as the Christ.
> And as Christians await the Second Coming, so the Jews await
> the Messiah, the Buddhists the fifth Buddha, the Moslims the
> Imam Mahdi, and the Hindus await Krishna. These are all
> names for one individual. His presence in the world guarantees
> there will be no third World War.

This stunning announcement sent shock waves throughout the
world, but those who had read and understood their Bibles immediately
knew that Maitreya was one of the false Christs Jesus warned about in
Scripture. The Bible makes it abundantly clear that Jesus Christ is the
one and only true Christ (John 14:6). The Bible also makes it clear that
believers will meet Him "in the air." Not "on the air"—as on television.
Not "through the air"—as on iPhones or the Internet. Not "in the
desert." Not "in the secret chambers"—like the "God within." Not on
the solid ground of planet Earth. We are to meet the Lord Jesus Christ
literally "in the air":

> For there shall arise false Christs, and false prophets, and
> shall show great signs and wonders; insomuch that, if it were
> possible, they shall deceive the very elect. Behold, I have told
> you before. Wherefore if they shall say unto you, Behold,

he is in the desert; go not forth: behold, he is in the secret chambers; believe it not. (Matthew 24:24-26)

For the Lord himself shall descend from heaven with a shout, with the voice of the archangel, and with the trump of God: and the dead in Christ shall rise first: Then we which are alive and remain shall be caught up together with them in the clouds, to meet the Lord in the air: and so shall we ever be with the Lord. Wherefore comfort one another with these words. (1 Thessalonians 4:16-18)

Maitreya's followers are very serious about what they are doing. They oversee the Share International organization that promotes Maitreya's teachings with main offices in London and Amsterdam. Maitreya "Transmission Meditation" groups are scattered throughout the United States and around the world. Today, almost forty years after those 1982 newspaper announcements, Share International continues to promote Maitreya as "the Christ" as he allegedly remains incognito in an undisclosed location, waiting for humanity to recognize their need for his intervention in their out-of-control world.

WHAT CAN WE LEARN FROM THIS FALSE CHRIST?

THE question we should be asking regarding Maitreya is—"What can we learn from this perennial false Christ figure? And why have most Christian leaders paid almost no attention to this deceptive Christ who has been around for so many years? Because his teachings are so completely in sync with those of the New Age and with what has been coming into the church, it is important for the church to become more familiar with Maitreya and what he teaches.

THE CHURCH'S STRANGE SILENCE

CONSISTENT with the 1982 newspaper ads and over the ensuing years, Maitreya has continued to state through his designated spokespeople that he will emerge one day from his present anonymity to publicly declare that he is "the Christ." Yet, for whatever reasons, most Christian leaders have never taken Maitreya or his New Age teachings very seriously—if at all. What's more, countless professing Christians today have never even heard of this false New Age Christ.

MESSAGES FROM MAITREYA

IT is clear that Maitreya's spiritual teachings are consistent with those of today's New Age leaders. This is one of the chief reasons why Maitreya is not only a probable prototype for Antichrist but why he also remains a viable candidate for the position himself.

Over the years, Maitreya maintained contact with the world through his longtime chief spokesman, British author, artist, esotericist and New Age channeler, Benjamin Creme (1922-2016). Maitreya's role as "the Christ" was definitively described in Creme's 1980 book, *The Reappearance of the Christ and the Masters of Wisdom*. Maitreya's expressed purpose is to teach humanity that we are all divine manifestations of "God's Dream"—and that we are all "One" because God is "in" everyone and everything. In his channeled book, *Messages from Maitreya the Christ*, Maitreya states:

I am your Purpose.[18]

I am with you as God's Representative, as the Spokesman for that Divine Being Whose dreams we are.[19]

God is within you and all around you.[20]

My name is Oneness.[21]

I make all men One.[22]

My Plan is God's Plan.[23]

My Coming brings peace.[24]

Because Maitreya teaches that we are all "One," he contends that we must learn to live in "right relationship" as brothers and sisters in our "One" great family. He teaches that the first step in recognizing this "Oneness" is to establish "sharing" as the way to eliminate poverty and starvation in the world. Sharing is the bottom line. Speaking for Maitreya, Benjamin Creme stated:

> He has come to teach humanity the need for sharing. "Sharing," He says, "is divine. When you share you recognize God in your brother."[25]

Channeling through Benjamin Creme, Maitreya emphatically stated that humanity "must share or die."

> My Teaching is, as ever, simple indeed. Men must share or die.[26]

Thus, in Maitreya's New World Religion, if you don't "share" by recognizing "God in your brother" then you must die. It is as simple and frank and brutally straightforward as that.

THE "MASTER JESUS" & THE MASTERS OF WISDOM

MAITREYA'S followers believe he is the emerging "Christ" and "World Teacher" who will return to help us to save ourselves and save our planet; and when enough people call for his "return," he will finally reveal himself on an internationally televised "Day of Declaration." Benjamin Creme stated:

> Maitreya will then be invited by the international media to speak directly to the entire world through the television networks linked together by satellites. On this Day of Declaration, we will see His face on the television screen wherever we have access. The Bible statement "All eyes will see Him" will be fulfilled.[27]

Maitreya's followers have reportedly included many past and present-day world leaders. Former Soviet Union leader Mikhail Gorbachev[28] and the late South African leader Nelson Mandela[29] are two prime examples. Many politicians, celebrities, and spiritual/religious leaders are also said to be secretly devoted to him and his teachings.

One of Maitreya's most deceptive spiritual devices is regarding his teachings about the "Master Jesus." In what would prove to be a cunningly clever counterfeit of Jesus' true return with His "mighty angels" (2 Thessalonians 1:7), Maitreya teaches that when he— Maitreya—comes as "the Christ," twelve disciples—his "Masters of Wisdom"—will also appear with him. Some of these "Masters" are said to already be physically present and active in the world under assumed names. Maitreya says that his "Masters of Wisdom" will work with him to teach humanity the "New Truth"[30] and the "new way"[31] of seeing God in the coming "New Age."[32] He said:

> They stand ready to greet the dawn of that New Age which beckons all into divinity.[33]

Benjamin Creme, again speaking for Maitreya, stated that one of the spiritual "Masters" who will "return" with Maitreya is the "Master Jesus." This "Master Jesus" is not described as the Christ, but rather as a "disciple" of Maitreya "the Christ." Maitreya is said to be the only person occupying the "office" of Christ and that he has occupied this "office" for over 2600 years. Creme alleges that it was Maitreya "the Christ" who overshadowed and worked through "the man" Jesus in Palestine back in the first century. Creme explained:

> In the esoteric tradition, the Christ is not the name of an individual but of an Office in the Hierarchy. The present holder of that Office, the Lord Maitreya, has held it for 2,600 years, and manifested in Palestine through His Disciple, Jesus, by the occult method of overshadowing, the most frequent form used for the manifestation of Avatars. He has never left the world, but for 2,000 years has waited and planned for this

180 / The Titanic and Today's Church

immediate future time, training His Disciples, and preparing Himself for the awesome task which awaits Him. He has made it known that this time, He Himself will come.[34]

In other words, Maitreya's "Master Jesus" is not the Lord, and he is not the Christ. He is a spiritual "Master" and "Master" only. Maitreya proclaims that he himself is "the Lord" and "the Christ." Benjamin Creme explained that the "Master Jesus" will be serving the "Lord Maitreya" by assuming "the Throne of St. Peter, in Rome." It is there in Rome that the "Master Jesus" will attempt to "reform" and "transform the Christian Churches" "to respond correctly" to the Lord Maitreya and the "new reality" his return creates.

This "Master Jesus" who says he is not "the Christ," is by the Bible's definition a counterfeit Jesus—"another Jesus" (2 Corinthians 11:4). And it is understood that a major part of this counterfeit Jesus' role will be to convince professing Christians they have misunderstood his person and his role and caused great problems in the world as a result. He will make sure that Christians understand that the "Master Jesus" is not the Christ—Maitreya is. Thus, the "Master Jesus" will be in charge of the New Reformation that will educate and reform the Christian churches. Speaking for Maitreya and turning the truth of the Bible upside down, Benjamin Creme stated:

> The Master Jesus is going to reform the Christian churches.[35]

> He is one of the Masters Who will very shortly return to outer work in the world, taking over the Throne of St. Peter, in Rome. He will seek to transform the Christian Churches, in so far as they are flexible enough to respond correctly to the new reality which the return of the Christ and the Masters will create.[36]

Once Maitreya's alleged reign is established, his role is to eventually bring all humanity to the feet of his "Father"—Sanat Kumara. Sanat Kumara is described as "God" and "Lord of the world."[37] It should be noted that Sanat is an anagram for Satan and that the Bible describes Satan as the "god of this world":

> In whom the god of this world hath blinded the minds of them which believe not, lest the light of the glorious gospel of Christ, who is the image of God, should shine unto them. For we preach not ourselves, but Christ Jesus the Lord; and ourselves your servants for Jesus' sake. (2 Corinthians 4:4-5)

Whether or not Maitreya is the actual Antichrist is not the concern here. What is of concern is that his New Age teachings are most likely a template—a blueprint—for the false Christ to come, whoever that may turn out to be. Scripture is very clear that we are not to be ignorant of Satan's devices, especially as he plies the world and the church with his antichrist leaven and false Christs like Maitreya (2 Corinthians 2:11).

MAITREYA'S PURPOSE & PLAN

IN looking at Maitreya as an Antichrist prototype and at his New Age teachings as a template for Antichrist, Maitreya seems to have a four-fold purpose and plan for the world and the church:

1. Bring peace to the world through his "reappearance" and return.

2. Establish a New Age/New World Religion by helping humanity to understand their "God within" "Oneness" with all creation.

3. Introduce and help to further radically progressive social, racial, economic, environmental, political, spiritual, and humanitarian projects around the world.

4. Lead mankind to the feet of the "Father," "Sanat Kumara," who is said to be "God" and the "Lord" of the World.

Immanence: The "God Within"

IT is important to note that Maitreya repeatedly presents the foundational teaching of the New Age movement—the "great heretical idea" of the "God within"—as the centerpiece of his "New Truth" for the coming "New Age." He states:

> My friends, God is nearer to you than you can imagine. God is yourself. God is within you and all around you.[38]

Benjamin Creme made it abundantly clear that Maitreya's New World Religion is based on this immanent "God within" teaching when he wrote:

> But eventually a new world religion will be inaugurated which will be a fusion and synthesis of the approach of the East and the approach of the West. The Christ will bring together, not simply Christianity and Buddhism, but the concept of God transcendent—outside of His creation—and also the concept of God immanent in all creation—in man and all creation.[39]

As previously noted, many prominent church figures have echoed Maitreya and the New Age by presenting this same God "in" everything teaching, along with other New Age concepts like "God's Dream."

"A Pentecostal Experience for All"

BENJAMIN Creme also described how Maitreya's "Day of Declaration"—his alleged "reappearance" and "return" as "the Christ"—will be a "Pentecostal" celebration—a spectacular event much like the original Pentecost—except it will be worldwide. Creme wrote:

> One day soon, men and women all over the world will gather round their radio and television sets to hear and see the Christ: to see His face, and to hear His words dropping silently into their minds—in their own language. In this way they will know that

He is truly the Christ, the World Teacher; and in this way too, we will see repeated, only now on a world scale, the happenings of Pentecost; and in celebration of this event Pentecost will become a major festival of the New World Religion.[40]

In addressing questions about Maitreya's ability to convince skeptical professing Christians that he is "the Christ," and not Antichrist, Creme described how Maitreya has been working behind the scenes for years with Christians "to soften them up."[41] He said that on the "Day of Declaration" there will be a powerful "overshadowing"—a "Pentecostal experience for all"—that will convince "even the fundamentalists" that Maitreya is "the Christ." Creme wrote:

> The fundamentalists, of course, are afraid that Maitreya might be the "'Antichrist," with which fallacy I have dealt many times, here and elsewhere. On the Day of Declaration, I submit, everyone—even the fundamentalists—will know, through the overshadowing of the minds of all humanity—a Pentecostal experience for all—that Maitreya is the Christ.[42]

In light of these statements, the church must ask some hard questions. Is an "unholy spirit"—the "spirit of Antichrist"—orchestrating spiritual experiences like "holy laughter" to "soften up" the church as described by Creme? Is "holy laughter" a dress rehearsal for the "Pentecostal experience for all" described by Creme? In short, are many of today's alleged revivals helping to prepare the way for the ultimate false Christ—someone like Maitreya?

SENDING "STRANGE FIRE"

ON February 23, 2019, 70,000 people gathered in Camping World Stadium in Orlando, Florida for what was called "The Send" conference. They were there to hear Rodney Howard-Browne, Benny Hinn, Bill Johnson, Todd White, Francis Chan, Lou Engle and other church figures give talks that reinforced conference leader

Lou Engle's longstanding belief in the concept of a "God's Dream" worldwide "revival" that would "change history."

In September 2019, a "revival" event titled "Light the Fire Again" was held in a large arena in Pensacola, Florida. Many of the featured speakers were "holy laughter" veterans who had been directly or indirectly involved with the Toronto Blessing and Brownsville "revivals" and the more recent "Send" conference in Orlando. Speakers included Lou Engle, Todd White, John Arnott, Heidi Baker, Dr. Michael Brown, and—once again—Rodney Howard-Browne. More "Send" and "Light the Fire" "revival" events are planned for the future.

HOLY LAUGHTER OR STRONG DELUSION?

IN a 1994 article titled "Holy Laughter or Strong Delusion?" I warned about Rodney Howard-Browne and his "holy laughter" "revival" meetings.[43] In that article, I noted how New Age leader Barbara Marx Hubbard, channeling the New Age Christ, described a future Planetary Pentecost that would be the result of a massive outpouring of "spirit" directed by this false Christ and how all "sensitive persons" would experience feelings of "uncontrollable joy" as "the joy of the force" flooded the "Earth" with feelings of "love and attraction." The false New Age Christ stated:

> The Planetary Smile is another name for the Planetary Pentecost. When enough of us share a common thought of our oneness with God, Spirit will be poured out on all flesh paying attention.[44]

> An uncontrollable joy will ripple through the thinking layer of Earth. . . . From within, all sensitive persons will feel the joy of the force, flooding their systems with love and attraction.[45]

In the article, I noted how the Planetary Pentecost/Planetary Smile with its "joy of the force" and feelings of "uncontrollable joy" sounded a lot like "holy laughter." In fact, as previously noted, the counterfeit

"Jesus" who channeled *A Course in Miracles* expressly stated that the world will not end in judgment but "in laughter." He said:

> The world will end in laughter.[46]

However, Jesus' last words on laughter do not offer much encouragement for laughing revivals and the world ending in laughter. He warns:

> Woe unto you that laugh now! for ye shall mourn and weep.
> (Luke 6:25)

ANTICHRIST WARNING

IN her 1888 book *The Secret Doctrine*, occult theosophist Helena Blavatsky, presented the foundational teachings of what would eventually become the New Age movement. In her frontal attack on biblical Christianity, she expounded upon the future coming of a mysterious "World Teacher" named Maitreya and how he would "return" one day to set the world straight—how he would clear up its many problems and help humanity evolve to a higher spiritual plane.

Ten years later, in 1898—fourteen years before the sinking of the *Titanic*—a Connecticut pastor named Samuel J. Andrews was very concerned about the state of the church. In response, he wrote a book titled *Christianity and Anti-Christianity in Their Final Conflict*. In it, he warned how Antichrist was preparing the way for his coming with false teachings like Blavatsky's Theosophy. Pastor Andrews didn't talk around the issue. He hit it straight on. He knew the Bible described a future "great deception"—not a future "great awakening." Quoting Scripture after Scripture, Andrews warned there would be no worldwide conversion to Jesus Christ—only worldwide hostility toward the true Christ and those who held to His biblical teachings. He wrote:

> This summary of the Lord's teaching shows us that anything like a conversion of the world before His return by the preaching of the gospel, was not in His thoughts.

Had it been, He could not have failed to comfort His mourning disciples, and encourage them to vigorous action by assurances of the success of their mission. But He persistently holds up before them hatred, persecution, death. His life on earth was prophetic of the history of the Church; and the greatest manifestation of hostility to her, as to Him, would be at the end.[47]

But most pastors and church leaders today don't talk about Antichrist and how New Age teachers have been preparing the way for this future world ruler. But thank God for discerning pastors today who, like Samuel Andrews, "have a love of the truth" and are concerned enough to warn about false New Age teachings and false Christs—like Maitreya.

Even him, whose coming is after the working

of Satan with all power and signs and lying

wonders, And with all deceivableness of

unrighteousness in them that perish; because

they received not the love of the truth, that they

might be saved. (2 Thessalonians 2:9-10)

❧11❧

CHRISTIANITY & ANTI-CHRISTIANITY

Some have laughed the Spirit of God out of Gospel meetings, and the one thing we are conscious of above all others in many meetings, is the lack of the deep sense of the presence and power of God.[1]

—Pastor John Harper
Titanic casualty

The man sitting beside me, Dwayne from California, roared like a wounded lion. The woman beside Dwayne started jerking so badly her hands struck her face. People fell like dominoes, collapsing chairs as they plunged to the carpeting.[2]

—*Toronto Life Magazine*
Article on the Toronto Blessing

❧THE TITANIC❧

After the *Titanic* collided with the fateful iceberg, most passengers still believed the ship to be unsinkable. A surprising number of people chose to remain on board the stricken vessel even when given the opportunity to leave on a lifeboat. Walter Lord wrote that "nearly everyone still expected to reach New York. At worst, they would all be transferred to other ships."[3]

With the ship's bright lights shining and Wallace Hartley and his eight-member band playing out on the forward part of the boat deck, many passengers felt safer on the doomed ship than on one of the lifeboats that could have saved their lives. As cited, John Jacob Astor originally dismissed the idea of boarding a lifeboat when he said, "We are safer here than in that little boat." And when William Carter had urged Harry Widener to have a go at one of the lifeboats, Widener spoke for many when he replied—"I think I'll stick to the big ship, Billy, and take a chance."

J. Bruce Ismay, the managing director of the White Star Line, was traveling on the ship's maiden voyage. After being informed by Captain Smith that the damage to the ship was beyond repair and that *Titanic* would soon sink, he helped load women and children into the departing lifeboats. When one of the last lifeboats was leaving with empty seats, he slipped in and took a seat. He was later vilified in the American press for saving himself while women and children were still aboard the ship. He was also singled out for being the one chiefly responsible for limiting the number of lifeboats on the ship. Though contrary to his later denial, he had, apparently, pressured Captain Smith to race the *Titanic* at nearly full speed that last day so they could reach New York and beat her sister ship *Olympic*'s maiden voyage time.

There were some other men like Ismay who, one way or another, were able to board the lifeboats meant for women and children. Dr. Henry William Frauenthal suddenly leaped into a lifeboat that was being lowered and landed on Mrs. Annie May Stengel's back, knocking her unconscious.[4] Another man made his way onto one of the lifeboats with a shawl over his head, passing for a woman. Several card sharps who had boarded the ship under assumed names to exploit unsuspecting passengers also found their way onto lifeboats. There were others also who were thinking only of themselves, but they were definitely the exception to the generally admirable behavior that prevailed as the disaster unfolded. In fact, many passengers, even as they faced an almost certain death, remained resolute—even heroic. Surviving passenger George Rheims recalled:

> We remained then, about 1500 persons, with no way to escape. It was sure death for all of us. I cannot say enough about the wonderful calm with which each one contemplated it. We said good-bye to all our friends and each one prepared himself to die decently.[5]

Reverend Robert Bateman told his sister-in-law as she got into a lifeboat:

> If I don't meet you again in this world, I will in the next.[6]

Surviving Second Officer Charles Lightoller, who was loading women and children into lifeboats on the port side of the ship, was impressed with a young American couple. He said her response to his invitation to board one of the lifeboats was "typical of the spirit throughout." With a "frank smile" and turning to her husband, she replied:

> Not on your life. We started together, and if need be, we'll finish together.[7]

It was much the same with Macy's department store founder and president Isidor Strauss and his wife. Refusing the offer of a lifeboat seat, Mrs. Strauss looked at her husband and said:

> We have been living together for many years, and where you go, I go.[8]

> I will not be separated from my husband. As we have lived, so we will die together.[9]

With that said, she and her husband stepped back from the lifeboats to quietly await their fate.

Dan Marvin coaxed his reluctant bride into one of the lifeboats and told her:

It's all right, little girl, you go, and I'll stay a while.[10]

When wealthy industrialist Benjamin Guggenheim realized that death was near, he and his personal secretary, Victor Giglio went back to their cabins and returned in their best evening attire. Guggenheim announced, "We've dressed up in our best and are prepared to go down like gentlemen."[11] He said, "No woman shall be left aboard this ship because Ben Guggenheim was a coward."[12] One of the last things he did was to convey a message that was to be given to his wife. He said, "If anything should happen to me, tell my wife I've done my best in doing my duty."[13] As reality settled in, these heart-wrenching dramas continued to play out.

With time winding down, the last of the ship's eight distress rockets was fired to alert possible ships in the area of their dire situation. The laughter and conviviality that had prevailed throughout the voyage and earlier that evening ceased—even as the band played on. Any remaining tendency to deny what was happening was now checked by reality. There were no more lifeboats, and all but a very few of the over 1500 people on board the sinking ship would soon die in the freezing ocean. And Scottish Pastor John Harper would be one of them.

Pastor John Harper (1872-1912)

SCOTTISH pastor John Harper was traveling on the *Titanic* from his home and church in London. He was on his way to the Moody Church in Chicago, Illinois where he had been asked to preach and conduct revival. He was accompanied by his six-year-old daughter Nana and his niece Jessica Leitch. Jessica had come to help him take care of his daughter after Harper's wife died soon after giving birth to Nana. Pastor Harper wrapped Nana in a blanket and safely saw the two of them into lifeboats.

Having almost drowned two other times in his life, and with his strong abiding faith, his desperate situation did not find him afraid. Sometime after his wife's death, looking back on his near drowning at age twenty-six, he had remarked, "The fear of death did not for one moment disturb me. I believed that sudden death would be sudden glory, but, there was a wee motherless girl in Glasgow."[14] But for his daughter, he would gladly depart to be with his Lord.

And while John Harper did not fear death, and his faith in God was sure, he also knew in those waning moments that his ministry was not over. Reportedly, he walked around the ship's deck calling out to those around him—"Let the women, children, and the unsaved into the lifeboats!"[15] After the disaster and reflecting on Pastor Harper's deep concern for the salvation of others, the *Moody Church Herald* published the following as part of its tribute to his life and ministry:

> Among the last of the survivors to leave the vessel was a Swedish sailor. He states that before he was swept overboard, a minister had gathered the people in a large circle upon the afterdeck himself kneeling in the center of the circle, with arms uplifted and a holy joy upon his face, was praying and pleading for the salvation of these people. We can well believe that this was our brother John Harper.[16]

As the presiding pastor of Walworth Road Church in London, John Harper had been invited back to Chicago's Moody Church after having conducted widely hailed revival meetings the previous winter. And while his daughter and niece were successfully rescued by the British ship *Carpathia*, Pastor Harper never made it back to Moody Church. However, his witnessing heroics—especially in the water after the ship sank—have been preserved by the Titanic Historical Society, at the Moody Church, and in a Gospel tract that recounts his actions that last night. He was also the subject of a book titled *Titanic's Last Hero* by Moody Adams.

The June 1998 Moody Church Radio Ministries monthly newsletter had an article about Pastor Harper written by the presiding Moody Church pastor, Erwin Lutzer. In the article, Lutzer recalled seeing the Harper Gospel tract years before in his native Canada. He wrote:

> I first heard the phenomenal story of John Harper, many years ago while growing up in Canada. My brother showed me a one-page tract titled I Was Harper's Last Convert. It was the story, told by a man, who floated next to Harper briefly in the icy waters of the Atlantic.[17]

A photocopy of the first page of a more extended English version of the Gospel tract was part of an article about Pastor Harper's life and ministry in a year 2000 issue of *The Titanic Commutator*, a quarterly magazine published by The Titanic Historical Society. The article was titled "A Passion for Souls." The photocopied tract contained the testimony of a *Titanic* survivor that Harper had reportedly witnessed to in the icy water after the ship sank. According to the tract, this man had stood up in a Canadian Gospel meeting at the Hamilton, Ontario Y.M.C.A., and introduced himself as John Harper's last convert. He said:

> I was a careless sinner on board when the *Titanic* went down, and with hundreds more I found myself struggling in the cold, dark waters of the Atlantic. I caught hold of something and clung to it for dear life, the wail of the perishing all around was ringing in my ears, when there floated by me a man who called to me, "Is your soul saved?" I said, "No, it is not."

> Back came the words, "Believe on the Lord Jesus Christ and thou shalt be saved;" we drifted apart, then seemed drifted together once more; "Is your soul saved?" again he cried out. "I fear it is not." "Then if you will believe on the Lord Jesus Christ your soul shall be saved." Again we were separated by

rolling currents; I heard him call out this message to others as they sank beneath the waters to eternity.

Then and there, with two miles of water beneath me, in my desperation I cried to Christ to save me. I believed and was saved.[18]

Pastor Harper was known to take every possible opportunity to talk about the Lord with whomever he met. His niece later described how he had witnessed to a young Englishman earlier that last day. She said:

The last day we spent on the *Titanic* was Sunday. Mr. Harper asked me to read the chapter at our morning family prayers, and later we went to the Sunday morning services. The day was quiet and pleasantly spent, and when Nana and I went to look for Mr. Harper at about 6 o'clock to go to dinner, I found him earnestly talking to a young Englishman whom he was seeking to lead to Christ.[19]

Pastor John Harper

A friend of twelve years, Pastor Malcolm Ferguson, praised Pastor Harper's passionate commitment to the Lord and described the inspirational revival meetings he held at his Paisley Road Church in Glasgow, Scotland before he moved to London:

> I was often there during 1905, when the news of the Welsh Revival spread. I did not go to Wales, but often saw scenes in Paisley Road Church similar to what we heard were going on there. The crowds were so great it was difficult to get in, and after getting in, still more difficult to get near the platform. Then, before anyone could speak ten minutes, souls were crying out for mercy under the mighty power of God. It was not excitement. It was the Holy Spirit convicting of sin.[20]

Pastor Ferguson recalled Pastor Harper lamenting on how some churches had "laughed the Spirit of God out of Gospel meetings." He recounted Harper once stating at a conference that the church wouldn't get many sinners convicted and converted through laughter. Harper had said:

> Some have laughed the Spirit of God out of Gospel meetings, and the one thing we are conscious of above all others in many meetings, is the lack of the deep sense of the presence and power of God.[21]

Pastor John Harper was a genuine revival pastor. Peers and others close to Harper, testified after his passing that he was a true man of God. His services were not humanly orchestrated or personality driven. There was no "take a drink, take a drink, fill, fill, fill" or "strange fire" being called down from heaven by a "holy ghost bartender." Souls truly and openly repented with godly sorrow as they earnestly cried out to God for His forgiveness and mercy.

John Harper was a man of God and faithful to the end. One of the rooms at the Moody Church today is named Harper Hall in honor of the way he glorified God in the many revival meetings he held at their Chicago church.

PASTOR SAMUEL J. ANDREWS (1817-1906)

IN 1899, thirteen years before the sinking of the *Titanic*, Connecticut pastor Samuel J. Andrews' book, *Christianity and Anti-Christianity in Their Final Conflict*, was reissued in a new more affordable edition for Christian workers and the Christian public at large. At the front of the book, serving as a foreword, was a powerful two-page "Commendation and an Appeal" written by James M. Gray of the Moody Bible Institute.

With "immanent" panentheistic God "in" everything teachings gaining momentum in the world and the church at that time, *Christianity and Anti-Christianity in Their Final Conflict* was a severe warning regarding the spiritual preparations being made to pave the way for Antichrist and his Antichrist system. Pastor Andrews stated that the church could ill-afford to ignore the "God within" foundation that was being carefully constructed for this coming world ruler. In the spirit of the apostle Paul, Pastor Andrews issued an urgent warning to the church to not be "ignorant" of Satan's deceptive "devices" (2 Corinthians 2:11). Andrews wrote:

> To ignore the Antichrist of whom she has been forewarned, is for the Church to expose herself defenseless to his wiles, deceptions, and attacks.[22]

Most particularly, Pastor Andrews warned about the Antichrist system's heretical "lie" regarding the "deification of man"—what New Age author Marilyn Ferguson would present eighty years later as the "great heretical idea." Pastor Andrews described how this "antichristian" "God within" leaven was preparing the way for Antichrist. He wrote:

> To understand the prophetic descriptions of the Antichrist, as claiming Divine homage, we must see how the prevalent philosophy tends to the deification of man, and so helps to prepare his way.[23]

> There is a "fullness of time" for his appearing, and this is not
> till the antichristian leaven has spread through Christendom.[24]

Amazingly, Pastor Andrews described this antichristian leaven as "new age" decades before the New Age became popularly known as "New Age." He wrote:

> Assuming here (what the examination of the Scriptures will soon show us) that the antichristian spirit, which has often had its partial representatives in the past, is to be finally summed up in a single person, who is distinctively the Antichrist—the last product of the antichristian tendencies—we are brought to the vital question, What will be the relations of the coming new age to him?[25]

Pastor Andrews not only anticipated the New Age movement but also the movement's future manipulation of science, with its emphatic but false declaration that humanity must take a "sudden leap" from its old age understandings to the seemingly scientific understandings of the "new age." He warned:

> With the spread of the new ideas, which dethrone God and His Christ, literature must take on itself more and more an antichristian character. Its prophets and its poets will unite in their jubilations on the speedy coming of the new age, when the superstitious and narrow beliefs of the past will give place to a rational and comprehensive religion based on science and glorifying the Divinity of man.[26]

Envisioning a future "quantum leap" into an occult/New Age "Quantum Christianity," Andrews asked:

> Why a new age? Are our old beliefs, our old institutions, outgrown? Are we about to break with the past, and take a sudden leap onward? . . .

When the new age has fully developed itself, what religion will it give us? Will it be some new phase of Christianity, or an eclectic religion, or something distinctly new?[27]

Samuel Andrews warned that this "new age" will come through "a Christianized civilization, and the enlargement of Christendom to embrace all nations."[28] The world will appear to be Christianized when, in reality, it has been cunningly universalized. And because Antichrist's New Age deception has crept into today's church with its Christianized terms and concepts, the church has missed what's going on. Thus, the church is moving toward a "New Age Christianity" that is not Christian at all.

Andrews also warned how the world was pressuring the church to re-examine its beliefs about God. They were insisting that a "new religion"—a "world religion"—with a "new conception of God" was needed for the "new age" that the world and the church were moving into. The forces that be were saying:

We have come to a new age, and a new age must bring with it a new religion, not a revivication of the past; one based upon a new conception of God, simple, comprehensive, and fitted to be a world religion.[29]

[T]he organism must be adjusted to its present environment. The Church, both as to its doctrine and polity and labours, must respond to the demands of the new age, and adapt itself to its needs.[30]

Pastor Andrews further warned about the attempt to deify man under unassuming labels like—"New Reformation," "New Orthodoxy," and "New Christianity"[31]—the same labels being used by a number of Christian leaders today.[32] Andrews was taking dead aim at the "God within" doctrinal leaven that had crept into popular books of his time, written by professing believers like William Stead and found in books like Stead's *After Death: Letters From Julia*. This was the same heretical "God within" leaven that would be put forward in the next century by Marilyn Ferguson, Oprah Winfrey, the whole New Age movement, and many undiscerning Christian authors and church leaders. This same "immanent," "God within" doctrine that Pastor Andrews warned about in the late 1800s continues to prepare the way today for the eventual coming of Antichrist. Andrews wrote:

> Do we see in its spirit and principles a preparation for him? . . . Are we to have a new religion in which the Saviour from sin can have no place, but will be supplanted by one who will present himself as the representative of a Divine humanity, and so an object of worship?[33]

> It is plain that the doctrine of the immanence of God in man, and that of a human element in God, each lays a broad basis for the deification of man, and so serves as a preparation for the Antichrist.[34]

Andrews described how this foundational leaven was making men equal to God as it "deposed" the true Jesus Christ and "prepares the way for Antichrist":

> This is the spirit that prepares the way for the Antichrist. Christ being deposed from His place as the only Godman; all men being as to nature equally with Him Godmen, the nations are prepared to welcome one who will prove to the deceived and wondering world his Divinity by his mighty acts, wrought in Satanic power; and will say, "This man is the great Power of God." As the representative of deified humanity, he will seat himself in the temple of God, and all "the children of pride" will worship Him. And thus the kingdom of Man will come, and the world will say, this is the kingdom of God, this is the King.[35]

Pastor Samuel Andrews' 1899 book, *Christianity and Anti-Christianity in Their Final Conflict* (published today by The Berean Call ministry) might have been overlooked by the average pastor and churchgoer of Andrews' day were it not for the strong endorsement and enthusiastic support of Pastor James M. Gray of the Moody Bible Institute.

PASTOR JAMES M. GRAY (1851-1935)

JAMES M. Gray D.D. understood the importance of Samuel Andrews' prophetic book. A long-time summer lecturer at the Moody Bible Institute in Chicago, Illinois, Gray was a well-respected pastor and teacher. He frequently preached alongside pastor and evangelist Dwight L. Moody during Moody's evangelistic campaigns in New York, Boston, and at Moody's popular Northfield summer conferences in Northfield, Massachusetts. D. L. Moody described two of Gray's sermons as ones he would never forget.[36]

In the restructuring of the Moody Bible Institute after Moody's passing, James Gray became dean of the institute and was later its first president. He was head of the institute when Pastor John Harper was invited to hold revival meetings at the Moody Church in 1911 and again in 1912. Gray was the author of many books, including *Satan and the Saint* and *The Concise Bible Commentary*. Torrey-Gray Hall, the main auditorium at The Moody Bible Institute today, is named in honor of the exemplary leadership of the institute by pastors R. A. Torrey and James M. Gray.

Gray knew the importance of defending, contending, and fighting for the faith when it is opposed by false teachings. He understood that preaching the Gospel means not only teaching who God *is*, but who God is *not*. He did not hesitate to preach and declare "all the counsel of God" (Acts 20:27)—especially in regard to what many in the church were referring to as "negative teaching."

James Gray knew that Samuel Andrews' book *Christianity and Anti-Christianity in Their Final Conflict* was a much-needed and urgent warning of how the world and the church were being spiritually prepared for the coming of Antichrist and his Antichrist system. Gray was passionate about Andrews' book and was primarily responsible for the publication of the new more affordable 1899 edition. He wanted to get this important information into the hands of as many pastors, missionaries, and Christian workers as possible. In writing his "Commendation and an Appeal" that served as a foreword to Pastor Andrews' book, he wrote:

> After the Bible, a concordance, a bible dictionary and, perhaps, an all-round work like Angus' "Bible Hand-Book," the next book I would recommend as indispensable for the library of the pastor, missionary or Christian worker of today is, *Christianity and Anti-Christianity in Their Final Conflict*, by Rev. Samuel J. Andrews.[37]

He continued his unequivocal endorsement by writing:

> Pastors, missionaries, Sunday-school teachers and social workers, bear with me if I say, you must read this book. By Divine grace, I have a large acquaintance among you, wherever the Gospel is preached, and I appeal to you, by whatever spiritual tie unites us, to become acquainted with what this prophet of the twentieth century has to teach. Here are no wild fancies, no foolish setting of times and seasons, no crude and sensational interpretations of prophecy, but a calm setting forth of *what the Bible says on the most important subject for these times.*[38] (italics his)

He concluded his "Commendation and an Appeal" by emphatically stating:

> The Christian leader who does not know these things is no leader, but the blind leading the blind. And, oh, there are so many of such leaders![39]

And, indeed, over the ensuing years, most church leaders have turned a blind eye to how the world and the professing church are being cunningly prepared for a false Christ and a New World Religion. Sadly, the biblical warnings of Samuel J. Andrews, James M. Gray, and other watchmen over the years, have been almost completely overlooked.

PASTOR HARRY IRONSIDE (1876-1951)

PASTOR Harry Ironside served as the pastor of the Moody Church from 1929-1948. He served his first five years while James M. Gray was still president of the Moody Bible Institute. Pastor Ironside's ministry was right in step with D. L. Moody and James Gray's emphasis on defending and contending for the faith. Ironside's classic treatise, "Exposing Error: Is It Worthwhile?," underlined what Samuel Andrews and James Gray were trying to communicate to pastors and other church leaders about the need to expose "damnable heresies"—like the "God within." Ironside wrote:

> Objection is often raised even by some sound in the faith regarding the exposure of error as being entirely negative and of no real edification. Of late, the hue and cry has been against any and all negative teaching. But the brethren who assume this attitude forget that a large part of the New Testament, both of the teaching of our blessed Lord Himself and the writings of the apostles, is made up of this very character of ministry—namely, showing the Satanic origin and, therefore, the unsettling results of the propagation of erroneous systems which Peter, in his second epistle, so definitely refers to as "damnable heresies."[40]

Pastor Ironside further warned of the "grievous wolves" who "alone and in packs, are not sparing even the most favored flocks." He reminded the church that we are not to stand idly by when error creeps into our midst. Pastors must preach and apply "the whole body of revealed truth." He said that we must "contend for the faith" and that "God's truth necessitates some negative teaching." He wrote:

> We are called upon to "contend earnestly for the faith once for all delivered to the saints," while we hold the truth in love. The faith means the whole body of revealed truth, and to contend for all of God's truth necessitates some negative teaching. . . . Paul likewise admonishes us to "have no fellowship with the unfruitful works of darkness, but rather reprove them" (Ephesians 5:11).[41]

Ironside warned that error was like leaven and must be exposed. He stated that "truth mixed with error," while appearing to be "more innocent-looking," is even "more dangerous." That it must be reproved and repudiated. He wrote:

> Error is like leaven, of which we read, "A little leaven leaveneth the whole lump." Truth mixed with error is equivalent to all error, except that it is more innocent looking and, therefore, more dangerous. God hates such a mixture! Any error, or any truth-and-error mixture, calls for definite exposure and repudiation. To condone such is to be unfaithful to God and His Word and treacherous to imperiled souls for whom Christ died.[42]

He finished his plea for biblical discernment by writing:

> Exposing error is most unpopular work. But from every true standpoint it is worthwhile work. To our Savior, it means that He receives from us, His blood-bought ones, the loyalty that is His due.[43]

❧TODAY'S CHURCH❧

ANTICHRIST'S NEW AGE ROOTS

There were not that many people coming out of New Age teachings and publicly warning about spiritual deception back in the 1980s and 1990s. But those who did were passionate in their books, talks, and interviews. We had a strong desire to warn the world and the church how the New Age was preparing the way for Antichrist and his New World Religion. It was what Samuel Andrews had written in his book *Christianity and Anti-Christianity in Their Final Conflict*. He described how "God within" leaven would provide the spiritual foundation for Antichrist to assume his role as the "Divine" head of a "Divine" humanity.

In 1990, Moody Press published then Moody Church pastor Erwin Lutzer's *Coming to Grips With Antichrist's New Age Roots*. Lutzer wrote:

> A massive worldwide crisis will trigger the emergence of the "New Age" of human destiny. As things begin to shake loose, worldwide changes will take place rapidly.[44]

Specifically regarding Antichrist, Lutzer wrote:

> As the notion that man is God gains widespread acceptance, we will soon live in a generation eager to accept the claims of a superman. If we are all God, then a particularly shrewd man can be a special God.[45]

> People are beginning to believe in the very doctrines that Antichrist will proclaim. A religious revolution is taking place that will make the spiritual aspects of Antichrist's rule welcomed by the world.[46]

> We will discover many parallels between his theology and that of the popular New Age movement that we are hearing so much about today.[47]

The *New* Age appears to be the preparation for the *Final* Age. And the Final Age will be the more terrifying than any that preceded it.[48] (italics his)

Thus, the New Age movement, which is actually based on old lies, will usher in the final age. That this will happen is certain; the *time* is not.[49] (italics his)

In 1992, two years after publishing Erwin Lutzer's book *Coming to Grips With Antichrist's New Age Roots*, Moody Press published my book *The Light That Was Dark*. In it, I warned from my own experience of how dangerous the New Age and its false Christ are to both the world and the church. At the end of my book, I asked:

Were we witnessing the great "falling away" predicted in the Bible (2 Thessalonians 2:3)? Was the "mystery of iniquity" talked about in the Scriptures already doing its deceptive work with "all power and signs and lying wonders" and "all deceivableness of unrighteousness" (2 Thessalonians 2: 7-10)? Would people calling themselves Christians abandon their faith in the Bible and the Bible's Christ (1 Timothy 4:1)? Would they join an ecumenical movement that in the name of love, God, unity, and peace would sacrifice the truth of the Bible and perhaps one day merge with the New Age itself? Jesus warned that such a faith would lead not to life but to ultimate destruction.[50]

In *Christianity and Anti-Christianity in Their Final Conflict*, Samuel Andrews warned about the Antichrist leaven that was coming into the world and into the church—the same leaven that is pouring into the church today. For a church leader like James Gray to strongly endorse Andrews' book was significant. For James Gray to endorse Andrews' book over the letterhead of The Moody Bible Institute was even more significant. It obviously meant that his commendation came with the blessing of the institute itself. However, what Samuel Andrews, James Gray, and The Moody Bible Institute saw so clearly well over a century ago, most church leadership does not see today. An Antichrist system has been put into place and is preparing the world and the church for a great deception—a deception foundationally based on the "great heretical idea" that God is "in" everyone and everything.

MOODY BIBLE INSTITUTE

OVER the years, Moody Bible Institute was held in high regard for its education, inspiration, and spiritual protection of the church; for upholding the ideals of its founder D. L. Moody and of God-fearing, spiritually discerning men like James M. Gray and Harry Ironside—men who loved God's Word and preached "all the counsel of God" (Acts 20:27). Men who contended, defended, and fought for the faith. Men who were prayerfully chosen to preach and teach and inspire revival at the Moody Bible Institute, Moody conferences, and Moody Church—men like Pastor John Harper.

However, The Moody Bible Institute has been challenged of late for having lost sight of those ideals—the ideals upon which they were originally founded.[51] And what has happened at Moody has happened with the greater church at large. Like the *Titanic*, complacency moved in as vigilance and spiritual discernment moved out. Sadly, an undiscerning church has placed its confidence in church leaders—not in their Savior. As a result, much of the church is unaware and unprepared for what is happening and what is going to happen.

BEAUTIFUL IN THE MORNING

MANY who were aboard the *Titanic* that fateful night were spiritually prepared for the disaster in which they suddenly found themselves. Pastor John Harper was one of them. He was ready because his spiritual assuredness came not from the words of other men, but from the Word of God and his relationship with the Lord. And while he knew he would probably not be physically saved that April night, he knew he was spiritually saved for the world to come. Thus, in his waning moments, his thoughts were not on himself but on those who were still lost and afraid—who were not prepared for what was taking place. In those cold dark waters, Harper continued to witness and share his faith with others. And his exhortation to "Repent and be saved" pierced the heart and saved the soul of at least one man Harper encountered in his last moments.

John Harper's niece, Jessica Leitch, later recalled how her uncle had stood on the deck and gazed out at the evening sky that last night. After a magnificent sunset, and with just a hint of red left on the horizon, he remarked, "It will be beautiful in the morning."[52] And so it would be, but not in the way that Harper thought at the time. Little did he know that it would be "beautiful in the morning" because having passed from this world to the next, he would be with his beautiful Savior.

Like the thief on the cross and John Harper's last convert in the water, it is never too late to get saved—even in the midst of disaster. As Harper said to the drowning man, "Believe on the Lord Jesus Christ and thou shalt be saved." This may seem like an easy way out to the disbelieving many, but it is *the* way out for those who have faith and choose to believe. And for those who do choose Jesus Christ and His free gift of salvation, John Harper's words will one day ring true for them as well:

"It will be beautiful in the morning."

Weeping may endure for a night, but joy

cometh in the morning. (Psalm 30:5)

⁓12⁓

RESCUE OPERATION

I am unable to find any possible explanation of what happened, except it may be the Captain of the vessel [Stanley Lord] was in ice for the first time and would not take the risk of going to the rescue of another vessel.[1]

—Sir Rufus Isaacs
British Inquiry regarding the *Californian*

Arthur Rostron was a man who would risk everything in the hope that he could reach the *Titanic* in time to save as many lives as he could.[2]

—Sir Rufus Isaacs
British Inquiry regarding the *Carpathia*

⁓THE TITANIC⁓

On Sunday, April 14, 1912, the day of the disaster, *Titanic's* scheduled boat drill was cancelled by Captain Smith for unknown reasons. Meanwhile, several church services were held on board for passengers, and things seemed to be taking their normal course. As noted, *Titanic* received six warnings that day from other ships about the heavy ice they were fast approaching. With most of those on board enjoying a pleasant passage, *Titanic* raced toward the fatal iceberg.

At 11:40 p.m., the ship struck the iceberg. Two hours and forty minutes later at 2:20 a.m. the *Titanic* had completely gone under. Over 1500 people were cast into the sea. William Stead, the man who had written stories about shipwrecks that didn't have enough lifeboats was now one of those he had once described as shipwrecked, "floundering in the water, and calling for help."[3]

After the ship sank, Colonel Archibald Gracie swam over to an auxiliary lifeboat that had slid off the sinking ship and was floating bottom-side-up in the water. He was one of the thirty or so men who stood on top of the overturned lifeboat, continually shifting their weight to keep the boat balanced and preventing them from toppling back into the ocean. Fortunate to have made it onto this lifeboat, Gracie listened in horror to those who were struggling in the water. He wrote:

> [T]here arose to the sky the most horrible sounds ever heard by mortal man except by those of us who survived this terrible tragedy. The agonizing cries of death from over a thousand throats, the wails and groans of the suffering, the shrieks of the terror-stricken and the awful gaspings for breath of those in the last throes of drowning, none of us will ever forget to our dying day.[4]

All the lifeboats were positioned away from any possibility of being sucked under when the ship went down. Tragically, only one of the many lifeboats with empty seats went back to try and rescue those in the water. Out of the over 1500 people in the water, very few made it out of the water into lifeboats even though there were over 470 empty and available seats. And roughly ten miles away stood the cargo ship *Californian* that had stopped for the night.

With various *Californian* crew members observing the eight distress rockets fired up into the sky by the *Titanic*, it didn't seem to occur to anyone—most especially the *Californian* captain—to wake up their wireless operator. All the radio man had to do was turn on his radio to find out what was happening.

❧THE CALIFORNIAN❧

The *Californian* was a Leland Line cargo ship traveling with no passengers from London, England to Boston, Massachusetts. On Sunday, April 14, Captain Stanley Lord had stopped his ship for the night after encountering one of the huge ice fields they had been warned about by other ships during the day. Choosing to be safe, they would wait until daylight to resume their journey. Aware that the *Titanic* was approaching this same area, Captain Lord instructed his lone radio operator, Cyril Evans, to warn the *Titanic* about the ice field they would soon encounter.

SHUT UP! SHUT UP!

AROUND 10:55 p.m. Cyril Evans wired the *Titanic* with his ice warning, "Say old man, we are surrounded by ice and stopped." However, as cited *Titanic*'s wireless operator, Jack Phillips, immediately cut him off, telling him to "Shut up! Shut up! I'm busy. I'm working Cape Race!" Phillips was in the midst of sending a back log of passenger wires to the Cape Race relay station. The messages had accumulated when *Titanic*'s telegraph set had broken down the day before. With the radio finally repaired and *Titanic* near enough to the mainland to relay messages, Phillips didn't appreciate the breach of ship etiquette of being interrupted while sending the messages. He was also irritated by the intensity of *Californian*'s signal as the two ships were so near each other. Because of the fractured communication, *Titanic* officers never received the *Californian*'s warning about the treacherous ice field that lay just forty-five minutes in front of them.

Having been rebuffed by Phillips, and tired after a long day, Cyril Evans finished his shift and shut off his radio around 11:30 p.m. After visiting a short while with Third Officer Charles Victor Groves, Evans went to bed. As he lay there, Jack Phillips sent *Titanic*'s first distress call at 12:15 a.m. Evans had no idea *Titanic* was sinking just ten or so miles away.

DISTRESS ROCKETS

AT 12:45 a.m., the *Titanic* sent up the first of eight distress rockets just as the first lifeboat was being lowered on the starboard side of the ship. After that first rocket was fired, *Californian* Second Officer Herbert Stone saw a sudden flash of white light burst over the strange ship he had been observing in the distance. He had been attempting to communicate with this unknown ship with his Morse lamp. Stone then saw four more white rockets burst in the sky after that. White rockets were commonly known as a sign of distress when fired from ships at sea.

Second Officer Stone spoke through the speaking tube to Captain Lord who was resting in the chart room at the time. Stone reported the white rockets he had seen. Dismissing the idea that they were distress signals, Captain Lord implied they were company rockets that were used by ships to identify themselves to other vessels. He instructed Stone to keep using the Morse lamp to try and make contact with the ship in question. He did not allow that the mystery ship might be the *Titanic*. And he did not tell Stone to wake up their telegraph operator to find out what was happening. Captain Lord then went back to sleep.

Apprentice Officer James Gibson joined Second Officer Stone on deck. As they observed the lights of the mystery ship in the distance, Stone said, "Look at her now; she looks very queer out of the water; her lights look queer."[5] After they watched the eighth and final rocket burst in the sky, Stone said that "a ship was not going to fire rockets at sea for nothing."[6] Acknowledging Stone, Gibson replied that "everything was not all right with her"—that there must be "trouble of some sort."[7]

Around 2:00 a.m., Gibson and Stone watched the lights of the mystery ship slowly fade in the distance. An uneasy Gibson woke Captain Lord and told him that the strange ship that had fired eight rockets seemed to be fading to the southwest. The captain acknowledged Gibson and went back to sleep. By 2:40 a.m. or so, the distant ship had completely disappeared. Stone got Captain Lord on the speaking tube again and told him the ship was gone from sight. Again, Captain Lord acknowledged the information but took no action and resumed sleeping. Meanwhile, Cyril Evans remained fast asleep with his radio turned off.

TITANIC GONE

CAPTAIN Lord was known to be a rather intimidating taskmaster. Because of this, his officers were probably hesitant to approach him about this matter anymore than they already had. However, when Chief Officer George Stewart arose and was briefed on all the early morning events, he woke up Cyril Evans and told him, "Sparks, there's a ship been firing rockets in the night. Will you see if you can find out what is wrong—what is the matter?"[8] When Evans turned his radio on, they were all shocked to hear about the *Titanic*. However, by this time, it was five hours or so after *Titanic's* initial distress call and since the first distress rocket was seen by Second Officer Stone.

When Captain Lord was given the news, the *Californian* finally set out for the disaster site. By the time they arrived, the rescue ship *Carpathia* was on the scene and had already taken everyone onto their ship from the lifeboats. As the *Carpathia* left the scene bound for New York City, the *Californian* did one final search of the area. No additional survivors were found.

QUESTIONS

TO this day, many questions remain regarding the *Californian* and its inexplicable passivity during those early morning hours. If Cyril Evans had been awakened after *Titanic's* first distress rocket and turned his radio on, he would have heard *Titanic's* call for help. If the *Californian* had departed immediately for the sinking ship, it has been estimated they would have arrived just after the *Titanic* sank. And while not all of the over 1500 people in the water would have been rescued, many more lives could have been conceivably saved.

At the United States and British inquiries, Captain Lord insisted that the *Californian* was over nineteen miles away and that the mysterious ship in the distance his crew had been observing was not the *Titanic*. However, after Robert Ballard's discovery of the *Titanic's* final resting place in 1985, it was estimated that the *Californian* was much closer to *Titanic* than what was reported by Captain Lord. The *Californian* may have been only five to ten miles away. Also disturbing, was the fact that none of the rockets seen by the *Californian* crew had been recorded in the ship's logbook. If they had been previously recorded, they had since been removed. All in all, the *Californian's* inaction amid this disaster has been a troubling subject throughout the years.

At the United States Senate Subcommittee Hearing, Captain Lord was held accountable for his unresponsiveness during this disaster. Even with the outcry raised by Captain Lord's supporters and family, one incontestable fact has remained—Captain Lord did not wake up his radio man when he was informed of the white distress rockets. Questions about his behavior that night would plague Captain Lord for the rest of his life.

THE SHIP THAT STOOD STILL

WHILE there is much debate and controversy about everything that happened in those early morning hours, it is generally agreed that the *Californian's* response to what was happening before them was very confused at best and tragically irresponsible at worst. While the ship could have played an important role in rescuing survivors, the *Californian* has come to be known as "The Ship That Stood Still."[9]

Sadly, the interactions between Captain Stanley Lord and his crew are reminiscent of today's church. Too often believers are intimidated by pastors and leaders who do not want to hear their concerns about a questionable book or a false teaching that has made its way into the church. Rebuffed and rejected, they are hesitant to bring up anything controversial again. And all too frequently, pastors and church leaders minimize or dismiss the observations and warnings of discernment ministries and individuals who are trying to expose deceptive teachings and trends that are impacting the church. But like the *Titanic* complacently disregarding those "last-day" warnings, and the *Californian* ignoring what was happening before them, today's church leaders are disregarding the many "last-days" warnings being given to them. Whether it is because the warnings don't fit with their theology, or they simply don't care, they are putting those who trust in their leadership and judgment in great jeopardy as a result. Somehow shepherds seem to have forgotten that one of their most important duties is to spiritually protect their flocks.

✥THE CARPATHIA✥

The RMS *Carpathia* was a transatlantic Cunard Line passenger steamship that departed New York City on April 11th bound for Gibraltar and other Mediterranean ports. On the night of the disaster, *Carpathia*'s sole telegraph operator, Harold Cottam, concluded his shift at midnight but kept his radio on as he took off his boots and got ready for bed. Before shutting his radio down, he decided to wire *Titanic*'s senior telegraph operator, Jack Phillips. He knew Phillips through their mutual telegraph work and wanted to let him know he had heard over the wires that the Cape Cod relay station had messages waiting for *Titanic*. Expecting an upbeat reply, Cottam was shocked when Phillips wired back SOS—"Come at once. We have struck a berg."[10]

58 MILES AWAY

HAROLD Cottam quickly notified the first officer, who in turn woke up Captain Arthur Rostron to inform him about the *Titanic*. Captain Rostron immediately gave the order to turn the ship around, and *Carpathia* bolted toward the coordinates provided to Cottam by *Titanic*'s Jack Phillips. Captain Rostron estimated they were 58 miles from the *Titanic*. Traveling as fast as safely possible, it would take the *Carpathia* an estimated four hours to get there. However, with the captain making some key adjustments, *Carpathia* reached the first lifeboat in just three-and-a-half hours.

Given the ice they would be encountering, Captain Rostron doubled his lookouts while maximizing the ship's engine efficiency to produce the absolute top speed. Every detail was anticipated and covered as Captain Rostron sped his ship toward the sinking *Titanic*. Doctors onboard were positioned in three separate rooms to minister aid to survivors needing medical assistance. Food was prepared, blankets were brought out, and Captain Rostron's own passengers were ready to help in whatever way they could.

The *Carpathia* arrived at the disaster site around 4 a.m.—about an hour-and-a-half after the *Titanic*'s sinking. In his autobiography, Captain Rostron described the huge icebergs that were all around them. He wrote:

> Daylight was just setting in and what a sight that new day gradually revealed! Everywhere were icebergs. . . . I instructed a junior officer to go to the wheel-house deck and count them. Twenty-five there were over two hundred feet in height and dozens ranging from a hundred and fifty down to fifty feet.[11]

Titanic **lifeboat approaching the** *Carpathia*

THE RESCUE

BY 9 a.m., just over 700 survivors had been removed from the lifeboats and brought aboard the *Carpathia*. Captain Rostron had high praise for the entire group. He said:

> As each boat came alongside, everyone was calm, and they kept perfectly still in their boats. They were quiet and orderly; and each person came up the ladder, or was pulled up in turn. . . . They behaved magnificently—every one of them.[12]

The weary survivors, many who had lost husbands, family, and friends, were calm but in obvious shock. *Carpathia* passengers assisted and supported them in every possible way. Many provided them with their own personal cabins. Captain Rostron wrote:

> The cream of human kindness was surely extended that morning and during the days that followed while we made New York, and through it all that quietness reigned—as though the disaster were so great that it silenced human emotion.[13]

Captain Rostron

Before *Carpathia* left the disaster site and headed to New York City, a brief memorial service was conducted in the first-class dining room. Captain Rostron said it was held "in memory of those who were lost and giving thanks for those who had been saved."[14]

Making their way past the ice fields, and then through some very challenging weather, the rescue ship reached New York City on the evening of April 18th. Anxious family and friends, and an eager press corps, were there to meet them.

COMMENDATIONS

DURING the United States Senate Subcommittee Hearing that began the next day, the chairman, Michigan Senator William Alden Smith, commended Captain Rostron's command as a "marvel of systematic preparation and completeness." He said:

> The committee deems the course followed by Captain Rostron of the *Carpathia* as deserving of the highest praise and worthy of especial recognition. . . . His detailed instructions issued in anticipation of the rescue of the *Titanic* are a marvel of systematic preparation and completeness, evincing such solicitude as calls for the highest commendation.[15]

Where Captain Stanley Lord was heavily criticized for his passivity and inaction, Captain Rostron received nothing but praise for his decisive and heroic actions. The *Carpathia* captain was given a heartfelt medal of appreciation from the *Titanic* survivors and was knighted by King George V of England. He was also presented with the Congressional Gold Medal at the White House by President William Howard Taft.

The *Carpathia*

❧TODAY'S CHURCH❧

The *Californian*'s inaction speaks directly to so many of today's church leaders. Like *Californian*'s Captain Lord, they have done almost nothing in response to the many warnings they have received over the years regarding spiritual deception. What has been ironic is how "revival" leaders in the New Apostolic Reformation have declared their "revivals" to be a "war on inaction." It is especially ironic because they have actually thrown open their doors to the very deception they should be taking action against.

Much like the *Titanic*, complacency and pride have settled in and taken their toll in today's church. Instead of taking action to protect the flock, church leaders, much like Captain Stanley Lord, seem to find ways to rationalize, explain away, or discredit the warnings brought to them. Over the last forty or more years, the warnings to church leaders have been largely dismissed, even as the Bible perfectly underscores and prophetically describes everything that is happening.

Time is running out. Much of today's professing church is sinking fast, and most of today's pastors, church leaders, and the church in general don't even know it. The *Titanic* could not be saved, but over seven hundred of its passengers were.

The Bible specifically warns how the world and a deceived church are being prepared for a great deception, not a "great revival." Men like Pastors Samuel Andrews and James Gray warned of this approaching disaster over a century ago. It was an "all hands-on deck" moment then; it is ever more so today. And while it was an "all hands-on deck moment" for the *Titanic*, all those assembled had to get off the deck and off the ship in order to be saved. And so it is today. People must get off the sinking ship that makes up so much of today's professing church—a deceived church that one NAR "revivalist" unwittingly linked to the *Titanic* by calling their "unsinkable" revival ship—the "Ship of Dreams."

TRUE GOSPEL SHIP

CAPTAIN Rostron and his *Carpathia* crew did everything they could to rescue those who had been able to leave the sinking *Titanic* in lifeboats. There is a comparable rescue operation in motion today. What will people do as the days grow even darker and more challenging? Will they stay onboard their "Ship of God's Dreams" because it seems safer and more secure?—brighter and more exciting with all of its signs and wonders and spiritual experiences like "holy laughter"? Or will they see through the complacency and spiritual deception by getting off the wayward ship, and then help others get off too?

HIS LIFEBOAT IS WAITING

LIKE the old Gospel song says, "Don't wait too late." Many say "Lord, Lord," but Jesus Christ is not the captain of a sinking ship. He is the Captain of our salvation (Hebrews 2:10) and the "anchor" of our soul (Hebrews 6:19). He is the way, the truth, and the life, and no one comes to the Father but through Him (John 14:6). If you sincerely ask Him, He will take you aboard His true Gospel Ship. He will get you safely to your destination—to the safe harbor of your heavenly home. His lifeboat is waiting.

O God of our salvation; who art the confidence

of all the ends of the earth, and of them that

are afar off upon the sea. (Psalm 65:5)

EPILOGUE

THE RETURN

IN 1915, three years after the sinking of the *Titanic*, the presiding head of the Moody Bible Institute, James Gray, released his *Concise Bible Commentary*—a respected work still in print today. Pertaining to true revival, Gray's discussion of 1 Samuel 7 is under the bold heading, "A National Revival and Its Results."

With Samuel Andrews' book and John Harper's revival meetings as a personal backdrop, James Gray described how the Israelites "lamented after the Lord" because they were "suffering the consequences" of God's "averted face"—how they were under God's judgment as they were forced to endure the longstanding "oppression of the Philistines." Gray explained that it was the prophet Samuel who counseled them on how to "find relief."[1] Samuel told them that for God to lift His judgment, they must "return" to the Lord with all of their hearts. And to accomplish this "return," they must repent and "put away the strange gods" that were in their midst and serve God only:

> And Samuel spake unto all the house of Israel, saying, If ye do return unto the LORD with all your hearts, then put away the strange gods and Ashtaroth from among you, and prepare your hearts unto the LORD, and serve him only: and he will deliver you out of the hand of the Philistines. (1 Samuel 7:3)

The Bible records that the Israelites did just that, and God's judgment was lifted. They put away their false gods and returned to the Lord with all of their hearts and served Him only:

> Then the children of Israel did put away Baalim and Ashtaroth, and served the LORD only. (1 Samuel 7:4)

However, today's deceived church has not put away its idols and false gods—most particularly, the false "God within."

SERIOUS WARNINGS

SHIPWRECKS happen when serious warnings are not taken seriously. It only took a little leaven the size of "two sidewalk squares" to shipwreck a seemingly unsinkable ship like the *Titanic*. And it only takes a little leaven—like the false teaching of "God within"—to shipwreck the seemingly unsinkable faith of today's deceived church. The *Titanic*—the "Ship of Dreams"—was shockingly unprepared for the disaster it encountered as it raced toward New York City to "make a record." Similarly, today's professing church—the "Ship of God's Dreams"—is shockingly unprepared for the disaster it will encounter as it races toward a deceptive "world revival" and "making history."

GREATEST AWAKENING OF ALL?

WHILE writing these final words, a friend sent me an online post from *Charisma* magazine. It was reputedly a "prophetic word" from a self-proclaimed "apostle" in today's professing church. He said the Lord told him we are not to be concerned with "what evil is doing."[2] Then, sounding more like William Stead's deceptive spirit "Julia" and today's New Age leaders, this "apostle" said we are to pray for a "third Great Awakening" that "is coming to the nations of the earth" and how it will be "the greatest awakening of all." He stated:

> We are going onto a reset and the spiritual turn around will continue, and a third Great Awakening—the greatest awakening of all—is coming to the nations of the earth.[3]

If Pastor Samuel Andrews were alive today, he would have much to say about today's professing church and its unbiblical declarations about a coming world revival. Andrews warned that the Bible says absolutely nothing about a great awakening that would be "coming to the nations of the earth" before Jesus' ultimate return. In fact, Scripture states just the opposite. Instead, it warns there will be the greatest hostility in history coming against His church before His return. As cited earlier, Pastor Andrews explained:

> This summary of the Lord's teaching shows us that anything like a conversion of the world before His return by the preaching of the gospel, was not in His thoughts. Had it been, He could not have failed to comfort His mourning disciples, and encourage them to vigorous action by assurances of the success of their mission. But He persistently holds up before them hatred, persecution, death. His life on earth was prophetic of the history of the Church; and the greatest manifestation of hostility to her, as to Him, would be at the end.[4]

CONVERGENCE

THE world, the New Age, and a deceived church are converging as "One" as they herald a "great awakening"—a coming "great revival." However, the Bible makes it clear that this "revival" will not be from God. Fueled by an unholy spirit, "strong delusion," and "signs and lying wonders," today's deceived church is walking into a spiritual trap. It is the iceberg and the Antichrist. It is the great deception. It is what Jesus warned would one day come.

And as he sat upon the mount of Olives, the disciples came unto him privately, saying, Tell us, when shall these things be? and what shall be the sign of thy coming, and of the end of the world? And Jesus answered and said unto them, Take heed that no man deceive you. (Matthew 24:3-4)

For Those in Peril on the Sea

Eternal Father, strong to save

Whose arm doth bind the restless wave,

Who bidd'st the mighty ocean deep

Its own appointed limits keep;

O hear us when we cry to Thee,

For those in peril on the sea![1]

Appendix

Disaster Plan

The Gospel of the True Jesus Christ

1. The true Jesus Christ said we must be born again.

That which is born of the flesh is flesh; and that which is born of the Spirit is spirit. Marvel not that I said unto thee, Ye must be born again. (John 3:6-7)

2. To be born again we must recognize we are lost, fall short of the glory of God, and are sinners.

For all have sinned, and come short of the glory of God. (Romans 3:23)

3. To remain a sinner is sure death. Believing in the true Jesus Christ brings eternal life and is a gift from God.

For the wages of sin is death; but the gift of God is eternal life through Jesus Christ our Lord. (Romans 6:23)

4. To save us from our sin, God sent His Son Jesus Christ to be our Savior.

For God so loved the world, that he gave his only begotten Son, that whosoever believeth in him should not perish, but have everlasting life. For God sent not his Son into the world to condemn the world; but that the world through him might be saved. (John 3:16-17)

5. The true Jesus Christ said we must repent of our sins.

[E]xcept ye repent, ye shall all likewise perish. (Luke 13:3)

6. To save us from our sin, the true Jesus Christ bore our sins and the sins of the whole world on the cross of Calvary.

But God commendeth his love toward us, in that, while we were yet sinners, Christ died for us. (Romans 5:8)

And he is the propitiation for our sins: and not for ours only, but also for the sins of the whole world. (1 John 2:2)

7. On the cross of Calvary, the true Jesus Christ defeated sin, evil, death—and the Devil himself.

Forasmuch then as the children are partakers of flesh and blood, he also himself likewise took part of the same; that through death he might destroy him that had the power of death, that is, the devil. (Hebrews 2:14)

8. If you confess with your mouth and believe in your heart that Jesus Christ is Lord and that God raised Him from the dead, you will be saved.

That if thou shalt confess with thy mouth the Lord Jesus, and shalt believe in thine heart that God hath raised him from the dead, thou shalt be saved. (Romans 10:9)

9. We are saved by the grace of the true Jesus Christ—not by our own works.

For by grace are ye saved through faith; and that not of yourselves: it is the gift of God: Not of works, lest any man should boast. (Ephesians 2:8-9)

10. True faith comes from hearing the Word of God.

So then faith cometh by hearing, and hearing by the word of God. (Romans 10:17)

11. Because of our faith in the finished work of the true Jesus Christ on the cross, we have peace with God.

Therefore being justified by faith, we have peace with God through our Lord Jesus Christ. (Romans 5:1)

12. We are the children of God by our faith in the true Jesus Christ.

For ye are all the children of God by faith in Christ Jesus. (Galatians 3:26)

13. If we believe in the true Jesus Christ and continue in His Word, then we are His disciples.

Then said Jesus to those Jews which believed on him, If ye continue in my word, then are ye my disciples indeed; And ye shall know the truth, and the truth shall make you free. (John 8:31-32)

14. The apostle Paul emphasized that we must stand on the truth and keep the Gospel of the true Jesus Christ.

Moreover, brethren, I declare unto you the gospel which I preached unto you, which also ye have received, and wherein ye stand; By which also ye are saved, if ye keep in memory what I preached unto you, unless ye have believed in vain. (1 Corinthians 15:1-2)

15. Whoever calls upon the Lord in sincerity and truth will be saved.

For whosoever shall call upon the name of the Lord shall be saved. (Romans 10:13)

Jesus saith unto him, I am the way, the truth, and the life: no man cometh unto the Father, but by me. (John 14:6)

Endnotes

Quote

1. Lawrence Beesley, *The Loss of the S.S. Titanic: Its Story and Its Lessons* (New York, NY: A Mariner Book, Houghton Mifflin Company, 1912, 2000), p. 3.

Prologue

1. Captain Stanley Lord, United States Senate Inquiry, Day 8; US Senate Hearings: STL285 (Titanic Inquiry Project, http://www.titanicinquiry.org/USInq/AmInq08Lord03.php).

Chapter 1: Dead Men Talking

1. William T. Stead, *How I Know That the Dead Return* (Boston, MA: The Ball Publishing Co., 1909), p. 49.

2. Steve and Sarah Berger, *Have Heart: Bridging the Gulf Between Heaven and Earth* (Franklin, TN: Grace Chapel, Inc., 2010), p. 100.

3. Morgan Robertson, *Futility or, the Wreck of the Titan* (originally published in 1898 under the title of *Futility*; now in the public domain), p. 1.

4. John Vess, *The Titan and the Titanic: The Life, Works and Incredible Foresight of Morgan Robertson* (Chapmansboro, TN: Pleasant Valley Publishers, 1990), p. 79.

5. Ibid.

6. Herbert B. Greenhouse, *Premonitions: A Leap Into the Future* (New York, NY: Bernard Geis Associates, 1971), p. 39.

7. Ibid.

8. William T. Stead, "How the Mail Steamer Went Down in Mid Atlantic by a Survivor" (*The Pall Mall Gazette*, March 22, 1886, W. T. Stead Resource Site: https://www.attackingthedevil.co.uk/pmg/steamer.php).

9. William T. Stead, "From the Old World to the New" (*The Review of Reviews*, December 1892, W. T. Stead Resource Site: https://www.attackingthedevil.co.uk/reviews/oldworld.php), chapters 7-8, pp. 39-50.

10. Herbert B. Greenhouse, *Premonitions: A Leap Into the Future*, op. cit., p. 31.

11. Estelle Wilson Stead, *My Father, Personal & Spiritual Reminiscences*

(London, England: William Heinemann,1913, reprinted by Hard Press Publishing), p. 170.

12. Ibid., pp. 177-193.

13. William Stead, *After Death: Letters From Julia* (Woodland, CA: Ancient Wisdom Communications, public domain, originally published 1905), p. 10.

14. Ibid., p. 21.

15. Estelle Wilson Stead, *My Father, Personal & Spiritual Reminiscences*, op. cit., p. 300.

16. William Stead, *After Death: Letters From Julia*, op. cit., p. 29.

17. Benjamin Creme, *The Reappearance of the Christ and the Masters of Wisdom* (London, England: The Tara Press, 1980), p. 88.

18. *A Course in Miracles: Combined Volume* (Glen Ellen, CA: Foundation for Inner Peace, 1975, 1992) (Workbook), p. 45.

19. Ibid. (Text), p. 585.

20. Estelle Wilson Stead, *My Father, Personal & Spiritual Reminiscences*, op. cit., p. 279.

21. Eyewitnesses, *The Welsh Revival & The Story of the Welsh Revival by Eyewitnesses* (Lawton, OK: Trumpet Press, 2015, originally this book was two independent books both published in 1905: William T. Stead authoring *The Welsh Revival* and "Eyewitnesses" authoring *The Story of the Welsh Revival*.

22. Estelle Wilson Stead, *My Father, Personal & Spiritual Reminiscences*, op. cit., p. 224.

23. Ibid., p. 225.

24. Mrs. Cecil M. Cook and Lloyd Kenyon Jones, *God's World* (Vol 1) (Whitefish, MT: Kessinger Legacy Reprints, originally published by The William T. Stead Memorial Center in1919), pp. i-v.

25. Ibid., p. v.

26. William T. Stead, *How I Know That the Dead Return*, op. cit., p. 49.

27. Steve and Sarah Berger, *Have Heart*, op. cit., pp. 99-100.

28. Ibid., pp. 100-101.

29. This information from my phone call with Jim Sterling was reconfirmed through a mutual friend's e-mail exchange with Mr. Sterling during the writing of this book.

30. *Pastors' Perspective* podcast, K-Wave radio, September 29, 2015 with Josh Turansky, Don Stewart, and Brian Brodersen. "Anne-Marie"

is the caller. Cited discussion begins at 23:50 minute mark and runs to 29:02 (https://www.youtube.com/watch?v=YpPoRdlTIhs; takes about 30 seconds to load).

31. "Endorsements and Contacting the Endorsers" (Spiritual Research Network, https://www.spiritualresearchnetwork.org/have-heart-bridging-the-gulf-between-heaven-and-earth-endorsements.html), per Chris Lawson, president of the Spiritual Research Network; telephone call with Pastor Steve Berger regarding *Have Heart.*

32. Ibid., per Chris Lawson, president of the Spiritual Research Network, pertaining to his telephone call with Pastor Greg Laurie's secretary about *Have Heart.*

33. William Stead, *After Death: Letters From Julia,* op. cit., p. 29.

34. James Redfield, *The Twelfth Insight: The Hour of Decision* (New York, NY: Grand Central publishing, 2011), p. 179.

35. Warren B. Smith, *The Light That Was Dark: From the New Age to Amazing Grace* (Magalia, CA: Mountain Stream Press, 1992, 2005), pp. 16-17.

Chapter 2: A Little Leaven

1. Knjazmilos, "Titanic, Myths, Legends, Truths and Facts" (Titanic-Titanic.com, June 13, 2019, https://www.titanic-titanic.com/titanic-myths-legends-truths-and-facts).

2. Samuel J. Andrews, *Christianity and Anti-Christianity in Their Final Conflict* (Bend, OR: The Berean Call edition, 2017, originally published in New York and London by G. P. Putnam's Sons in 1898, 1899), p. xx.

3. William J. Broad, "Toppling Theories, Scientists Find 6 Slits, Not Big Gash, Sank Titanic" (*New York Times,* April 8, 1997, https://www.nytimes.com/1997/04/08/science/toppling-theories-scientists-find-6-slits-not-big-gash-sank-titanic.html).

4. Marilyn Ferguson, *The Aquarian Conspiracy: Personal and Social Transformation in the 1980s* (Los Angeles, CA: J. P. Tarcher, Inc., 1980), p. 27.

5. Ibid., p. 382.

6. Ibid., p. 45.

7. Scott Ventureyra, "Challenging the Rehabilitation of Pierre Teilhard de Chardin" (*Crisis Magazine,* January 20, 2015, https://www.crisismagazine.com/2015/challenging-rehabilitation-pierre-teilhard-de-chardin).

8. Marilyn Ferguson, *The Aquarian Conspiracy*, op. cit., p. 25.

9. Ibid., p. 34.

10. Ibid.

11. *The Oprah Winfrey Show*, # W265, "The New Age Movement," Program date: September 18, 1987 (official transcript).

12. *A Course in Miracles: Combined Volume* (Workbook), op. cit., p. 183.

13. Ibid. (Text), p. 38.

14. Ibid. (Text), pp. 49-50.

15. Ibid. (Text), p. 52.

16. Ibid. (Text), p. 425.

17. Ibid. (Workbook), p. 45.

18. *The Oprah Winfrey Show*, January 2002, "Memorable Thinkers."

19. Neale Donald Walsch, *The New Revelations: A Conversation with God* (New York, NY: Atria Books, 2002), p. 157.

20. Neale Donald Walsch, *Tomorrow's God: Our Greatest Spiritual Challenge* (New York, NY: Atria Books, 2004), pp. 167-168.

21. Benjamin Creme, *Maitreya's Mission* (Volume Two) (London, England: Share International Foundation, 1993), p. 7.

22. *Messages from Maitreya the Christ: One Hundred Forty Messages* (Los Angeles, CA: Share International Foundation, 1980, 1992), p. 88.

23. Benjamin Creme, *The Reappearance of the Christ and the Masters of Wisdom*, op. cit., p. 88.

24. Alice Bailey, *The Reappearance of the Christ* (London, UK: Lucis Publishing Company, 1948, 1996), p. 150.

25. William Thomas Stead, "Character Sketch: October, Mrs. Annie Besant" (*The Review of Reviews*, October, 1891, Vol. IV. No. 22), pp. 349-367, taken from Nabu Public Domain Reprints.

26. Marilyn Ferguson, *The Aquarian Conspiracy*, op. cit., p. 45.

27. Norman Vincent Peale, *The Power of Positive Thinking* (New York, NY: Prentice-Hall, Inc., Sixteenth Printing, 1955), p. 40.

28. Robert H. Schuller, *Self-Love* (New York, NY: Jove Books, The Berkeley Publishing Group, 1969, 1978), p. 43.

29. M. Scott Peck, *The Road Less Traveled: A New Psychology of Love, Traditional Values and Spiritual Growth* (New York, NY: Simon & Schuster, 1978), p. 281.

30. Leonard Sweet, *Quantum Spirituality: A Postmodern Apologetic*

(Dayton, OH: Whaleprints for SpiritVenture Ministries, Inc., 1991, 1994), p. 125.

31. Betty J. Eadie, *Embraced by the Light* (Placerville, CA: Gold Leaf Press, 1992), p. 81.

32. Sue Monk Kidd, *The Dance of the Dissident Daughter: A Woman's Journey From Christian Tradition to the Sacred Feminine* (New York, NY: Harper Collins Publishers Inc., 1992), p. 160.

33. Jack Canfield and Mark Victor Hansen, *Chicken Soup for the Soul: 101 Stories to Open the Heart and Rekindle the Spirit* (Deerfield Beach, FL: Health Communications, Inc., 1993), p. 71.

34. Eugene Peterson, *The Message: The New Testament in Contemporary Language* (Colorado Springs, CO: NavPress, 1993, 2003), pp. 21-22.

35. *Catechism of the Catholic Church* (New York, NY: Doubleday, 1995), #460.

36. Ibid., #795.

37. Henri Nouwen, *Here and Now* (New York, NY: The Crossroad Publishing Company, 1997), p. 22.

38. Rick Warren, *The Purpose Driven Life: What on Earth am I Here For?* (Grand Rapids, MI: Zondervan, 2002), p. 88.

39. Robert H. Schuller, "God's Word: Rebuild, Renew, Restore," (*Hour of Power,* Program #1762, November 9, 2003, https://web.archive.org/web/20031210012744/http://www.hourofpower.org/booklets/booklet-detail.cfm?ArticleID=2107).

40. Sarah Young, J*esus Calling: Enjoying Peace in His Presence* (Nashville, TN: Thomas Nelson, 2004), p. 199.

41. William P. Young, *The Shack: Where Tragedy Confronts Eternity* (Newbury Park, CA: Windblown Media, 2007), p. 112.

42. Glenn Beck and Dr. Keith Ablow, *The Seven Wonders That Will Change Your Life* (New York, NY: Penguin Books, 2011), p. 58.

43. Ibid., p. 24.

44. Cindy Wooden, "Pope Francis Offers Six New Beatitudes for the Modern Christian" (*America: The Jesuit Review*, Catholic News Service, November 1, 2016, https://www.americamagazine.org/faith/2016/11/01/pope-francis-offers-six-new-beatitudes-modern-christian).

45. Roma Downey interviewed by Lorna Dueck (2018, https://m.youtube.com/watch?v=q2RXVCZm01k), beginning at 1 minute 40 second mark.

46. Walter Lord, *The Night Lives On* (New York, NY: Avon Books, 1986, 1987), p. 1.

Chapter 3: Smart Ship, Smart Church
1. Walter Lord, *A Night to Remember* (New York, NY: St. Martin's Griffin, 1955, 1983), p. 95.
2. *What the Bleep Do We Know!?* (20th Century Fox film, 2004, http://www.whatthebleep.com), transcribed by author, on file.
3. Annette Capps, *Quantum Faith* (England, AR: Capps Publishing, 2003), p. 6.
4. Walter Lord, *The Night Lives On*, op. cit., p. 12.
5. Steven Biel, editor, *Titanica: The Disaster of the Century in Poetry, Song, and Prose* (New York, NY: W.W. Norton & Company, 1998), pp. 25-26.
6. Wyn Craig Wade, *The Titanic: End of a Dream* (New York: NY: Penguin Books, 1979, 1986), p. 1.
7. Ibid., p. 3.
8. Ibid.
9. Jeanne Whalen, "The Quantum Revolution Is Coming, and Chinese Scientists Are at the Forefront" (*The Washington Post*, August 18, 2019, https://www.washingtonpost.com/business/2019/08/18/quantum-revolution-is-coming-chinese-scientists-are-forefront).
10. Barbara Marx Hubbard, *The Revelation: A Message of Hope for the New Millennium* (Novato, CA: Nataraj Publishing, 1995), p. 125.
11. Ibid., p. 132.
12. Fritjof Capra, *The Tao of Physics: An Exploration of the Parallels between Modern Physics and Eastern Mysticism* (Boston, MA: Shambhala Publications, Inc., 1999), p. 11.
13. Ibid., pp. 324-325.
14. Ibid., p. 330.
15. Ibid., p. 341.
16. *What the Bleep Do We Know!?*, op. cit.
17. Annette Capps, *Quantum Faith*, op. cit., p. 6.
18. Gary Zukav, *The Dancing Wu Li Masters: An Overview of the New Physics* (New York, NY: HarperCollins Publishers Inc., Perennial Classics, 1979, 2001), p. 346.
19. Judy Franklin and Ellyn Davis, *The Physics of Heaven: Exploring*

God's Mysteries of Sound, Light, Energy, Vibrations, and Quantum Physics (Shippensburg, PA: Destiny Image Publishers, Inc., 2012), pp. 16-17.

20. Ibid., p. 15.

21. Leonard Sweet, *Quantum Spirituality*, op. cit., p. viii.

22. Ibid., p. 125.

23. Ibid., p. 113.

24. Scott Ventureyra "Challenging the Rehabilitation of Pierre Teilhard de Chardin," op. cit.

25. Leonard Sweet, *Quantum Spirituality*, op. cit., p. 106.

26. Leonard Sweet, *soulTsunami: Sink or Swim in New Millennium Culture* (Grand Rapids, MI: Zondervan Publishing House, 1999), p. 28.

27. William P. Young, *The Shack*, op. cit., p. 95.

28. Ibid., p. 112.

29. Sarah Young, *Jesus Calling*, op. cit., p. 199.

30. Ibid., p. 285.

31. Adam Milton Barker, "How CERN Plan to Use the Large Hadron Collider to Open Portals to Other Dimensions, and Possibly Already Have" (Techbubble, 5/4/15, https://www.techbubble.info/blog/quantum-physics/entry/how-cern-plan-to-use-the-large-hydrogen-collider-to-open-portals-to-other-dimensions).

32. Mark Cartwright, "Shiva Nataraja-Lord of the Dance" (*Ancient History Encyclopedia*, https://www.ancient.eu/article/831/shiva-nataraja—lord-of-the-dance).

Chapter 4: Ship of Dreams/Ship of God's Dreams

1. Robert Plant, *Titanic: The Ship of Dreams* (Scotland, UK: Christian Focus Publications, 2011), back cover.

2. Faith Marie Baczko, "God's Armada Is Now Moving Out to Sea!" (Word of Power, October 5, 2017, https://faithmariebaczko.com/2017/10/05/gods-armada-is-now-moving-out-to-sea).

3. Hugh Brewster and Laurie Coulter, *882 1/2 Amazing Answers to Your Questions About the Titanic* (Aurora, Ontario: Madison Press Books, 1998), p. 6.

4. Eric Caren and Steve Goldman, *Extra Titanic: The Story of the Disaster in the Newspapers of the Day* (Edison, NJ: CastleBooks, 1998), p. 4, from the newspaper article titled, "The Titanic Tears Steamship From Pier by Suction" from *The New York Herald*, April 11, 1912.

5. Rick Warren, Saddleback Church e-mail, October 27, 2003, "God's Dream for You—And the World!" Also in Warren B. Smith's *Deceived on Purpose: The New Age Implications of the Purpose Driven Church* (Magalia, CA: Mountain Stream Press, 2004), pp. 131-132.

6. Katherine Tingley, editor, "Practical Theosophy" (*New Century Path, Volume Vll No. XlV*, 1904, New Century Corporation, http://iapsop.com/archive/materials/century_path/new_century_path_v7_nov_1903-nov_1904.pdf), p. 922.

7. N. L., "Reincarnation" (*The Theosophical Path, Volume X, No. 2*, February 1916), p. 159, New Century Corporation, Point Loma, CA., Katherine Tingley, editor, https://www.theosociety.org/pasadena/ttp/ttp_v10n02.pdf.

8. *Britannica* online: https://www.britannica.com/topic/theosophy.

9. William Thomas Stead, "Character Sketch: October, Mrs. Annie Besant," op. cit., pp. 349-367.

10. N. L., "Reincarnation," *The Theosophical Path* (Volume X, No. 2, February 1916, op. cit., p. 159.

11. Paramahansa Yogananda, *Journey to Self-Realization: Collected Talks and Essays on Realizing God in Daily Life, Volume 111* (Los Angeles, CA: Self-Realization Fellowship, 1997, 2005), p. 34.

12. Sri Chinmoy, *The Vision of God's Dawn*, taken from an extract called "God's Dream and God's Reality," https://www.yogaofsrichinmoy.com/the-higher-worlds/dream/godsdreamreality.

13. *A Course in Miracles* (Text), op. cit., pp. 584-585.

14. Ibid., p. 584.

15. Dutch Sheets, "God Will Redeem His Dream" (https://m.youtube.com/watch?v=UKsEwBj8pXE), start at 3 minute 20 second mark.

16. Conrad Hanson, personal notes from author Johanna Michaelsen's telephone call to Crystal Cathedral on October 3, 1985, used with permission. More detail in Warren B. Smith's book *Deceived on Purpose: The New Age Implications of the Purpose Driven Church* (Magalia, CA: Mountain Stream Press, Second Edition, 2004), pp. 92-93.

17. "Reverend Sun Myung Moon Speaks on New Morning of Glory" (January 22, 1978 at Belvedere, New York, http://www.unification.net/1978/780122.html).

18. *Messages from Maitreya the Christ: One Hundred Forty Messages*, op. cit., p. 42.

19. Wayne Dyer, *You'll See It When You Believe It: The Way to Your Personal Transformation* (New York: NY: HarperCollins, First Quill Edition, 2001), pp. 108-109.

20. Neale Donald Walsch, "Should We Let Go of Our Dreams—A Message From God Channeled by Neale Donald Walsch" (Spirit Library, May 1, 2008, https://spiritlibrary.com/neale-donald-walsch/should-we-let-go-of-our-dreams).

21. Ann Oldenburg, "The Divine Miss Winfrey" (*USA Today*, May 11, 2006, posted at www.religionnewsblog.com/14801/the-divine-miss-winfrey).

22. Oprah at the 2016 Essence Festival, New Orleans, Louisiana (https://www.youtube.com/watch?v=wUPKMiIeGhA).

23. Robert H. Schuller, *Your Church Has Real Possibilities* (Glendale, CA: Regal Book Division, G/L Publications, 1974), p. 177.

24. Robert H. Schuller, *Discover Your Possibilities* (New York, NY: Ballentine Books, 1978, 1990), p. 100.

25. Robert H. Schuller, *Self-Esteem: The New Reformation* (Waco, TX: Word Books, 1982), p. 75.

26. Ibid., p. 104.

27. Ibid., p. 112.

28. Richard Abanes, *Rick Warren and the Purpose That Drives Him: An Insider Looks at the Phenomenal Bestseller* (Eugene, OR: Harvest House Publishers, 2005), p. 94.

29. Rick Warren's Saddleback Church e-mail, October 27, 2003, "God's Dream for You—And the World!," op. cit.

30. Rick Warren, "How You Can Realize God's Dream for Your Life" (*Charisma* magazine, August 1, 2016, https://www.charismamag.com/spirit/spiritual-growth/27170--how-you-can-realize-god-s-dream-for-life).

31. Rick Warren, "Dream Big" (*Daily Hope With Rick Warren*, July 30, 2016, https://www.crosswalk.com/devotionals/daily-hope-with-rick-warren/daily-hope-with-rick-warren-july-30-2016.html).

32. Ibid.

33. Rick Warren, "Dreaming the Future God Wants for You" (Saddleback Church sermon, February 16, 2020, https://saddleback.com/watch/time-to-dream/dreaming-the-future-god-wants-for-you), start at 38 minute 10 second mark.

34. Ibid., sermon notes on right-hand side of page.

35. Saddleback Church, October 26, 2003, Internet broadcast from Saddleback Church, transcribed by author, on file.

36. Bruce Wilkinson, *The Dream Giver* (Sisters, OR: Multnomah Publishers, Inc., 2003), p. 77.

37. Sarah Young, *Jesus Calling: Enjoying Peace in His Presence*, op. cit., p. 6.

38. Sarah Young (adapted by Tama Fortner), *Jesus Calling: 365 Devotions for Kids* (Nashville, TN: Tommy Nelson, 2010), p. 7.

39. Brian D. McLaren, *The Secret Message of Jesus: Uncovering the Truth That Could Change Everything* (Nashville, TN: W. Publishing Group, a Division of Thomas Nelson Inc., 2006), p. 142.

40. Ibid.

41. Shane Claiborne, *Jesus for President* (Grand Rapids, MI: Zondervan, 2008), p. 307.

42. Ravi Zacharias, keynote address at The Cannon House in Washington, D.C (National Day of Prayer Address on May 1, 2008, https://rzim. org/read/just-thinking-magazine/national-day-of-prayer-address).

43. Ruth Malhotra, "Ravi Zacharias Participates in 67th Annual National Day of Prayer Observation in Washington, D.C." (RZIM website, https://www.rzim.org/read/rzim-updates/ravi-zacharias-67th-national-day-of-prayer).

44. Catherine Meeks, editor, *Living Into God's Dream: Dismantling Racism in America* (New York, NY: Morehouse Publishing, 2016), p. vi.

45. Joel Osteen, "God's Dream for Your Life" (January 17, 2020, https://sermons-online.org/joel-osteen/joel-osteen-supersized).

46. Ann Schneible, "Synod Must Serve God's Dream, Not Try to 'Take Over,' Pope Says" (*Catholic News Agency*, October 5, 2014, https://www. catholicnewsagency.com/news/synod-must-serve-gods-dream-not-try-to-take-over-pope-says-37495).

47. Carol Glatz, "Pope Francis: God Wants People to Dream Big, Not Listen to Cynics" (*America Magazine: The Jesuit Review*, August 30, 2017, https://www.americamagazine.org/faith/2017/08/30/pope-francis-god-wants-people-to-dream-big-not-listen-cynics).

48. Pope Francis, "Lent with Pope Francis: "God's Dream for Us" (Franciscan Media, 3/18/18, https://blog.franciscanmedia.org/franciscan-spirit/lent-with-pope-francis-gods-dream-for-us?hs-amp=true).

49. Dr. Alan Keyes, "God's Dream for Us Is Better" (ChurchMilitant. com, June 9, 2020, https://www.churchmilitant.com/news/article/gods-dream-for-us-is-better).

50. Chip Ingram, "God's Dream for Your Life" (Living on the Edge, https://livingontheedge.org/broadcast/gods-dream-for-your-life).

51. Mark Batterson, *Chase the Lion: If Your Dream Doesn't Scare You, It's Too Small* (Sisters, OR: Multnomah, 2016, 2019), p. 4.

52. James Robison, "The Greatest Dream" (*The Stream*, April 4, 2018, https://stream.org/the-greatest-dream).

53. Sally Lloyd-Jones, *The Jesus Storybook Bible: Every Story Whispers His Name* (Grand Rapids, MI: Zonderkidz, 2007), p. 25.

54. Kenneth Copeland, "Dream Big Dreams" (Kenneth Copeland Ministries, Ministry Minute, https://blog.kcm.org/ministry-minute-dream-big-dreams).

55. Leonard Sweet, *soulTsunami*, op. cit., p. 34.

56. Richard Abanes, *Rick Warren and the Purpose That Drives Him*, op. cit., p. 94.

57. Bill Johnson, *Dreaming With God: Co-laboring With God for Cultural Transformation* (Shippensburg, PA: Destiny Image Publishers, Inc., 2006), p. 39.

58. Ibid., p. 21.

59. "God's Dream? A Kingdom Building Dream" (July 17, 2008, https://herescope.blogspot.com/2008/07/gods-dream.html?m=1).

60. Lou Engle Ministries (https://louengle.com).

61. Ibid.

62. Sean Feucht, *Fire and Fragrance* (Destiny Image Publishers, September 2010, Kindle edition), p. 198, Kindle location: 2387.

63. https://www.fireandfragrance.ca/about.html.

64. https://www.burn24-7.com/about.

65. Faith Marie Baczko, "God's Armada is Now Moving Out to Sea!," op. cit.

Chapter 5: The Launch

1. "Titanic Launch" (Titanic Facts, https://titanicfacts.net/titanic-launch).

2. Randy Clark, *Lighting Fires* (Global Awakening, 1998), p. 125.

3. "Titanic Launch," op. cit.

4. George Behe, *Titanic: Psychic Forewarnings of a Tragedy* (Wellingborough, England: Patrick Stephens Limited, 1988), p. 11.

5. Ibid., p. 120.

6. "Dream Kept Man Off Titanic" (*The Denver Post*, April 18, 1912); cited in *Titanic: The Story of the Disaster in the Newspapers of the Day*, op. cit., p. 52.

7. Geoff Tibballs, editor, *Voices From the Titanic: The Epic Story of the Tragedy From the People Who Were There* (New York, NY: Skyhorse Publishing, 2012), p. 33.

8. Robert Hough, "God Is Alive and Well and Saving Souls on Dixon Road" (*Toronto Life Magazine*, February, 1995), p. 31; cited in James A. Beverley, *Holy Laughter and The Toronto Blessing: An Investigative Report* (Grand Rapids, MI: Zondervan Publishing House, 1995), p. 12.

9. Randy Clark, *Lighting Fires*, op. cit., p. 81.

10. Ibid.

11. James A. Beverley, *Holy Laughter & The Toronto Blessing: An Investigative Report*, op. cit., p. 54.

12. Sid Roth interview w/Rodney Howard-Browne (*It's Supernatural!*, February 3, 2014, https://sidroth.org/television/tv-archives/rodney-howard-browne-0-2).

13. Ibid.

14. Rodney M. Howard-Browne, *The Coming Revival* (Tampa, FL: Revival Ministries International, 1991), p. 6.

15. Sid Roth interview w/Rodney Howard-Browne on February 3, 2014, op. cit., at 6 minute 30 second mark.

16. John Arnott, "The Toronto Blessing: What Is It?" (John & Carol, December 31, 1999, www.johnandcarol.org/updates/the-toronto-blessing-what-is-it).

17. From the Desk of Steve Schultz (The Elijah List, March 5, 2018, https://www.elijahlist.com/mobile/display_word.html?ID=19772).

18. Tamara Hartzell, *In the Name of Purpose: Sacrificing Truth on the Altar of Unity* (Xlibris, 2007).

19. Michael L. Brown, *From Holy Laughter to Holy Fire: America on the Edge of Revival* (Shippensburg, PA: Destiny Image Publishers, Inc., 1996), p. 18.

20. William Stead, *After Death: Letters From Julia*, op. cit., p. 29.

21. Barbara Marx Hubbard, *The Revelation*, op. cit., pp. 157, 172-173.

22. Chris Mitchell, "Spirit-Empowered Believers Praying for a Second Pentecostal Outpouring" (*Charisma* magazine, https://www. charismamag.com/spirit/revival/20088-spirit-empowered-believers-praying-for-second-pentecostal-outpouring).

23. Barbara Marx Hubbard, *Teachings From the Inner Christ: For Founders of a New Order of the Future (A Work in Progress): A Compliment to the Book of Co-Creation* (Greenbrae, CA: Foundation For Conscious Evolution, 1994), p. 79.

24. Barbara Marx Hubbard, *The Revelation*, op. cit., p. 243.

25. Ibid., pp. 95-96.

26. Benjamin Creme, *Maitreya's Mission: Volume 2*, op. cit., p. 250.

27. *A Course in Miracles* (Manual for Teachers), op., cit., Section 14, p. 37.

28. Barbara Marx Hubbard, *The Revelation*, op. cit., p. 115.

29. Ibid., p. 132.

30. Ibid., pp. 298-299.

31. Ibid., p. 43.

32. Ibid., p. 262.

33. Faith Marie Baczko, "The Greater Glory & the Dance of Mahanaim" (Word Of Power, https://faithmariebaczko.com/2015/01/01/the-dance-of-mahanaim-the-greater-glory).

34. Ibid.

35. Faith Marie Baczko "God's Armada is Now Moving Out to Sea!," op. cit.

Chapter 6: Ark of Safety/Ark of Oneness

1. "Analysis of Titanic's Safety Features and Failures" (ultimatetitanic. com, https://www.ultimatetitanic.com/titanics-safety-features).

2. Tamara Hartzell, "Are You Being Led Away With the Error of the Wicked to the New Age Ark of Oneness?" (https://web.archive.org/web/20151223002956/http://www.inthenameofpurpose.org/arkofoneness.pdf), p. 11.

3. Leonard Sweet, *soulTsunami*, op., cit., p. 23.

4. Tim Maltin with Eloise Aston, *101 Things You Thought You Knew About the Titanic . . . but Didn't!* (New York: NY: Penguin Books, 2010), p. 10, citing *Shipbuilder* magazine, 1911.

5. Walter Lord, A *Night to Remember*, op. cit., p. 36.

6. Eric Caren and Steve Goldman, *Extra Titanic: The Story of the Disaster in the Newspapers of the Day*, op. cit., p. 32, citing the article, "Captain Smith Believed the Titanic Unsinkable" (*New York Herald*, April 16, 1912).

7. *A Course in Miracles: Combined Volume*, op. cit. (Text), p. 147.

8. Ibid.

9. Ibid. (Text) p. 125.

10. Ibid. (Workbook) p. 461.

11. Ibid. (Text) p. 433.

12. Ibid. (Text) p. 605.

13. Helena P. Blavatsky, "The New Cycle" (*La Revue Theosophique Magazine*, March 21, 1889, https://web.archive.org/web/20090627070150/https://www.blavatsky.net/blavatsky/arts/NewCycle.htm).

14. Deepak Chopra, "A Letter from Deepak Chopra to Mythic Journeys" (Mythic Passages newsletter, May 2005, http://www.mythicjourneys.org/passages/may2005/ALetterFromDeepakChopra.pdf).

15. Tamara Hartzell, "Are You Being Led Away With the Error of the Wicked to the New Age Ark of Oneness?," op. cit., p. 18.

16. Ibid.

17. Barbara Marx Hubbard, *The Revelation: A Message of Hope for the New Millennium*, op. cit., p. 233.

18. Ibid., p. 255.

19. Ibid., p. 240.

20. Ibid., p. 303.

21. *Messages From Maitreya*, op. cit., p. 248.

22. Tamara Hartzell, "Are You Being Led Away with the Error of the Wicked to the New Age Ark of Oneness?," op. cit., p. 5

23. Ibid.

24. Ibid., pp. 5-6.

25. Ronald S. Miller and the editors of the *New Age Journal*, *As Above, So Below: Paths to Spiritual Renewal in Daily Life* (Los Angeles, CA: Jeremy P. Tarcher, Inc., 1992), p. xi.

26. Leonard Sweet, *Quantum Spirituality*, op. cit., p. 106.

27. Leonard Sweet, *AquaChurch: Essential Leadership Arts for Piloting Your Church in Today's Fluid Culture* (Loveland, CO: Group Publishing, Inc., 1999), p. 39.

28. Ibid.

29. Leonard Sweet, *soulTsunami*, op., cit., p. 28.

30. Leonard Sweet, *Quantum Spirituality*, op. cit., p. 125.

31. Ibid., p. 13.

32. Leonard Sweet, *soulTsunami*, op. cit., p. 198.

33. "The Tides of Change: Riding the Next Wave in Ministry" (A 1995 audio presentation with Leonard Sweet and Rick Warren that was part of an ongoing series called "Choice Voices for Church Leadership," distributed by Abington Press), transcribed by Lighthouse Trails Publishing and on file with them.

34. Pierre Teilhard de Chardin, *Toward the Future* (New York, NY: Harcourt, Inc., 1973, 1975), pp. 86-87.

35. Warren B. Smith, *A "Wonderful" Deception: The Further New Age Implications of the Emerging Purpose Driven Movement* (Magalia, CA: Mountain Stream Press, 2009, 2011), p. 106.

36. Richard Abanes, "Leonard Sweet, Rick Warren, and the New Age" (https://web.archive.org/web/20080214224312/http://abanes.com/warren_sweet.html).

37. Dr. Harry Ironside, "Exposing Error: Is it Worthwhile?" (The Berean Call, April 2008, https://www.thebereancall.org/content/april-2008-extra-exposing-error).

38. Leonard Sweet, *soulTsunami*, op., cit., p. 23.

39. Ibid.

40. Ibid., p. 34.

41. Ibid.

42. Leonard Sweet, *Quantum Spirituality*, op. cit., p. 13.

Chapter 7: False Confidence, Complacency, & Denial

1. Wyn Craig Wade, *The Titanic: End of a Dream*, op. cit., p. 38

2. Rick Warren, *The Purpose Driven Life*, op. cit., p. 203.

3. Walter Lord, *A Night to Remember*, op. cit., p. 95.

4. Eric Caren and Steve Goldman, *Extra Titanic: The Story of the Disaster in the Newspapers of the Day*, op. cit., p. 51, citing the newspaper article, "Titanic Can't Sink, Smith Told Friend," *Denver Post*, April 18, 1912, p. 3.

5. Wyn Craig Wade, *The Titanic: End of a Dream*, op. cit., p. 38.

6. Tim Maltin with Eloise Aston, *101 Things You Thought You Knew About the Titanic . . . but Didn't!*, op. cit., p. 12.

7. Wyn Craig Wade, *The Titanic: End of a Dream*, op. cit., p. 35.

8. Lawrence Beesley, *The Loss of the S.S. Titanic: Its Story and Its Lessons,* op. cit., p. 31.

9. Don Lynch (Text) and Ken Marschall (Paintings), *Titanic: An Illustrated History* (Toronto, Ontario: Madison Press Books, 1992), p. 82.

10. Nick Barratt, *Lost Voices From the Titanic: The Definitive Oral History* (New York, NY: Palgrave Macmillan, 2010), p. 160.

11. Walter Lord, *A Night to Remember,* op. cit., p. 52.

12. Walter Lord, *The Night Lives On,* op. cit., p. 33.

13. Ibid.

14. Wyn Craig Wade, *The Titanic: End of a Dream,* op. cit., p. 49.

15. Don Lynch (Text) and Ken Marschall (Paintings), *Titanic: An Illustrated History,* op. cit., p. 216.

16. Wyn Craig Wade, *The Titanic: End of a Dream,* op. cit., p. 39.

17. Ibid.

18. Eva Hart, *Shadow of the Titanic: A Survivor's Story* (Dartford, UK: Greenwich University Press, 1994, 1995), p. 19.

19. Ibid., p. 24.

20. Robert H. Schuller, *Discover Your Possibilities,* op. cit., p. 61.

21. Promo for 2004 Robert H. Schuller Institute, Powerlines: Monthly news for *Hour of Power* Spiritual Shareholders and Friends (https://web.archive.org/web/20031017043658/http://www.hourofpower.org/powerlines/09.03/2004_robert_schuller_institute.cfm); cited in Warren B. Smith, *Deceived on Purpose,* op. cit., p. 80.

22. Rick Warren, *The Purpose Driven Life,* op. cit., p. 203.

23. Alice A. Bailey, *The Reappearance of the Christ,* op. cit. p. 188.

24. Rick Warren, *The Purpose Driven Life,* op. cit., pp. 285-286.

25. Brian D. McLaren, *The Secret Message of Jesus: Uncovering the Truth That Could Change Everything,* op. cit., p. 171.

26. Warren B. Smith, *Deceived on Purpose,* op. cit., p. 147.

27. "A Call to Faith" (*Orange County Register,* September 3, 2006, https://www.ocregister.com/2006/09/03/a-call-to-faith).

28. "Jim Jones Receives the Martin Luther King, Jr. Humanitarian Award" (https://commons.m.wikimedia.org/wiki/File:Jim_Jones_receives_the_Martin_Luther_King,_Jr._Humanitarian_Award_-_January_1977.jpg).

Chapter 8: Wasted Warnings

1. Walter Lord, *A Night to Remember,* op. cit., p. 87.

2. Casey Sabella, *Titanic Warning: Hearing the Voice of God in This Modern Age* (Green Forest, AR: New Leaf Press, Inc., 1994), p. 49; note: Well into the research and writing of *The Titanic and Today's Church*, I came upon Pastor Casey Sabella's 1994 book *Titanic Warning*. I was intrigued by the fact that Sabella used the *Titanic* from a pastor's perspective to warn about the need for godly church leadership, whereas I used the *Titanic* from the perspective of a former New Ager to warn about the need for spiritual discernment. While our books are vastly different in scope, there are a number of interesting parallels. This wake-up call to the body of Christ statement made by Pastor Sabella over twenty-five years ago remains just as urgent today—both from his perspective and from mine.

3. British Wreck Commissioner's Inquiry (Titanic Inquiry Project, https://www.titanicinquiry.org/BOTInq/BOTReport/botRepRoute. php).

4. April 18, 1912 letter sent to the *New York Evening Post*; cited in Wyn Craig Wade, *The Titanic: End of a Dream*, op. cit., p. 40.

5. Walter Lord, *The Night Lives On*, op. cit., p. 48.

6. Ibid.

7. John P. Eaton and Charles A. Haas, *Titanic: Triumph and Tragedy* (UK: Haynes Publishing, 2011), pp. 118-120; Don Lynch (Text) and Ken Marschall (Paintings), *Titanic: An Illustrated History*, op. cit., pp. 71-83.

8. Don Lynch (Text) and Ken Marschall (Paintings), *Titanic: An Illustrated History*, op. cit., p. 83.

9. Rabindranath R. Maharaj with Dave Hunt, *Death of a Guru: A Hindu Comes to Christ* (New York, NY: A. J. Holman Company, 1977), p. 170; republished by Harvest House in 1984.

10. Johanna Michaelsen, *The Beautiful Side of Evil* (Eugene, OR: Harvest House Publishers, 1982), p. 165.

11. Constance Cumbey, *The Hidden Dangers of the Rainbow: The New Age Movement and Our Coming Age of Barbarism* (Shreveport, LA: Huntington House, Inc., 1983), p. 7.

12. Dave Hunt and T. A. McMahon, *The Seduction of Christianity: Spiritual Discernment in the Last Days* (Eugene, OR: Harvest House Publishers, 1985), p. 91 (republished by The Berean Call in 2013).

13. Ibid., p. 213.

14. Caryl Matrisciana, *Gods of the New Age* (Eugene, OR: Harvest House Publishers, 1985), pp. 214-215.

15. Randall N. Baer, *Inside the New Age Nightmare: A Former Top New Age Leader Takes You on a Dramatic Journey* (Lafayette, LA: Huntington House, Inc., 1989), p. 83.

16. Warren B. Smith, *False Christ Coming: Does Anybody Care?* (Magalia, CA: Mountain Stream Press, 2011), pp. 117-118.

17. "Francis Chan Warns Those Who Criticize Christian Leaders: God Will Destroy You" (Lighthouse Trails blog, April 9, 2018, www.lighthousetrailsresearch.com/blog/?p=28116).

18. Richard Abanes, *Rick Warren and the Purpose That Drives Him*, op. cit., p. 96.

19. *Lookout Training Handbook* (NAVEDTRA 12968-D, Special Publication, February 2007, Navybmr.com/study%20material/NAVEDTRA%2012968A.pdf).

20. Tim Maltin, *101 Things You Thought You Knew About the Titanic . . . But Didn't!*, op. cit., pp. 78-79.

21. Warren B. Smith, *False Christ Coming: Does Anybody Care?*, op. cit., pp. 119-120; Formerly published as: Warren Smith, *Reinventing Jesus Christ: The New Gospel* (Ravenna, Ohio: Conscience Press, 2002), p. 68. (RJC book free online at newagetoamazinggrace.com).

Chapter 9: Racing Toward Disaster

1. Wyn Craig Wade, *The Titanic: The End of a Dream*, op. cit., p. 45.

2. Leonard Sweet, *soulTsunami*, op. cit., p. 34.

3. Bill Johnson, *Dreaming With God*, op. cit., p. 179.

4. United States Senate Inquiry (Titanic Inquiry Project, under heading: "Ice Both to Northward and Southward of Steamship 'Titanic's' Track," https://www.titanicinquiry.org/USInq/USReport/AmInqRep04.php).

5. Ibid. (under heading: "Speed").

6. "Wreck of the White Star Liner Titanic: How the World's Greatest Steamship Went Down With 1,600 Souls" (*Scientific American*, April 27, 1912, Vol. CVI, No. 17, https://www.scientificamerican.com/article/archive-titanic-wreck-white-star-liner); cited in Stephen Spignesi, *The Titanic for Dummies* (Hoboken, NJ: John Wiley & Sons, Inc., 2012), p. 160.

7. John P. Eaton and Charles A. Haas, *Titanic: Destination Disaster: The Legends and the Reality* (New York, NY: W. W. Norton & Company Inc., 1987, 1996), p. 9. Cited in Casey Sabella, *Titanic Warning: Hearing the Voice of God in This Modern Age*, op. cit., p. 36.

8. Geoff Tibballs, editor, *Voices From the Titanic: The Epic Story of the Tragedy From the People Who Were There*, op. cit., p. 327.

9. George Behe, *Titanic: Safety, Speed and Sacrifice* (Polo, IL: Transportation Trails, 1997), p. 23.

10. Ibid., p. 24.

11. Nick Barratt, *Lost Voices From the Titanic: The Definitive Oral History*, op. cit., pp. 131-132.

12. Ibid., p. 132.

13. Wyn Craig Wade, *Titanic: The End of a Dream*, op. cit., pp. 174-175.

14. Tim Maltin with Eloise Aston, *101 Things You Thought You Knew About the Titanic . . . but Didn't!*, op. cit., p. 110.

15. Walter Lord, *A Night to Remember*, op. cit., p. 4.

16. *New York World*, April 19, 1912. Cited in Geoff Tibballs, editor, *Voices From the Titanic*, op. cit., p. 62.

17. Ibid., p. 63.

18. "Edith Russell: My Experiences on the Titanic" (April 14, 1970, BBC Interview, https://www.youtube.com/watch?v=EMGkGr2TQUM).

19. Walter Lord, *A Night to Remember*, op. cit., p. 11.

20. Ibid., p. 13.

21. Geoff Tibballs, editor, *Voices From the Titanic*, op. cit., p. 67.

22. Lawrence Beesley, *The Loss of the S.S. Titanic*, op. cit., p. 109.

23. Walter Lord, *A Night to Remember*, op. cit., p. 13.

24. Geoff Tibballs, editor, *Voices From the Titanic*, op. cit., p. 59.

25. Walter Lord, *A Night to Remember*, op. cit., p. 12.

26. Geoff Tibballs, editor, *Voices From the Titanic*, op. cit., p. 81.

27. Walter Lord, *A Night to Remember*, op. cit., p. 12.

28. Ibid., p. 21.

29. Ibid., p. 37.

30. Andrew Wilson, *Shadow of the Titanic: The Extraordinary Stories of Those Who Survived* (New York, NY: Atria Books, 2011), p. 328.

31. Lawrence Beesley, *The Loss of the S.S. Titanic*, op. cit., p. 157.

32. Leonard Sweet, *soulTsunami*, op. cit., p. 23.

33. Ibid., p. 34.

34. Leonard Sweet, *Quantum Spirituality*, op. cit., p. 46.

35. Marilyn Ferguson, *The Aquarian Conspiracy*, op. cit., p. 128.

36. Warren B. Smith, *Deceived on Purpose*, op. cit., p. 124.

37. Rick Warren's Saddleback Church e-mail, October 27, 2003, "God's Dream for You—And the World!" op. cit.

38. Brian D. McLaren, *Everything Must Change: Jesus, Global Crises, and a Revolution of Hope* (Nashville: TN: Thomas Nelson, 2007), p. 21.

39. "God's Dream? A Kingdom Building Dream," op. cit.

40. Lou Engle website: https://louengle.com.

41. Sean Feucht, *Fire and Fragrance* (Destiny Image Publishers, September 2010, Kindle edition), p. 137, Kindle location: 1638.

42. https://www.burn24-7.com/about.

43. Bill Johnson, *Dreaming With God: Co-laboring With God for Cultural Transformation*, op. cit., p. 179.

44. Ibid., p. 21.

45. Catherine Meeks, editor, *Living Into God's Dream*, op. cit., p. vi.

46. Faith Marie Baczko, "God's Armada is Now Moving Out to Sea!," op. cit.

47. Faith Marie Baczko, "The Greater Glory & the Dance of Mahanaim," op. cit.

48. Faith Marie Baczko, "Can You Hold the Ground God Wants to Give You?" (Headstone Ministries, https://headstoneministries.com/can-you-hold-the-ground-god-wants-to-give-you).

49. Marilyn Ferguson, *The Aquarian Conspiracy*, op. cit., p. 34.

50. Maitreya, *Messages from Maitreya*, op. cit., p. 42.

51. Benjamin Creme, *Maitreya's Mission: Volume Three* (Los Angeles, CA: Share International Foundation, 1997), p. 1.

52. Julia Duin, "Praise the Lord and Pass the New Wine" (*Charisma* magazine, August 1994).

53. Randy Clark, *Lighting Fires*, op. cit., p. 93.

54. Ibid.

55. Brian McLaren, *The Secret Message of Jesus*, op. cit., p. 144.

56. Leonard Sweet, *soulTsunami*, op. cit., p. 34.

57. Ibid.

58. Michael Brown, *Holy Laughter to Holy Fire: America on the Edge of Revival*, op. cit., p. 18.

Chapter 10: The Iceberg & The Antichrist

1. Randall Baer, *Inside the New Age Nightmare: A Former Top New Age Leader Takes You on a Dramatic Journey*, op. cit., p. 76.

2. This statement taken from the body of the text in chapter ten of *The Titanic and Today's Church: A Tale of Two Shipwrecks.*

3. Steven Biel, editor, *Titanica: The Disaster of the Century in Poetry, Song, and Prose*, op. cit., pp. 25-26.

4. *Your Dictionary* (https://www.yourdictionary.com/convergence).

5. Pierre Teilhard de Chardin, *Christianity and Evolution* (New York, NY: Harcourt Brace Jovanivich, Inc., 1971), p. 130.

6. Leonard Sweet, *Quantum Spirituality*, op. cit., p. 106.

7. Leonard Sweet, *soulTsunami*, op. cit., front cover. The front cover contains the following endorsement by Rick Warren: "'SoulTsunami' shows us why these are the greatest days for evangelism since the first century!"

8. Ibid., p. 23.

9. Leonard Sweet, *AquaChurch*, op. cit., taken from subtitle.

10. Wyn Craig Wade, *The Titanic: End of a Dream*, op. cit., p. 119; taken from United States Senate Inquiry Report: Titanic Inquiry Project (titanicinquiry.org).

11. Ibid.

12. Ibid.

13. "Did the *Titanic* Sink Because of an Optical Illusion?" (*Smithsonian Magazine*; March 1, 2012, https://www.smithsonianmag.com/science-nature/did-the-titanic-sink-because-of-an-optical-illusion-102040309). This article is citing the research by Tim Maltin in his book *Titanic: A Very Deceiving Night* (Great Britain: Malt House Publishing, 2012), which states atmospheric conditions were ripe for super refraction bending of light causing miraging.

14. United States Senate Inquiry Report (Titanic Inquiry Project, Day 4, line 5214, https://www.titanicinquiry.org/USInq2/AmInq04Fleet01.php).

15. Walter Lord, *A Night to Remember*, op. cit., p. 2.

16. Warren Smith, *Reinventing Jesus Christ: The New Gospel*, op. cit., (online update for Chapter 11: https://www.spiritualresearchnetwork. org/reinventing-jesus-christ-book.html).

17. April 25, 1982: *New York Times* and many other major newspapers around the world.

18. Maitreya, *Messages from Maitreya the Christ*, op. cit., p. 123.

19. Ibid., p. 42.

20. Ibid., p. 88.

21. Ibid., p. 203.

22. Ibid., p. 142.

23. Ibid., p. 218.

24. Ibid., p. 150.

25. Benjamin Creme, *Maitreya's Mission: Volume Two*, op. cit., p. 8.

26. Maitreya, *Messages from Maitreya the Christ*, op. cit., p. 272.

27. Benjamin Creme, *Maitreya's Mission: Volume Two*, op. cit., p. 11.

28. Wayne S. Peterson, *Extraordinary Times, Extraordinary Beings: Experiences of an American Diplomat With Maitreya and the Masters of Wisdom* (Henderson, NV: Emergence Press, 2001, 2003), pp. 100-101.

29. Wayne S. Peterson interviewed on *Bridging Heaven & Earth*, a weekly talk show broadcast on Cox Communications' public access channel 17 in Santa Barbara, California on November 9, 2001 (https:// web.archive.org/web/20020203123135/http://www.heaventoearth. com/guests.html).

30. *Messages from Maitreya the Christ*, op. cit., p. 6.

31. Ibid., p. 248.

32. Ibid., p. 7.

33. Ibid., p. 238.

34. Benjamin Creme, *The Reappearance of the Christ*, op. cit. p. 30.

35. Ibid., p. 85.

36. Ibid., p. 46.

37. Ibid., p. 135.

38. Maitreya, *Messages from Maitreya*, op. cit. p. 88.

39. Benjamin Creme, *The Reappearance of the Christ*, op. cit., p. 88.

40. Ibid., p. 37.

41. Maitreya's Appearances, FAQ (Share International, first published in April 1999, modified on October 15, 2005, https://www.share-international.org/archives/M_appearances/faq_M_appearances.htm).

42. Benjamin Creme, *Maitreya's Mission: Volume Two*, op. cit., p. 250.

43. Warren B. Smith, "False Revival Coming: Holy Laughter or Strong Delusion?" (Eureka, MT: Lighthouse Trails Publishing, 2015); from original article by Warren Smith, "Holy Laughter or Strong Delusion?" SCP newsletter, Berkeley, CA, 1994.

44. Barbara Marx Hubbard, *Teachings From the Inner Christ: For Founders of a New Order of the Future (A Work in Progress)*, op. cit., p. 79.

45. Barbara Marx Hubbard, *The Revelation*, op. cit., p. 243.

46. *A Course in Miracles: Combined Volume* (Teachers Manual), op. cit., p. 37.

47. Samuel J. Andrews, *Christianity and Anti-Christianity in Their Final Conflict*, op. cit., p. 17.

Chapter 11: Christianity & Anti-Christianity

1. Moody Adams, *The Titanic's Last Hero* (West Columbia, SC: The Olive Press, a division of Midnight Call Ministries, 1997), p. 101.

2. Robert Hough, "God Is Alive and Well and Saving Souls on Dixon Road" (*Toronto Life Magazine*, February, 1995), p. 31. Cited in James A. Beverley, *Holy Laughter & The Toronto Blessing: An Investigative Report*, op. cit., p. 12.

3. Walter Lord, *A Night to Remember*, op. cit., p. 39.

4. John P. Eaton and Charles A. Haas, *Titanic: Triumph and Tragedy*, op. cit., p. 154.

5. Nick Barratt, *Lost Voices From the Titanic*, op. cit., p. 85.

6. *Encyclopedia Titanica* (https://www.encyclopedia-titanica.org/titanic-victim/robert-james-bateman.html).

7. Jack Winocour, editor, *The Story of the Titanic as Told by Its Survivors* (New York, NY: Dover Publications, Inc., 1960), p. 293.

8. Don Lynch (Text) and Ken Marschall (Paintings), *Titanic: An Illustrated History*, op. cit., p. 112.

9. Ibid.

10. Walter Lord, *A Night to Remember*, op. cit., p. 47.

11. *Encyclopedia Titanica* (https://www.encyclopedia-titanica.org/titanic-victim/benjamin-guggenheim.html).

12 . Wyn Craig Wade, *The Titanic: End of a Dream*, op. cit., p. 57.

13. *Encyclopedia Titanica* (https://www.encyclopedia-titanica.org/titanic-victim/benjamin-guggenheim.html).

14. Moody Adams, *The Titanic's Last Hero*, op. cit., p. 17.

15. *The Titanic Commutator* (The official journal of the Titanic Historical Society, Vol. 24, Number 152, 2000, Rev. Mick Steiner, "Pastor John Harper and the Titanic"), p. 260.

16. Ibid., p. 261.

17. Erwin Lutzer, "Harper's Last Convert" (The Moody Church Radio Ministries monthly letter, June 1998, https://www.sermonsearch.com/sermon-illustrations/7089/harpers-last-convert).

18. *The Titanic Commutator*, op. cit., p. 262.

19. Ibid., p. 259.

20. Moody Adams, *The Titanic's Last Hero*, op. cit., p. 100.

21. Ibid., p. 101.

22. Samuel J. Andrews, *Christianity and Anti-Christianity in Their Final Conflict*, op. cit., p. x.

23. Ibid., p. xxi.

24. Ibid., p. xx.

25. Ibid., pp. xvii-xviii.

26. Ibid., p. 207.

27. Ibid., pp. xiv-xv.

28. Ibid., p. xv.

29. Ibid., p. xvi.

30. Ibid., pp. xv-xvi.

31. Ibid., p. 132.

32. For example, Robert Schuller's book *Self-Esteem: The New Reformation* and Rick Warren's frequent use of the term. Emergent church leader Tony Jones' book *The New Christianity* and Brian McLaren's *A Generous Orthodoxy* are a fulfillment of Pastor Samuel Andrews nineteenth-century warnings.

33. Samuel J. Andrews, *Christianity and Anti-Christianity in Their Final Conflict*, op. cit., p. xviii.

34. Ibid., p. 150.

35. Ibid., p. 159.

36. Biography of James M. Gray (Moody Bible Institute, https://library.moody.edu/archives/biographies/james-m-gray).

37. Samuel J. Andrews, *Christianity and Anti-Christianity in Their Final Conflict*, op. cit., p. v.

38. Ibid., p. vi.

39. Ibid.

40. Harry Ironside, "Exposing Error: Is it Worthwhile?," op. cit.

41. Ibid.

42. Ibid.

43. Ibid.

44. Erwin W. Lutzer, *Coming to Grips With the Antichrist's New Age Roots* (Chicago, IL: Moody Press, 1990), pp. 13-14.

45. Ibid., p. 26

46. Ibid., p. 15.

47. Ibid.

48. Ibid., p. 17.

49. Ibid., p. 41.

50. Warren B. Smith, *The Light That Was Dark: A Spiritual Journey* (Chicago: Moody Press, Northfield imprint, 1992), p. 150; current edition: Warren B. Smith, *The Light That Was Dark: From the New Age to Amazing Grace* (Magalia, CA: Mountain Stream Press, 2006), pp. 160-161.

51. Bob Ditmer, "Top Leaders Leave Moody Bible Institute Over 'Crisis of Leadership'" (*Church Leaders*, January 11, 2018, https://churchleaders.com/news/317364-moody-bible-institute-facing-crisis-leadership.html). Also see: Julie Roys, "Moody Bible Institute Facing Unprecedented Crisis. Please Pray!" (January 4, 2018, julieroys.com/moody-bible-institute-facing-unprecedented-crisis-please-pray).

52. Don Lynch (Text) and Ken Marschall (Paintings), *Titanic: An Illustrated History*, op. cit., p. 76.

Chapter 12: Rescue Operation

1. Daniel Allen Butler, *The Other Side of the Night: The Carpathia, the Californian, and the Night the Titanic Was Lost* (Havertown, PA: Casemate Publishers, 2009), p. 206.

2. Ibid.

3. Herbert B. Greenhouse, *Premonitions: A Leap Into the Future*, op. cit., p. 31.

4. Colonel Archibald Gracie, *Titanic: A Survivor's Story* (Gloucestershire, England: The History Press, 2008), p. 48. First published in 1913 with the title *The Truth About Titanic*.

5. British Wreck Commissioner's Inquiry (Titanic Inquiry Project, Day 7, line 7515, https://www.titanicinquiry.org/BOTInq/BOTInq-07Gibson01.php).

6. Ibid., line 7529.

7. Ibid., lines 7538-39.

8. Daniel Allen Butler, *"Unsinkable": The Full Story of the RMS Titanic* (Boston, MA: Da Capo Press, 2002, 2012), p. 176.

9. Leslie Reade, *The Ship That Stood Still: The Californian and Her Mysterious Role in the Titanic Disaster* (New York, NY: W. W. Norton & Co. Inc., 1993).

10. Daniel Allen Butler, *The Other Side of the Night*, op. cit., p. 63.

11. Arthur Rostron, *Titanic Hero: The Autobiography of Captain Rostron of the Carpathia* (Gloucestershire, UK: Amberley Publishing, 2011), p. 41, originally published as *Home From the Sea*, 1931.

12. Wyn Craig Wade, *The Titanic: End of a Dream*, op. cit., p. 120.

13. Arthur Rostron, *Titanic Hero: The Autobiography of Captain Rostron of the Carpathia*, op. cit., p. 45.

14. Ibid., p. 41.

15. United States Senate Inquiry Report (Titanic Inquiry Project, https://www.titanicinquiry.org/USInq/USReport/AmInqRep08.php).

Epilogue

1. James M. Gray, *Concise Bible Commentary* (Peabody, MA: Hendrickson Publishers, 1999), p. 262.

2. Dutch Sheets, "Prophetic Word: The Lord Says, 'Don't Look for the Antichrist Right Now'" (*Charisma* magazine, July 11, 2020, https://www.charismanews.com/opinion/81835-prophetic-word-the-lord-says-don-t-look-for-the-antichrist-right-now).

3. Ibid.

4.. Samuel J. Andrews, *Christianity and Anti-Christianity in Their Final Conflict*, op. cit., p. 17.

Appendix

1. Hymn also titled "Eternal Father, Strong to Save"; written in 1860 by William Whiting.

PHOTO CREDITS

Page 8: Public domain; engraving done in 1912 by Willy Stöwer: Der Untergang der *Titanic* (The Sinking of the *Titanic*); https://commons. wikimedia.org/wiki/File:St%C3%B6wer_Titanic.jpg.

Page 10: Public domain; "Titanic in Southampton"; photographer unknown; https://commons.wikimedia.org/wiki/File:Titanic_in_Southampton.jpg.

Page 12: From Maurice Savage / Alamy Stock Photo; alamy.com; used with permission.

Page 18: From Karen Black / Alamy Stock Photo; alamy.com; used with permission.

Page 24: Public domain; Bain News Service, publisher, taken in 1909; https://commons.wikimedia.org/wiki/File:William_Thomas_Stead_1909.jpg.

Page 41: Scanned copy from Chris Lawson's private collection.

Page 80: Photo from Warren Smith's private collection.

Page 87: Public domain; photo by Robert John Welch (1859-1936), official photographer for Harland & Wolff (https://commons.wikimedia.org/wiki/File:RMS_Titanic_ready_for_launch,_1911.jpg); taken in 1911.

Page 122: Public domain; from the National Archives; https://commons.wikimedia.org/wiki/File:RMS_Titanic_sea_trials_April_2,_1912_(cropped).jpg; taken April 2, 1912.

Page 135: Public domain; photo taken by the chief steward of the liner Prinz Adalbert, April 15, 1912; https://commons.wikimedia.org/wiki/File:Titanic_iceberg.jpg.

Page 151: Public domain; photographer unknown (see Simon Adams's *Titanic* book "credit" section); first published in British and American newspapers following *Titanic* Sinking in 1912; https://commons.wikimedia.org/wiki/File:J._Bruce_Ismay.jpeg.

Page 152: Public domain; taken by the *New York Times* in April 1912; https://eo.wikipedia.org/wiki/Dosiero:Edward_J._Smith.jpg.

Page 154: Public domain; photographer unknown; taken on April 10, 1912; http://carnet-maritime.com/photographie/frederick-fleet-titanic-1912.html.

Page 193: Public domain; photograher and date unknown; from *Encyclopedia Titanica*; https://www.encyclopedia-titanica.org/revd-john-harper-portrait.html.

Page 214: Public domain; taken by a passenger of the *Carpathia;* April 15, 1912; https://commons.wikimedia.org/wiki/File:Titanic_lifeboat.jpg.

Page 215: Public domain; taken on April 20, 1912 when he was receiving an award from *Titanic* survivor, Margaret Brown; https://commons.wikimedia.org/wiki/File:RostronandBrown.jpg.

Page 216: From alamy.com; Scrap of letterhead stationery from RMS *Carpathia* with a small engraving of ship, ca. 1912; used with permission.

Index

OTHER BOOKS BY WARREN B. SMITH

The Light That Was Dark: From the New Age to Amazing Grace

False Christ Coming—Does Anybody Care?: What New Age Leaders Really Have in Store for America, the Church, and the World

Deceived on Purpose: The New Age Implications of the Purpose-Driven Church

A "Wonderful" Deception: The Further New Age Implications of the Emerging Purpose Driven Movement

"Another Jesus" Calling: How Sarah Young's False Christ is Deceiving the Church

Pressing On Through It All: Scriptural Encouragement for These Last Days

Watering the Greyhound Garden: Stories From the Streets of San Francisco

Warren B. Smith
c/o Mountain Stream Press
P.O. Box 269
Fortine, MT 59918

E-mail: warren@mountainstreampress.org
Website: www.newagetoamazinggrace.com
YouTube: https://www.youtube.com/warrenbsmith

Warren B. Smith's books can be ordered through most bookstores and major outlets, including Amazon and Barnes & Noble. Digital formats also available. For toll free ordering, call 866-876-3910.